# Feminism in th

*Feminism in the United States: A Concise Introduction* presents readers with the key debates and ideas central to contemporary US feminism. With a focus on intersectionality, the book highlights the goals, tactics, and varieties of feminism.

This engaging, clear, and accessible text includes current examples, case studies, profiles of key figures in the movement, and opportunities/resources to gather more information. The reader will learn how to employ a feminist lens as an informed conversationalist, social media user, news consumer, and if so desired, activist. Readers will learn about the varieties of contemporary US feminism and how different strands of feminism emerge; the heterogeneity of the movement as it endures over generations in hospitable and inhospitable climates alike; and the inequalities addressed and tactics used by feminists to create lasting social change.

*Feminism in the United States* is ideal for undergraduate students, particularly those enrolled in introductory classes in feminist, gender, and sexuality studies and related programs, as well as for anyone seeking to explore feminism for the first time.

**Alison Dahl Crossley**, PhD, is the Executive Director of the Michelle R. Clayman Institute for Gender Research at Stanford University. She is the author of *Finding Feminism: Millennial Activists and the Unfinished Gender Revolution.*

# Feminism in the United States
## A Concise Introduction

Alison Dahl Crossley

Routledge
Taylor & Francis Group

LONDON AND NEW YORK

First published 2024
by Routledge
4 Park Square, Milton Park, Abingdon, Oxon OX14 4RN

and by Routledge
605 Third Avenue, New York, NY 10158

*Routledge is an imprint of the Taylor & Francis Group, an informa business*

*British Library Cataloguing-in-Publication Data*
A catalogue record for this book is available from the British Library

*Library of Congress Cataloging-in-Publication Data*
Names: Crossley, Alison Dahl, author.
Title: Feminism in the United States : a concise introduction / Alison Dahl Crossley.
Description: Abingdon, Oxon ; New York, NY : Routledge, 2024. | Includes bibliographical references and index.
Identifiers: LCCN 2024016722 (print) |
LCCN 2024016723 (ebook) |
Subjects: LCSH: Feminism--United States.
Classification: LCC HQ1426 .C76 2024 (print) |
LCC HQ1426 (ebook) | DDC 305.420973--dc23/eng/20240411
LC record available at https://lccn.loc.gov/2024016722
LC ebook record available at https://lccn.loc.gov/2024016723

ISBN: 978-1-032-31724-3 (hbk)
ISBN: 978-1-032-31719-9 (pbk)
ISBN: 978-1-003-31099-0 (ebk)

DOI: 10.4324/9781003310990

Typeset in Sabon
by Taylor & Francis Books

# Contents

*List of Figures*                                                    viii
*Acknowledgments*                                                      ix

Introduction                                                           1

   *Key Things to Pay Attention to in the Book 2*
   *Desired Outcomes of the Book 3*

1   What is Feminism, and Who is a Feminist?                        4

   *Definition of Feminism 5*
   *Intersectionality 7*
   *Intersectional Feminisms 8*
   *Case Study, Missing White Woman Syndrome 12*
   *Feminist Identities 14*
   *Case Study, Sandberg and hooks 18*
   *Pathways to Feminism 21*
   *Men and Feminism 22*
   *Trans-inclusive Feminism 24*
   *Global Feminisms 24*
   *Chapter 1 Mini Toolkit: #SayHerName 26*
   *Chapter 1 Dive Deeper 28*

2   Varieties of Feminisms                                      34

    *Women of Color Feminisms 35*
    *The Emergence of Black, Indigenous, Asian American,*
      *and Chicana Feminisms 37*
    *Black Feminism 39*
    *Spotlight on an Organization 41*
    *Asian American Feminism 45*
    *Indigenous Feminism 49*
    *Chicana Feminism 58*
    *Whitewashed Feminisms 62*
    *Lesbian, Queer, and Trans Feminisms 64*
    *Chapter 2 Mini Toolkit: Audre Lorde and Feminist*
      *Poetry as Transformation 70*
    *Chapter 2 Dive Deeper 71*

3   Waveless Feminism and Movement Persistence                  79

    *The Persistence of Feminism 80*
    *Between the Surges: The Abeyance Theory 83*
    *Waveless vs. Wave Feminism 86*
    *Waveless Feminism 87*
    *Feminist Wave Framework 88*
    *Analyses of Feminisms' Ancillary Trends 91*
    *Case Study, Girl Boss Era 95*
    *Chapter 3 Mini Toolkit: Feminist Community and*
      *Black Joy Farm 98*
    *Chapter 3 Dive Deeper 99*

4   What do Feminists Care About?                               103

    *Wages and the Wage Gap 104*
    *Case Study, Wage Gap and Trucking 109*
    *Gender-Based Violence 109*
    *Health Disparities 114*
    *Reproductive Health Care 118*
    *Spotlight: The Jane Collective 121*

*Prison Industrial Complex 122*
*Climate Change and Environmental Inequalities 124*
*Childcare Insecurity 125*
*Inequality in Technology and Online Harassment 127*
*Media Inequality 130*
*Political Representation 132*
*Chapter 4 Mini Toolkit: Non-Disclosure Agreements 134*
*Chapter 4 Dive Deeper 136*

5   How do Feminists Create Change?                          152

*Feminist Methods for Social Change 153*
*Tactic #1: Online Feminisms 154*
*Tactic #2: Everyday Feminism 160*
*Tactic #3: Feminist Organizations 165*
*Tactic #4: Street Protest and Civil Disobedience 170*
*Tactic #5: Consciousness-Raising Groups and*
 *Collective Identity 173*
*Case Study, CR 173*
*Tactic #6: Feminist Legal Advances 176*
*Tactic #7: Academia and Student Activism 182*
*Tactic #8: Media 186*
*Tactics #9: Music and Art 193*
*Chapter 5 Mini Toolkit: Guerrilla Girls 196*
*Chapter 5 Dive Deeper 197*

6   What is the Future of Feminism, and How Can I Live a
     Feminist Life?                                          207

*Visions for Feminist Futures 207*
*Living a Feminist Life: Quotidian Feminisms 210*
*A Feminist Lens 213*
*Chapter 6 Dive Deeper 213*

*Index*                                                      215

# Figures

2.1 LaDonna Brave Bull Allard 57
3.1 UCSB students marching in Isla Vista, CA protesting gender-based violence after the May 2014 shootings 83
5.1 Feminista Jones 157
5.2 "5 Femicides a Day," Feminist Collages NYC 172
6.1 Feminist community and collectivity has always fueled the movement. Resistance Revival Chorus at the Women's Convention, October 28, 2017, Detroit, MI 208

# Acknowledgments

Thank you to all of my colleagues at the Clayman Institute for Gender Research, who are a source of feminist community and intellectual growth. Especially to Adrian Daub, Claire Urbanski, Laura Goode, Bethany Nichols, Arghavan Salles, and the Clayman Institute staff. Thank you to Lily Forman, Olivia Ziegler, Maria Thereza Rios Hortencio, and Meagan Khoury; and to Ariel (Hong Lam) Chan, Hana/Connor Yankowitz, and Isabel Sieh. With appreciation to my gender research colleagues and collaborators near and far who have provided valuable feedback and comments, Heather Hurwitz, Fatima Suarez, Melissa C. Brown, Brooke Mascagni, Anna Sorensen, and Saidah Grayson Dill.

Thank you to Charlotte Taylor and Jodie Collins at Routledge. Thank you also to copyeditor Driss Fatih.

Finally, thank you to my family and friends, who go way above and beyond in their support and kindness. This book is dedicated to the one and only ADC.

# Introduction

In the last decade, feminism has become a buzzword like never before. From Beyoncé to "white feminism," it has been embraced, rejected, discussed, and made headlines the world over.

What is feminism? Who is a feminist? What do feminists do? How has feminist activism changed US society? How has feminism evolved over time? By answering these questions, this book introduces students and the general public to the key terms, debates, and ideas central to contemporary US feminism. Although the feminist movement has been vibrant and influential for generations, attention to it has been renewed. In response, a concise take on feminism is necessary for those who are enrolled in a course or who wish to be well-informed citizens. With everyone from Hollywood stars to politicians sharing their takes on feminism (some more informed than others), it is especially relevant and timely to offer a comprehensive, concise, and easy to understand book about feminism. Much of the information circulating out there could use a research and historic framework as a correction.

As you will see, intersectional feminism is the primary theoretical framework employed in the book. By this I mean feminists are driven to eliminate gender inequality connected to the inequalities of racism, classism, homophobia, ableism, etc. Feminism is a movement to make visible, and dismantle, power structures that have, throughout history, harmed all women. Since women are a very large and heterogeneous group, the interests of one group of women may be different from the interests of another group of women. Because of this, there are multiple ways of "doing" feminism. With this in mind, I emphasize the complexity of feminism and

DOI: 10.4324/9781003310990-1

the divergent ways in which feminism has been adopted in different communities and contexts. Throughout the book I refer to feminisms with an 's'.

This book highlights the contributions of racially diverse feminists, including Black feminists, Asian American feminists, Indigenous feminists, queer feminists, and Chicana feminists. It also acknowledges the conflicts between privileged white feminists and feminists with less material resources, revealing that the dismantling of power hierarchies is as complex and multifaceted as the power structures themselves. The intersectional orientation used in this book is essential from a pedagogical standpoint, and simply affords the most accurate and comprehensive account of the movement, as feminism has always been advanced by women from a wide spectrum of backgrounds with intersectional concerns.

The book is about feminism as a social movement (rather than as a theory, for example). The book affirms the ways in which individuals and collectives have created feminist campaigns, feminist change, and feminist communities. In addition to providing a research-based foundation of feminism as a social movement, I expand on how the reader may live a feminist life. This perspective is woven throughout the book by including research about how individuals integrate feminist principles in their everyday lives, and by providing online and offline resources for further reading.

In this action-oriented book, *Feminism in the United States: A Concise Introduction* will summarize scholarly research, use real world examples, and feature the key thinkers and leaders of the movement. The book illustrates the vibrancy and breadth of the US feminist movement from the 1960s to today. I paint a picture of feminism as a movement with nuance and complexity, and one that continues to be tremendously impactful.

## Key Things to Pay Attention to in the Book

The mini toolkits at the end of each chapter are exercises for readers to a. understand the application of feminist ideologies (tools to translate feminism into their own lives) and b. understand how dominant structures all around us are steeped in patriarchy, and how feminists have pushed back (tools that help build more egalitarian communities). A mini toolkit is not a lesson plan per se (although the entire book could be the outline of a syllabus, should that be helpful to an instructor), nor is it a course project (although research and reflection prompts are featured throughout the book). Rather, the toolkit is the most concrete way to address how students can "live feminism," as students have requested. It encourages them to learn about feminist issues around them, to spur their interest and to give them examples of other feminists who have successfully incorporated feminism into their lives and communities.

Any book of this nature is but a slice of a large topic. Particularly with a topic such as feminism in which there are so many different views and contributions, this book does not represent the full spectrum of feminist thought. The perspectives and main points of this book will not resonate with all readers, and indeed many might give rise to disagreements. Moreover, looking forward, feminist terminology, expressions, and contexts will undoubtedly shift. That is expected and completely acceptable. This book brings up provocative questions that are meant to engage, pique curiosity, and even lead to debate. It is my hope that you open the book in that spirit.

## Desired Outcomes of the Book

- To educate readers about the primary grievances, goals and tactics of the feminist movement, as well as its successes and challenges
- To impart a clear understanding of intersectional feminism and its centrality to the movement
- To impart to readers the varieties of contemporary feminisms and how different strands of feminism emerge and shape each other
- To provide readers with a full understanding of how the feminist movement has endured over generations in hospitable and inhospitable climates alike
- To understand the role of individuals and organizations in perpetuating feminism
- To provide readers additional resources about feminism
- To provide readers with information about how to get involved in feminism
- To allow readers to be informed conversationalists, social media users, news consumers, and activists

# 1 What is Feminism, and Who is a Feminist?

- Raising millions of dollars for reproductive justice and abortion services
- Marching for climate change policy in Washington DC
- Distributing menstrual products to end period poverty
- Convening community groups to support those experiencing postpartum depression
- Joining city wide guerrilla art projects drawing attention to street harassment
- Protesting the epidemic of gender-based violence on a college campus
- Distributing resources to queer and trans individuals experiencing housing insecurity
- Educating medical students about health care for queer and gender non-conforming populations
- Contributing to a social media campaign drawing attention to Black women victims of police violence

These are recent examples of feminist organizing, drawing attention to the variety of ways that feminism is enacted by individuals and communities. However, these examples are just a tiny fraction of a massive feminist movement. Over generations and continuing today, feminists across the world have consistently organized, confronted inequalities, created feminist communities, and advanced a more just society for women of all different backgrounds. Feminism also evolves and changes over time to remain relevant and to respond to current events. Many

DOI: 10.4324/9781003310990-2

advancements that we might not even appreciate, or that we take for granted, are the results of feminist organizing.

Why has feminism continued over such a long period of time? Gender inequality and interrelated inequalities (based on race, class, sexuality, ability, etc.) are persistent and what scholars call *durable* (Tilly, 1998). That means that these inequalities hold up over time, over changes in our culture and society, despite organizing and activism. Also contributing to the movement's longevity is that feminism is a broad movement addressing inequalities impacting over half the population, so its goals and constituencies are vast and varied. To be sure, feminists and other social movement participants have had major successes in creating a more equal world. Indeed, research finds that most adults agree feminists have "done at least a fair amount to advance women's rights" (Horowitz and Igielnik, 2020). However, there continue to be more injustices to fight, and new ways in which they will spring up.

In this chapter you will learn about feminisms and feminist identities, and the concerns, debates, and concepts central to feminisms. I refer to feminisms, plural, because there are many different types of feminism. At times, distinct forms of feminism can be at odds with each other, or even contradict each other. The intersectional feminist framework employed throughout the book is also laid out here. Note that although feminism is a global movement, this book is about US feminisms.

## Definition of Feminism

Feminism is a movement to end gender inequality and interrelated inequalities. While feminism has been defined in a number of different ways, Black lesbian feminist Barbara Smith (1980) wrote: "Feminism is the political theory and practice that struggles to free *all* women...Anything less than this vision of total freedom is not feminism, but merely female self-aggrandizement" (p. 48).

### Spotlight on Barbara Smith

Barbara Smith is an American feminist, writer, and scholar known for her significant contributions to Black feminism and intersectionality. Smith was instrumental in fostering greater awareness of the complexities of oppression and advocating for recognition of these intersections to understand the nuanced dynamics of inequality.

She co-founded the Combahee River Collective in Boston in 1974, a Black feminist organization that laid the foundation for contemporary Black feminist thought, and the *Kitchen Table: Women of Color Press* in 1980, which published works by and about Women of Color. This press played a crucial role in amplifying the voices of marginalized women.

**Who is a feminist?** Anyone who works individually or within a group to end gender inequality and interrelated inequalities.

How exactly is feminism a social movement? First, feminism as a social movement means it involves groups of people working to confront and change power hierarchies. These groups could be small community partnerships, grassroots collectives, large national or transnational organizations, and everything in between. Second, individuals themselves are also feminist and can uphold feminist ideals and incorporate feminist changes in their own personal lives.

Although major feminist successes occur primarily when collectives or organizations or community groups come together, individual feminist relationships and actions can accomplish change as well. Relatedly, feminism is also a viewpoint that informs individual choices and perspectives on current events and popular culture. The feminist perspective, which will also be developed throughout the book, centers consideration of justice and equality. Taken all together, this book addresses how individuals and groups work to change their communities and societies to make them more feminist.

**Roxane Gay**, professor and author of New York Times bestselling book, *Bad Feminist* (2014), writes:

"At its basis, I just don't believe that women should be treated like [expletive] for being women. But as you begin to expand the definition, it's that women deserve to have full and satisfying lives in the same way that men do. I'm very committed to making sure that we do get there somehow."

## Intersectionality

Because feminism is all about fighting inequality, it is important to have a good foundation for understanding the inequalities that feminists are motivated to change. The central approach to understanding the interrelated nature of inequalities is through *intersectionality*, the main framework of this book. Initially theorized by feminist organization the Combahee River Collective in 1974 and coined by Kimberlé Crenshaw in 1989, intersectionality highlights power structures and the interconnection of identity categories. Intersectionality emphasizes that race, gender, class, and sexuality, for example, cannot be separated from each other, and that these categories intersect to create individual/group experiences. We cannot truly understand an individual's gender without also incorporating understandings of their race, class, sexuality, ability, immigration status, and other identity categories. Thus, a person's experience as a woman is dependent on other elements of her identity. She will experience being a woman differently whether she is Black, or Latinx, or queer, or wealthy or poor. Depending on the full spectrum of her identity, expectations of her as a woman, worker, mother, daughter, or partner will vary.

However, more than simply acknowledging that identity categories intersect to create different experiences for people of diverse backgrounds, what truly distinguishes the perspective of intersectionality from other feminist perspectives is that of *power*. Intersectionality draws attention to the power and inequality generated as a result of the interconnectedness of different categories. Connections of race and gender, for example, generate distinct experiences in the hierarchy of power. To illustrate, women of different racial backgrounds do not experience interactions with the police in the same way: Women of Color are more likely to experience violence, mistreatment and sexual misconduct from police officers than white women (Harper, Gover, and Mages, 2021; Ritchie, 2017). Related to the intersection of gender, sexuality, and race, Black sexual minority and gender diverse women may experience sexism, as well as homophobia and racism (Page, Cerezo, and Ross, 2022). To provide another example, women who wear the hijab (a veil covering the hair) for religious reasons experience discrimination related to their race, gender and religion (Ahmed and Gorey, 2023). When immigration status is considered as an additional identity dimension, another layer of power and inequality becomes clear (Patrón, 2020).

Thus, individual everyday experiences with privilege and power are significantly shaped by gender, race, and sexuality, and other categories. Considering the interaction of these identities is the only way we can truly understand an individual's life experiences. The point is not to create a "hierarchy of oppressions," as per Audre Lorde, but rather to acknowledge that seeing only one identity category, such as only gender or only race, will inevitably miss a big part of the picture.

## Intersectional Feminisms

So what does intersectionality mean for feminism? Sometimes, when people think of or define feminism, they think of women's rights. But there is no universal category or definition of women. Women and their life experiences vary significantly and are shaped by other elements of their identities. When we embrace an intersectional perspective, we can understand that there is no one representative woman. Rather, women of different ethnicities, races, sexualities, and abilities, are part of and valuable to the feminist movement. As such, there are many ways of being feminist and many strands of feminisms with different goals and constituents. Thus, it makes sense to reference feminisms, plural, throughout this book. Because we are acknowledging the complexities and multiplicities of the movement, it is important to also note that feminism is not always harmonious, solidarity-defined, or without flaws and tensions.

### Spotlight on Cherríe Moraga

Cherríe Moraga is a famous and influential Chicana feminist. She is a poet, playwright, director, and educator, perhaps most known for co-editing with Gloria Anzaldúa the seminal feminist text *This Bridge Called My Back: Writings by Radical Women of*

*Color* (1981). Here, in a classic text (originally written in 1979), she illustrates the nuances of intersectionality and the problems with thinking that one form of inequality is worse than another.

Cherríe Moraga, "La Güera":

"In this country, lesbianism is a poverty- as is being brown, as is being a woman, as is being just plain poor. The danger lies in ranking the oppressions. *The danger lies in failing to acknowledge the specificity of the oppression.* The danger lies in attempting to deal with oppression purely from a theoretical base. Without an emotional, heartfelt grappling with the source of our own oppression, without naming the enemy within ourselves and outside of us, no authentic, non-hierarchical connection among oppressed groups can take place."

(1981, p. 29)

Building upon the concept of intersectionality, feminisms incorporate considerations of the complexity of gender, including its intersections with race, class, gender identity, sexuality, ability, or immigration status. Intersectional feminisms are so important because they lead us to the most precise and useful approach to understanding inequalities. By understanding the complicated dimensions of inequalities, feminists can more effectively combat them. Also, through intersectional feminism, feminists can reach and recruit a broad range of supporters for its activism and campaigns.

Let's think about issues that affect or potentially affect all women, such as sexual harassment, and how intersectional feminism informs a response. In a nationally representative study, 81 percent of women have reported experiencing sexual harassment in their lifetime (Kearl, Johns, and Raj, 2019).

Owing to racism and gendered and racial stereotypes, women will experience sexual harassment differently and at different rates (Buchanan et al., 2018). As a result of homophobia and entrenchment of binary gender norms, trans-identified individuals will experience harassment differently from cisgender women. Women's experiences of sexual harassment are also shaped by their occupations. Someone who works in the service sector (such as being a server, bartender, or flight attendant) will experience sexual harassment differently from someone who works in an office or corporate setting. The highest rates of sexual harassment charges filed are in public-facing (Stewart, 2017) and service sector jobs (Frye, 2017) dominated by women of low socioeconomic statuses, many of whom are Women of Color. Thus, as feminists consider how to combat sexual harassment, an intersectional understanding of the situation informs how complex it is and encourages targeted actions that are sensitive to these nuances.

**Cisgender**: a person whose gender identity aligns with the sex they were assigned at birth. A cisgender person is someone who identifies with the same gender as the one typically associated with their biological or physical sex characteristics. For example, a person who is assigned female at birth and identifies as a woman is considered cisgender.

**Women of Color**: a broad category used to describe women who identify as Black, brown, or other racial identities that are not white. Racial minorities often experience discrimination based on their skin color and racial identities. As such, the category Women of Color is a way for individuals and groups to signal their shared, although diverse, experiences. While some may find the term too universal, many women find it meaningful to uplift a community of women who are marginalized by race. Women of Color may also connect with a more specific racial identity (i.e. Black, South Asian, multiracial, etc.)

Intersectional feminists know that to fully understand inequality and how to fight it effectively, we need an intersectional perspective. An intersectional feminist campaign against sexual harassment is sensitive to different experiences with harassment, and different responses available to different women (California Coalition Against Sexual Assault [CALCASA], 2017; Cole and Duncan, 2023). Women of Color and women with limited financial resources have been found to be more vulnerable to sexual harassment (Cantalupo,

2019; Uggen and Blackstone, 2004). Because many women who report sexual harassment lose their jobs or are maligned in their workplace, an individual with robust financial resources may be more able to risk her career by disclosing an experience of harassment. In contrast, an undocumented individual or one who lives paycheck to paycheck may be silent when it comes to reporting harassment, for fear she would be fired. Since intersectional feminists also recognize that power dynamics occur in all sectors of society, they may consider how harassment also occurs outside of the workplace. Research has found, for example, that race, class and gender inequalities shape the experiences of women who are sexually harassed by their landlords, and that these women are silenced in large part due to their housing vulnerability and the institutional authority of the perpetrator (Tester, 2008). An intersectional feminist activist in this case might consider coalitioning with tenants' rights groups, given the intersection of gender, race, and class inequalities with the issue of housing insecurity. Overall, intersectional feminists appreciate and recognize the numerous nuances and complexities in activism.

Scholar Heather McKee Hurwitz (2020) defines three criteria central to activists' effectively incorporating intersectionality in social justice work: "(1) they address multiple forms of inequality with specificity, (2) they depict the lives and stories of people who are multiply marginalized, and (3) they encourage coalition building with other groups and movements from outside the main movement" (p. 145). For the feminist movement, this "intersectional imperative" (ibid) means that activists are motivated by very tangible, measurable and specific interlocking inequalities, have the desire to promote inclusivity, highlight and uplift Women of Color and women who have a variety of life experiences, and build broad and wide coalitions.

Readers should be aware that a feminism that only focuses on gender is likely a feminism that centers on whiteness by default. One person's feminism might indeed marginalize other women. Non-intersectional feminist movements do exist. For example, campaigns for the right of women to vote were primarily led by white women. They focused on the rights of white women, isolating Women of Color to the detriment of the movement. For many women, including Black women, Latinx women, and Indigenous women, voting restrictions kept them from the polls for years after white women were allowed to vote. In contrast, intersectional feminists are motivated to understand and act upon gender inequality with an eye toward how it relates to other inequalities. An intersectional feminist campaign for voting rights considers all dimensions of the barriers to democratic participation including race, class, and gender (Montoya, 2020).

This comparison highlights that when we only talk about gender and feminism—and not other intersecting categories—it probably means that the conversation is centering on white people and assumes racial privilege. Whiteness is often invisible and unmarked. Be wary of or question a universal feminism that does not integrate intersectional perspectives.

Legendary activist and scholar **Angela Davis** highlights the plurality of the movement and its need for inclusiveness:

"I rarely talk about feminism in the singular. I talk about feminisms. And, even when I myself refused to identify with feminism, I realized that it was a certain kind of feminism... It was a feminism of those women who weren't really concerned with equality for all women..."

(2019)

Intersectional feminism is the primary mode by which we may understand feminism and be involved in feminism. It is the most accurate lens to use to understand feminism of the past as well as in moving forward. In fact, research supports that self-identified feminists are concerned with intersectional issues of social justice, and not only a narrow focus on gender (Kelly et al., 2016).

## Case Study, Missing White Woman Syndrome

One of the clearest and most powerful examples of the usefulness of intersectional feminist perspectives is "Missing white woman syndrome." Coined by Gwen Ifill in 2004, "missing white woman syndrome" occurs when young, attractive, white women who go missing draw sustained national media attention (Demby, 2017). In contrast, when Women of Color go missing, sometimes even from the same city or state, they draw very little attention. Research has found that Black women and Indigenous women, for example, go missing at higher proportions than white women, although they garner less attention. In 2020 a total of 268,884 women in the US were reported missing. Fully one-third of those were Black women and girls, which is larger than their proportion of the population (National Crime Information Center, 2021; Pruitt-Young, 2021). Scholars Danielle Slakoff and Henry Fradella (2019) have conducted research on this topic and found that missing white women receive more initial and more sustained media attention.

Moreover, white women are portrayed in the media as good, honest, and wholesome people; their disappearance is an unimaginable tragedy. In contrast, their research has found that Women of Color who go missing are more likely reported to have been in dangerous situations, subtly blaming them for, and even normalizing their disappearances (Slakoff and Fradella, 2019).

While any woman or girl who goes missing is undeniably tragic, there are complex dimensions of inequality within this phenomenon that warrant attention. If we were to examine missing girls and women from only a gendered perspective, of the missing women as women only, we wouldn't see missing white woman syndrome. It is only through an intersectional analysis that we can understand the racial and gendered dimensions of missing persons, and fully address the problem.

### Why does this matter?

Abundant resources and attention help find missing persons. More attention, more people keeping their eyes out for a missing person or organizing search parties, raises the likelihood of the person being found. Much of this is done through the media. Without mainstream media attention, families of missing girls and Women of Color need to galvanize their own networks and communities, which is inevitably going to reach fewer people. It also matters because we as a population are learning whose lives to value and whose lives are dispensable. This reinforces a gendered racial hierarchy.

### What can I do?

The missing women epidemic is deeply related to inequality. It should not be normalized or acceptable. Educate yourself about your own community's missing women. Share with your friends what you have learned about the intersectional inequalities that shape missing white woman syndrome. Also, consider your social media feed. Whose voices and stories are you amplifying? Observe the news and your news feed. Whose stories are taking center stage? Consider diversifying your news and social media feeds, or even asking sources in your news landscape to highlight the stories of missing Women of Color.

## Feminist Identities

Feminism, perhaps more than other movements, is dynamic and complex. The feminist movement endures because of its heterogeneity, and its continuing relevance to ongoing debates, inequalities, and timely events. There are an abundance of opportunities for individuals to define their feminisms– their feminist grievances, philosophies, goals, and approaches to change. Owing to its plurality, there are many ways in which feminist identities have been measured.

Over decades, the majority of women in the US (approximately 61 percent) have identified as feminist (Barroso, 2020). Young women aged 18–29 have been found to have the highest rates of feminist identity (Barroso, 2020). In particular, white men and women who associate feminism with negative characteristics (polarizing and outdated) (Barroso, 2020) are less likely to identify as feminists (Cole & Zuker, 2007). Over time, a significant body of research, including a study by Elizabeth Cole and Alyssa Zucker (2007), has found that Women of Color are more likely to identify as feminist than white women. This has typically been attributed to the fact that since Black and Latina women and other Women of Color experience and observe inequality from a young age, they are more readily able to notice inequalities that are related to gender. In contrast, white heterosexual women, particularly those from higher socioeconomic backgrounds who also enjoy white privilege, may not come to understand the gender inequality that shapes their lives until there is a profound moment in their development- such as learning that a male co-worker in the same position is making more money (wage gap), experiencing inequality in an intimate relationship, or encountering lack of support while raising a child.

**White privilege** encompasses the advantages white individuals and communities experience. The term highlights systemic disparities based on race, and its roots in historical racial biases. For example, Pew research has noted that the majority of Americans believe that being white helps people "get ahead," at least to some extent, providing them with easier access to opportunities (Horowitz, Brown & Cox 2019). White individuals also experience more positive representation in media and culture– even when people of color are represented, they often have stereotyped roles (World Economic Forum, 2021). Additionally, white individuals receive greater levels of trust and respect (Evangelist, 2022).

While most studies agree that Women of Color identify as feminists at higher rates than white women, there are some qualifications. Studies that focus on different ages, or different ethnic groups, have mixed findings. One study of college students found that white women had higher rates of feminist identities than participants in other ethnic groups, which the authors suspect could be related to the exclusion of African American women from some modes of feminism (Robnett and Anderson, 2017). At the same time, labeling oneself as feminist specifically may not tell us a lot about someone's beliefs, as there are a variety of other movements and labels that have some of the core tenets of feminism. For example, research has found that Black women specifically are more likely (or equally) to identify with *womanism* (Brewer, 2020), a movement created by Alice Walker in the early 1980s, that advocates for the unique interests and rights of Black women (more about womanism in Chapter 2). Moreover, many scholars find that for Black women "feminism is inherent in an anti-racist struggle," and that the allegiance to or identity of feminist is not of immense concern (Roth, 2004, 79; Giddings, 1984).

**White feminism**: term used to describe a brand of feminism that primarily focuses on the struggles and issues faced by white women while often neglecting or marginalizing the concerns of Women of Color. It is characterized by a lack of awareness and advocacy for the unique challenges that women of different racial, ethnic, and socioeconomic backgrounds face, and can inadvertently perpetuate systemic inequalities. White feminism tends to lack intersectional approaches to gender oppression.

**Womanism**: a social and political movement and term created by writer and activist Alice Walker that advocates for the unique interests and rights of Black women from an intersectional perspective. Womanism aims to be more inclusive and holistic than some other forms of feminism, recognizing that the liberation of Black women is essential for the liberation of all people. (Brewer, 2020)

There are also individuals who ascribe to and hold feminist beliefs and/or support women's rights who would not consider themselves feminist. Some of these people would rather identify as humanist, indicating they believe in equality for all people (Crossley, 2017), or as individuals who believe in feminism but do not wish to be part of any specific social movement at all.

You may ask, why does it matter whether a person identifies as feminist or not? The act of identifying as a feminist is important for several reasons. First, if you take the step of identifying as a feminist then you are aligning yourself with other people who also identify as feminist. Finding other like-minded people is likely to lead to taking part in feminist community and discussion. Second, in the big picture, the movement can only forge ahead if there are those in large numbers who believe in the movement and embrace the identity. In other words, a movement's continuity relies on some people being inside the movement and others being outside the movement (Taylor and Whittier, 1992).

As you have learned, feminism is a shape-shifting movement. It looks different in different contexts and among different populations of women. Far from being a weakness of the movement, this ability to adapt and change to local contexts, all while maintaining the core value of eradicating gender inequality and interrelated inequalities, is a strength which has allowed the movement to persevere over generations.

Key priorities of feminists in the US today include:

- Wage gap
- Gender-based violence
- Health disparities
- Reproductive health care
- Prison industrial complex
- Climate change
- Childcare insecurity
- Inequality in tech
- Media inequality
- Political representation

Feminist concerns vary by population and are not interchangeable. In a study of millennials (GenForward, 2018), white, Latinx, and Black respondents said the most important problem facing women today was "ending sexual harassment and sexual assault," while the most common response of Asian respondents was "equal treatment and opportunity in the workplace." In terms of educational levels, encompassing all racial categories, GenFoward's research (2018) also shows: those with no high school diploma were the group most likely to respond with "ending sexual harassment and sexual assault." The most educated participants (BA or above) were most likely to respond with "equal treatment and opportunity in the workplace."

A core feminist principle is valuing and uplifting a range of types of knowledge, including those developed outside of traditional institutions of learning. This is especially important as social inequalities shape many barriers to higher education. The broader women's movement of the 1970s, however, developed in tandem with many advancements in higher education, such as the inclusion of women's expertise in academic canons and the inception of women's studies, ethnic studies, and gender research centers. Much of the development of the research about feminism, intersectionality, and inequality has occurred in gender research institutes and interdisciplinary academic departments/programs within colleges and universities. Nonetheless, a substantial body of feminist research and intellectual perspectives have been created, developed, and circulated outside of academia. The prominent feminist thinkers and leaders quoted throughout this book are scholars, students, and activists within and outside of the academy.

## Case Study, Sandberg and hooks

Feminism, as it is complex and intersectional, is not a one-size-fits-all movement. Because women from different backgrounds experience their gender differently, as outlined previously, they are involved in various ways with feminism. What is in the interest of some feminists may be not in the interests of other feminists. Here is a case study to illustrate this.

One clear example of two different approaches to feminism involve Sheryl Sandberg and bell hooks. Sandberg is a well-respected executive, author, and philanthropist. She was formerly Chief Operating Officer of Meta (formerly Facebook), and is also a billionaire. At the beginning of her career, she was an economist at the World Bank and chief of staff to Larry Summers, who at the time was the US Treasury Secretary. In this midst of her time at Facebook, she wrote a book called *Lean In: Women, Work, and the Will to Lead*, and it marked a major moment in discussions of women in the workplace, and feminism. Published in 2013, it was on *The New York Times* bestseller list for over a year, sold over 4 million books worldwide within five years of its release, has been translated into many different languages, and even has a version for recent college graduates with additional chapters about entering the workforce (Newman, 2018). As Sandberg describes in her book, feminism is an approach by which women are encouraged to take their seat at the table, join in and advocate for themselves and other women, and not be afraid to "lean in" to their career and ambition. The audience for the book is primarily professional or corporate women. The book contains research about gender inequality at work and home, and provides research-based advice to women on succeeding in their careers. She urges women to take control of their careers. Fans of the book saw it as a manifesto for working women and gender equality, and applauded her for using her very visible platform to address feminism.

The views of bell hooks are in contrast to Sandberg's thinking. The late bell hooks was a famous and influential Black queer feminist writer and activist. hooks is a lauded and well-published feminist leader, whose writing for both academic and non-academic audiences has been a benchmark for contemporary feminist thinking. Famous quotes of hooks include "feminism is for everybody" and "patriarchy has no gender." She wrote over thirty books on topics such as feminism, race, class, love, patriarchy, capitalism, and inequality, interrogating the connections between racism, classism, and sexism. hooks was a faculty member and also a public intellectual. After her passing in 2021, her legacy lives on at the bell hooks center at Berea College.

hooks wrote an essay about Sandberg's *Lean In* that was widely discussed in feminist circles. hooks found *Lean In* a less than desirable representation of feminism. In her essay, hooks (2013) writes:

> "Her [Sandberg's] unwillingness to consider a vision that would include all women rather than white women from privileged classes is one of the flaws in her representation of herself as a voice for feminism. Certainly, she is a powerful figure for fiscally conservative white feminist elites."
>
> (pp. 671–672)

hooks' main issue with *Lean In* is that Sandberg and her optimism for change doesn't fundamentally recognize that most workplaces are patriarchal and sexist institutions in which solidarity between women, or a loosening of male privilege, is near impossible. hooks' view is that holding women themselves accountable for pushing through a workplace that is not set up for them is not only a likely unattainable goal, but one that then ultimately places the blame on women themselves if they don't succeed in breaking through these barriers. hooks (2013) concludes her essay by writing:

> "we all need to remember that visionary feminist goal which is not of a woman running the world as is, but a women [sic] doing our part to change the world so that freedom and justice, the opportunity to have optimal well-being—can be equally shared by everyone, female and male"
>
> (p. 674)

Given hooks' and Sandberg's proclivities, goals for feminism, and particular orientations to the world, they certainly have very different views of what feminism is. So what do we make of this debate? Sandberg and hooks are examples of two feminist women, both well-known in their respective fields, disagreeing about the basic tenets of feminism. But they are both feminist. So what sense do we make of this? The point is that hooks and Sandberg are engaging with feminism by viewing social change and economic advancement using different feminist lenses.

For Sandberg, a white woman executive in a field dominated by men, there is merit in encouraging women to rise in the ranks of their corporations and to give them the tools to do so. Putting weight into diversifying corporate America might, in the long run, benefit many employees and companies. In this context, however, feminism is about advancing women in professional spheres, within organizations that oftentimes uphold and perpetuate inequalities. It is also clearly focused on individual women changing their behaviors, rather than imploring organizations and structures to change. In comparison, hooks diverges in her approach to economic advancement and equality. Because hooks, like many intersectional feminists, is particularly attuned to the nuances of and connections between inequalities, she is critical of the way that power and institutions operate, as well as of calls for social change that emphasize individual action rather than broader structural change. In her essay she questions the capitalist systems and workplaces that uphold and mask many inequalities. Moreover, hooks is wary about a racially and economically privileged woman who seemingly represents feminism so broadly and publically. This has been a long-standing tension in contemporary feminist discourse. For many feminists such as hooks, promulgating a feminism that is not inclusive is dangerous, and sustains the racial and gender hierarchies that many feminists wish to dismantle. In some ways, they fundamentally disagree about feminism. In other ways, they are speaking two totally different languages.

*Lean In* ultimately drove conversations about women in the workplace to an unprecedented level and galvanized attention and awareness of gender inequality in a way that really had not happened before. Because of Sandberg's high profile and vast reach, she was able to normalize and encourage conversations about gender in settings that had previously been uninterested at best, or hostile at least to topics of feminism. Her book was very clearly written for professional or corporate audiences of women in the US who are statistically more likely to be white than any other race. That said, because of the massive attention to *Lean In,* Sandberg became a famous representative of feminism at the time. Whatever you think of Sandberg's argument, due both to the book's content and to the subsequent debates and conversations in feminist communities, we cannot deny its importance in the evolution of contemporary feminism.

The Sandberg and hooks story is but one example of a long history of these types of debates in feminism. While it is important to interrogate power and privilege in any movement, especially feminist, it is not particularly useful to police different forms of feminism, or have a barometer of what makes something "truly feminist." Rather, for our sake it is more productive to use these examples such as hooks and Sandberg to think about the complexities of feminism, the representatives of feminism, and the strands of feminism and issues of power and privilege in the movement.

**Reflection:** What do you think of Sandberg's and hooks' arguments? Have you heard these arguments before? Do you know of anyone who might be considered a feminist role model?

## Pathways to Feminism

Individuals come to identify as feminist and participate in the feminist movement in a variety of ways, although they follow some main pathways. One is through personal experiences, such as encountering or observing injustice, such as sexism, racism, ableism, transphobia or homophobia. Having first-hand experience with injustice is an important foundation and driver to embracing a feminist identity. The second is through relationships, often with mothers, grandmothers, sisters, teachers, or friends who identify as feminists and who speak about the importance of identifying as a feminist. The third is through information, such as reading about feminism in school or outside of school, seeing feminists or feminism in the news, or following feminists and feminist accounts on social media. Social media has broadened on and offline feminist communities and expanded the circulation of feminist knowledge, important avenues to feminist identities. (Crossley, 2017)

**Ableism:** discrimination, prejudice, and social bias against individuals with disabilities.

Context and community are pivotal in terms of one adopting a feminist identity. There are some contexts and communities in which feminism is not accepted, or in which there is a negative perception of feminism. When feminism is seen as anti-men rather than pro-equality, for example, feminism is stigmatized. Sometimes, when an individual is in a community with few people who outwardly define themselves as feminists, it may be difficult to learn about feminism, understand feminism, or aspire to identify as feminist. In other communities or settings in which there are girls' empowerment groups or leadership opportunities for women and girls, it is more common and less of a leap to identify as a feminist.

## Men and Feminism

Many people ask "what is the role of men in the feminist movement?". Men have never been central to the feminist movement and the movement has historically been led by and guided by women-identified individuals. Although one study found that 40 percent of US men identify as feminist, only 9 percent say "feminist" describes them "very well", and 31 percent "somewhat well" (Pew Research Center, 2020). Men do not have the same perspective on gender inequality as women: research has found that men have a harder time identifying gender inequality and that they are less likely than women to believe that instances of sexism are serious (Drury and Kaiser, 2014).

Because feminism requires reorganizing, or at least questioning, gender hierarchies that place men at the top, men may neither recognize nor have a vested interest in confronting the structures that bestow privilege onto them. At the same time, when men confront or address sexism, they are taken more seriously than women because they are advocating for a group other than themselves (Drury and Kaiser, 2014). Moreover, there are fewer negative consequences for men who espouse feminist beliefs. While women are seen as complainers when confronting sexism, men are less so (ibid, 642).

There are certainly men who identify as feminist and who advance feminist movements. One challenge to men's effective involvement in feminism is the danger in replicating gendered hierarchies within a movement. Men might be paternalistic, or even man-splainers. In other words, men may recreate the inequalities that they are also trying to combat.

**What is a man-splainer?** It is a derivative of the word "explain" and refers to when a man explains something to a woman in a patronizing, dismissive, or condescending way. This happens in many settings. One very clear and insulting example is when a man incorrectly assumes that the woman he is speaking to doesn't know anything about a topic, when in fact she does.

Because feminism seeks to disrupt the power hierarchy of male privilege that generally centers men and marginalizes women, trans people, and gender expansive people, men may also feel neutrality at best or animosity at worst toward feminists and feminism. Feminists are not inherently anti-men. Lifting up one group (women) does not necessarily have to be at the expense of another group (men), although the success of feminism does mean that men would have to share the spotlight, power, and control with women. Moreover, as patriarchy perpetuates many harmful and unrealistic expectations of men, a feminist dismantling of these gendered expectations could also benefit men. Some attributes that men are socialized to have can ultimately be detrimental to them, such as hiding their emotions, or being solitary, strong, and stoic. An intersectional perspective reminds us that the rewards and penalties for adhering to or disrupting expected notions of gendered behavior will vary according to one's identities. To the extent that feminism seeks to question and dismantle rigid gender expectations, it could benefit all people, in addition to the fact that a world that is more equal would be better for all.

## Trans-inclusive Feminism

An intersectional feminist approach incorporates concerns of all women and gender marginalized people. Throughout history, there have certainly been a lot of trans-inclusive feminists. However, there are also feminists who have marginalized or sought to exclude transgender individuals. In the 1980s and 1990s there were debates about whether or how to include transgender women in "women only" organizations, spaces, and festivals. This tension has been ongoing, and was a precursor to the current strain of feminists known as "TERFS" (trans-exclusive radical feminists), who wish to exclude transgender women from feminism with the claim that only cisgender women are women (Butler, 2024). These transphobic organizers, predominantly in Britain, engage in their activism online and in-person, deriding transgender women with transphobic remarks. While these so-called "TERFS" are not feminist based on this book's definition of feminism, and are a fringe group, they have gained traction and following particularly in online settings. Notwithstanding, intersectional feminism is inclusive of concerns and lives of trans individuals.

> **Transgender:** term for those whose gender identity differs from that associated with the sex assigned to them at birth, determined by their biological or physical characteristics.
> Many US feminist groups believe in and work for the inclusion of all trans and gender non-binary individuals. Most national feminist groups, like the National Organization of Women, Planned Parenthood, National Black Women's Justice Institute, and National Women's Law Center, have explicitly stated that they are trans-inclusive.

## Global Feminisms

Feminism is practiced across the world, and is certainly a global movement. Even within a US focused analysis of feminism, it is important to also understand feminisms in different parts of the world. Moreover, the US certainly does not exist in a vacuum, and many policies of and approaches to global relations by the US impact inequalities in other countries. 59 percent of men and women in a large global study agree very much or somewhat that they identify as feminist (Ipsos, 2017). While different geographical, national, and political contexts shape feminisms, there are dominant themes in global feminisms. These include environmental health (safe drinking water, clean air, climate change); economic freedom; safety (i.e. war/militarism, gender-based violence); and political representation/leadership.

Feminists across the world organize on the ground with other feminists in their own national contexts. For example, feminists in Mexico and across Latin America have recently protested high rates of femicide (killing of women) and the government's failure to protect women in their countries and communities (Miller, 2022). Feminists have a long history of protesting and organizing against war. In Russia, feminists mobilized against Putin and his invasion of Ukraine. Russian feminists wrote an article for *Jacobin* (2022) linking feminism to anti-war struggles: "Feminism as a political force cannot be on the side of a war of aggression and military occupation. The feminist movement in Russia struggles for vulnerable groups and the development of a just society with equal opportunities and prospects, in which there can be no place for violence and military conflicts" and "war exacerbates gender inequality and sets back gains for human rights by many years." Across Russia, feminists have staged anti-war protests (*The Moscow Times*, 2022).

One major opportunity for global feminisms is International Women's Day, which occurs on March 8 every year. Across the world, feminists both celebrate their communities and protest injustices. Examples include: women in Turkey protesting withdrawal from the Istanbul convention, women in Myanmar protesting the military coup, women in Nigeria protesting the government's failure to pass bills protecting women, women in South Korea protesting the wage gap (Owen, 2022). These examples show that despite contextual differences, many experiences with inequality are shared by women across the world.

Since the 1980s, there has been a long track record of Transnational feminist networking (TFNs). Defined as "groups of women's rights advocates from three or more countries who mobilize and coalesce around a common set of grievances and goals"

(Moghadam, 2021), TFNs grew with the prioritization of women's rights in the UN and other international women's groups. In addition to being global in focus, TFNs can also be regional in nature, such as those organized across countries in Latin America or sub-Saharan Africa (Moghadam, 2021). Ongoing concerns of TFNs include the consequences of globalization, climate change, militarism, and lack of women representation in government and politics, all of which feminists worldwide are organizing against.

**Research Reflection:** The #MeToo movement and its focus on gender-based violence, sexual harassment, and sexual assault resonated with women across the world. It was adapted within occupational, national, religious, or political contexts. Research international and transnational #MeToo campaigns such as: #MosqueMeToo, #BalanceTonPorc, #YoTambién, #Quella-VoltaChe (Ghadery, 2019). What are their main concerns? How are they similar to and different from each other?

Transnational feminist networks have been established and developed over generations (Rupp, 1997) and feminists communicated by letter writing, faxes, and other modes of communication. Online feminisms have allowed feminists across the world to connect in ways they couldn't previously, although access to the Internet remains unavailable and challenging for many women in the US and abroad as a result of cost, hardware availability, and lack of infrastructure. For those who do have access to the Internet, it allows feminists to connect with each other, learn from one another, and create organizations in some cases.

## Chapter 1 Mini Toolkit: #SayHerName

Police violence and brutality are epidemics, mainly affecting Black communities. With the murders of Michael Brown in 2014 and George Floyd in 2020, the country experienced racial reckonings that spurred protests and mass mobilization. But what you might not have known is that police brutality against Black men gets much more attention (disproportionate to statistics about incidents) than police brutality against Black women and gender non-conforming Black individuals. According to a YWCA report (2020), Black women and girls are 13 percent of the population (U.S. Census Bureau, 2019), but 19 percent of those shot by police from January 1, 2015 to June 20, 2020 (Fatal Force, 2020). Transgender people of color were six times more likely to experience physical violence by police compared to white cisgender people (National Coalition of Anti-Violence Programs, 2013).

The collective erasure of this violence against Black women and gender non-confirming individuals overlooks, silences and makes invisible their experiences, and all but cancels their existence. These sorts of messages teach us whose lives are valued and whose are not. They also erase any opportunity to mourn the lives of these women that are tragically cut short (Khaleeli, 2016).

In 2014 Kimberlé Crenshaw, the law professor who developed the term "intersectionality", along with collaborators from African American Policy Forum (AAPF) and the Center for Intersectionality and Social Policy Studies (CISPS), started an online campaign called #SayHerName (Crenshaw and African American Policy Forum, 2023). In 2015 the AAPF and CISPS, with Andrea Ritchie, published a report, "Say Her Name: Resisting Police Brutality Against Black Women", discussing the goals for the movement. The movement is a call to action, for us to say the names of the women who have been victims of police brutality. As much as "George", "Freddie", and "Michael" are shorthand for police brutality, so too should be "Breonna," "Sandra," and "Reika." By imploring all of us on social media to draw attention to the Black women who have been killed, Crenshaw and her collaborators created an intersectional feminist campaign to change the way society sees the problem of police violence, at the same time uplifting Black women. This reflects the argument of the Combahee River Collective (1977), which is that if Black women are free, everyone is free because all systems of oppression would be eliminated.

To get involved and to learn more about #SayHerName:

- #SayHerName: Black Women's Stories of Police Violence and Public Silence (Crenshaw and African American Policy Forum, 2023)
- #SayHerName: why Kimberlé Crenshaw is fighting for forgotten women (Khaleeli, 2016, *The Guardian*)

- The urgency of intersectionality, Kimberlé Crenshaw (TED TALKS, Crenshaw, 2016)
- Incite! Toolkit
- Search #SayHerName on social media

## Chapter 1 Dive Deeper

*Feminism is for Everybody* (bell hooks)
*Pleasure Activism: The Politics of Feeling Good (Emergent Strategy, 1)* (adrienne maree brown)
*Women, Culture and Politics* (Angela Davis)
*Bad Feminist: Essays* (Roxane Gay)
*Gender Outlaw: On Men, Women, and the Rest of Us* (Kate Bornstein)
*The Oppositional Gaze: Black Female Spectators* (bell hooks)
*#SayHerName: a case study of intersectional social media activism* (Melissa Brown, Rashawn Ray, Ed Summers and Neil Fraistat)
*Feminist Theory: From Margin to Center* (bell hooks)
*Black Feminist Thought in the Matrix of Domination* (Patricia Hill Collins)
*Age, Race, Class, and Sex: Women Redefining Difference* (Audre Lorde)

## References

Ahmed, S. & Gorey, K.M. (2023) Employment discrimination faced by Muslim women wearing the hijab: exploratory meta-analysis, *Journal of Ethnic & Cultural Diversity in Social Work*, 32(3), 115–123. doi:10.1080/15313204.2020.1870601.

Barroso, A. (2020). "61% of U.S. women say 'feminist' describes them well; many see feminism as empowering, polarizing." www.pewresearch.org/short-reads/2020/07/07/61-of-u-s-women-say-feminist-describes-them-well-many-see-feminism-as-empowering-polarizing.

Brewer, R.M. (2020). Black Feminism and Womanism. In Naples, N. (Ed.), *Companion to Feminist Studies Feminist Epistemology and Its Discontents* (pp. 91–104). Wiley Online Books. doi:10.1002/9781119314967.ch6.

brown, a.m. (2019). *Pleasure activism: The Politics of Feeling Good (Emergent Strategy, 1)*. AK Press.

Brown, M., Ray, R., Summers, E., & Fraistat, N. (2017). #SayHerName: A case study of intersectional social media activism. *Ethnic and Racial Studies*, 40(11), 1831–1846. doi:10.1080/01419870.2017.1334934.

Buchanan, N.T., Settles, I.H., Wu, I.H.C., & Hayashino, D.S. (2018). Sexual Harassment, Racial Harassment, and Well-being among Asian American Women: An Intersectional Approach. *Women and Therapy.* doi:10.1080/02703149.2018.1425030.

Butler, J. (2024). *Who's Afraid of Gender?* Macmillan.

California Coalition Against Sexual Assault (CALCASA). (2017). Ending Sexual Violence: An Intersectional Approach [Toolkit]. www.calcasa. org/wp-content/uploads/2017/03/SAAM-2017-reduced-size-edited.pdf.

Cantalupo, N.C. (2019). And even more of us are brave: intersectionality & sexual harassment of women students of color. *Harvard Journal of Law and Gender*, 42(1), 1–81. https://ssrn.com/abstract=3168909.

Charan, M.L. (2022). Predictors of feminist identity utilizing an intersectional lens with a focus on non-Hispanic white, Hispanic, and African American MSW students. *Affilia*, 37(1), 97–117. doi:10.1177/0886109920963013.

Combahee River Collective. (1977). The Combahee River Collective Statement. Retrieved November 8, 2023, from https://www.loc.gov/item/lcwaN0028151/.

Connell, R. (2005). *Masculinities* (2nd ed.). Routledge. doi:10.4324/9781003116479.

Cole, E.R. & Zucker, A.N. (2007). Black and white women's perspectives on femininity. *Cultural Diversity and Ethnic Minority Psychology*, 13(1), 1–9. doi:10.1037/1099-9809.13.1.1.

Cole, E.R. & Duncan, L.E. (2023). Better policy interventions through intersectionality. *Social Issues and Policy Review*, 17, 62–78. doi:10.1111/sipr.12090.

Crenshaw, K. (1989). Demarginalizing the Intersection of Race and Sex: A Black Feminist Critique of Antidiscrimination Doctrine, Feminist Theory and Antiracist Politics. *University of Chicago Legal Forum* Iss. 1, Article 8.

Crenshaw, K. (2016). The urgency of intersectionality [Video]. TED Talks. www.ted.com/talks/kimberle_crenshaw_the_urgency_of_intersectionality.

Crenshaw, K. & African American Policy Forum. (2023). *#SayHerName: Black Women's Stories of Police Violence and Public Silence*. Chicago, IL: Haymarket.

Crenshaw, K.W. & Ritchie, A.J. (2015). Say Her Name: Resisting Police Brutality Against Black Women. From www.aapf.org/_files/ugd/62e126_9223ee35c2694ac3bd3f2171504ca3f7.pdf.

Crossley, A.D. (2017). *Finding Feminism: Millennial Activists and the Unfinished Gender Revolution*. NYU Press. doi:10.2307/j.ctt1ggjjdg.

Davis, A. (1989). *Women, Culture and Politics*. Vintage Books.

Davis, A. (2019, August 5). Oral History Interview. National Museum of African American History and Culture. Retrieved November 7, 2018, from https://nmaahc.si.edu/explore/stories/revolutionary-practice-black-feminisms.

Demby, G. (2017, April 13). What We Know (And Don't Know) About 'Missing White Women Syndrome'. *NPR*. Retrieved November 10, 2023, from www.npr.org/sections/codeswitch/2017/04/13/523769303/what-we-know-and-dont-know-about-missing-white-women-syndrome.

Drury, B.J. & Kaiser, C.R. (2014). Allies against Sexism: The Role of Men in Confronting Sexism. *Journal of Social Issues*, 70, 637–652. doi:10.1111/josi.12083.

Evangelist, M. (2022). Narrowing Racial Differences in Trust: How Discrimination Shapes Trust in a Racialized Society. *Social Problems*, 69(4), 1109–1136. doi:10.1093/socpro/spab011.

*Fatal Force: Police shootings database*. (2020, January 22). From www.washingtonpost.com/graphics/investigations/police-shootings-database.

Feminist Anti-War Resistance. (2022, February 27). Russia's Feminists Are in the Streets Protesting Putin's War. *Jacobin*. Retrieved November 8, 2023, https://jacobin.com/2022/02/russian-feminist-antiwar-resistance-ukraine-putin.

Frye, J. (2017, November 20). Not Just the Rich and Famous: The Pervasiveness of Sexual Harassment Across Industries Affects All Workers. *American Progress*. Retrieved November 9, 2023 from www.americanprogress.org/article/not-just-rich-famous.

Gay, R. (2014). *Bad Feminist: Essays*. Harper Perennial.

GenForward. (May, 2018). Data—Gender & Sexuality (May 2018). Retrieved November 1, 2023 from https://genforwardsurvey.com/2018/06/01/gender-sexuality/?question=Q32.

Ghadery, F. (2019). #Metoo—Has the 'sisterhood' finally become global or just another product of neoliberal feminism? *Transnational Legal Theory*, 10(2), 252–274. doi:10.1080/20414005.2019.1630169.

Giddings, P. (1984). *When and Where I Enter: The Impact of Black Women on Race and Sex in America*. New York: Bantam Books.

Gross, J. (2014, July 25). Roxane Gay's 'Bad' Feminism. *The New York Times Magazine*, [Talk]. Retrieved November 8, 2023, from www.nytimes.com/2014/07/27/magazine/roxane-gays-bad-feminism.html.

Hall, L.K. (2009). Navigating Our Own "Sea of Islands": Remapping a Theoretical Space for Hawaiian Women and Indigenous Feminism. *Wicazo Sa Review*, 24(2), 15–38. www.jstor.org/stable/40587779.

Harper, S. Gover, A., & Mages, I. (2021). Interactions between law enforcement and women of color at high-risk of lethal intimate partner violence: An application of interpersonal justice theory. *Criminal Justice Studies*, 34(3), 268–288. doi:10.1080/1478601X.2021.1965286.

Hill Collins, P. (1990). Black feminist thought in the matrix of domination. In P.H. Collins (Ed.), *Black Feminist Thought: Knowledge, Consciousness, and the Politics of Empowerment* (Vol. 21). Sage Publishing.

hooks, b. (1984). *Feminist Theory: From Margin to Center.* Pluto Press.

hooks, b. (2013, October 28). Dig deep: Beyond Lean In. *The Feminist Wire.* Retrieved November 1, 2023, from https://thefeministwire.com/2013/10/17973.

Horowitz, J.M. & Igielnik, R. (2020). A Century After Women Gained the Right To Vote, Majority of Americans See Work To Do on Gender Equality. *Pew.* From www.pewresearch.org/social-trends/2020/07/07/a-century-after-women-gained-the-right-to-vote-majority-of-americans-see-work-to-do-on-gender-equality.

Horowitz, J.M., Brown, A., & Cox, K. (2019). Race in America 2019. *Pew.* From https://www.pewresearch.org/social-trends/2019/04/09/race-in-america-2019.

Hurwitz, H.M.K. (2020). *Are we the 99%?: the occupy movement feminism and intersectionality.* Temple University Press.

Ipsos. (2017). Feminism and Gender Equality Around the World. Retrieved November 1, 2023, from www.ipsos.com/sites/default/files/2017-03/global-advisor-feminism-charts-2017.pdf.

Kearl, H., Johnson, N.E., & Raj, A. (2019). Measuring #MeToo: A National Study on Sexual Harassment and Assault. From https://stopstreetharassment.org/wp-content/uploads/2012/08/2019-MeToo-National-Sexual-Harassment-and-Assault-Report.pdf.

Kelly, M. & Gauchat, G. (2016). Feminist Identity, Feminist Politics: U.S. Feminists' Attitudes toward Social Policies. *Sociological Perspectives*, 59 (4), 855–872. doi:10.1177/0731121415594281.

Khaleeli, H. (2016, May 30). #SayHerName: Why Kimberlé Crenshaw is Fighting for Forgotten Women. *The Guardian.* Retrieved November 8, 2023, from www.theguardian.com/lifeandstyle/2016/may/30/sayhername-why-kimberle-crenshaw-is-fighting-for-forgotten-women.

Lorde, A. (2021). Age, Race, class, and sex: women redefining difference. In Routledge eBooks (pp. 191–198). doi:10.4324/9780429038556-22.

Miller, L. (2022, March 8). Thousands of feminists march in Mexico City: 'I am scared to simply be a woman in Mexico'. *Los Angeles Times.* Retrieved November 8, 2023, from www.latimes.com/world-nation/story/2022-03-08/mexico-womens-day-protest#:~:text=%E2%80%9CI%20am%20scared%20to%20go,be%20a%20woman%20in%20Mexico.%E2%80%9D&text=Leslie%20Garin%2C%20a%2025%2Dyear,her%20boyfriend%20several%20years%20ago.

Moghadam, V.M. (2021, April 21). Transnational Feminist Networks and Contemporary Crises. *E-International Relations.* Retrieved November 8,

2023, from www.e-ir.info/2021/04/06/transnational-feminist-networks-a
nd-contemporary-crises.

Montoya, C. (2020). Intersectionality and voting rights. *PS: Political Science & Politics*, 53(3), 484–489. doi:10.1017/S104909652000030X.

Moraga, C. and Anzaldúa, G. (1981). *This Bridge Called My Back: Writings By Radical Women of Color*. Watertown, MA: Persephone Press.

*The Moscow Times*. (2022). Russian Feminists Stage Anti-War Protests in 100 Cities. From www.themoscowtimes.com/2022/03/09/russian-fem inists-stage-anti-war-protests-in-100-cities-a76832.

National Coalition of Anti-Violence Programs. (2013). Lesbian, Gay, Bisexual, Transgender, Queer, and HIV-Affected Hate Violence in 2013 [Report]. http s://avp.org/wp-content/uploads/2017/04/2013_ncavp_hvreport_final.pdf.

National Crime Information Center. (2021). 2020 NCIC Missing Person and Unidentified Person Statistics. Retrieved November 10, 2023, from www.fbi.gov/file-repository/2020-ncic-missing-person-and-unidentified-p erson-statistics.pdf/view.

Newman, J. (2018). 'Lean In:' Five Years Later. *The New York Times*, March 16.

Nielsen, C. (2021, November 21). Women of Color and the Wage Gap. *American Progress*. Retrieved November 10, 2023, from www.americanp rogress.org/article/women-of-color-and-the-wage-gap.

Owens, L. (2022, March 9). International Women's Day: From celebrations to anti-war protests. *BBC News*. Retrieved November 10, 2023, from www.bbc.com/news/world-60677051.

Patrón, O.E. (2021) 'That hat means a lot more than a hat for some of us': Gay Latino collegians in the era of Trump. *Race Ethnicity and Education*, 24(6), 737–754. doi:10.1080/13613324.2021.1924135.

Page, K.V., Cerezo, A., & Ross, A. (2022). Creating space for ourselves: Black sexual minority women and gender diverse individuals countering anti-Black racism and heterosexism. *Psychology of Sexual Orientation and Gender Diversity*, 9(2), 131–140.

Pruitt-Young, S. (2021). Tens Of Thousands Of Black Women Vanish Each Year. This Website Tells Their Stories. *NPR*. From www.npr.org/2021/ 09/24/1040048967/missing-black-women-girls-left-out-media-ignored.

Ritchie, A.J. (2017). *Invisible no more: police violence against Black women and women of color*. Beacon Press.

Robnett, R.D. & Anderson, K.J. (2017). Feminist identity among women and men from four ethnic groups. *Cultural Diversity and Ethnic Minority Psychology*, 23(1), 134–142. doi:10.1037/cdp0000095.

Roth, B. (2004). *Separate Roads to Feminism: Black, Chicana, and White Feminist Movements in America's Second Wave*. Cambridge University Press. doi:10.1017/CBO9780511815201.

Rupp, L.J. (1997) *Worlds of women: the making of an international women's movement.* Princeton University Press.

Slakoff, D.C. & Fradella, H.F. (2019). Media messages surrounding missing women and girls: The "missing white woman syndrome" and other factors that influence newsworthiness. *Criminology, Crim. Just. L & Society*, 20(3), 80–102.

Smith, B. (1980). Racism and Women's Studies. *Frontiers: A Journal of Women's Studies*, 5(1),48–49.

Tester, G. (2008). An Intersectional Analysis of Sexual Harassment in Housing. *Gender & Society*, 22(3), 349–366. doi:10.1177/0891243208317827.

*Taylor, V. & Whittier, N.E. (1992). Collective identity in social movement communities: Lesbian feminist mobilization. In A.D. Morris & C.M. Mueller (Eds), Frontiers in social movement theory (pp. 104–129). Yale University Press.*

Thwaites, R. (2016). Making a choice or taking a stand? Choice feminism, political engagement and the contemporary feminist movement. *Feminist Theory*, 18(1), 55–68. doi:10.1177/1464700116683657.

Tilly, C. (1998). *Durable inequality.* University of California Press.

Uggen, C. & Blackstone, A. (2004). Sexual Harassment as a Gendered Expression of Power. *American Sociological Review*, 69(1), 64–92. www.jstor.org/stable/3593075.

U.S. Census Bureau. (2019). Annual Estimates of the Resident Population by Sex, Race, and Hispanic Origin for the United States, States, and Counties: April 1, 2010 to July 1, 2018.

World Economic Forum. (2021, September). Reflecting society: the state of diverse representation in media and entertainment. Retrieved November 8, 2023, from www3.weforum.org/docs/WEF_The_State_of_Diverse_Rep resentation_in_Media_and_Entertainment_2021.pdf.

YWCA. (2020, September). We Still Deserve Safety: Renewing the Call to End the Criminalization of Women and Girls of Color. From https://static1.squa respace.com/static/64d2df2225d0880d22000dca/t/6554edd763ed4d3925d28cf 4/1700064728876/20200909-WeStillDeserveSafety-FINALREPORT.pdf.

# 2  Varieties of Feminisms

Feminism is a singular social movement, although it takes many forms. In this chapter, you will learn about the varieties of feminisms that drive the movement. These include feminisms that serve different populations and communities of women, some with differing aims and objectives. As you will see, there is considerable overlap in many of these feminisms. Strands of feminism included in this chapter have defined the movement: Women of Color feminism, Black feminism, Asian American feminism, Chicana feminism, Indigenous feminism, and lesbian, queer and trans feminism. There are many more types of feminisms that could be addressed (e.g. ecofeminism, abolitionist feminism, Marxist feminism). All of these feminisms have transformed communities and our overall society, and have collectively created what we know as the feminist movement.

This chapter also highlights the scholars, activists, and organizations that have made the movement what it is, such as Cherríe Moraga, Patricia Hill Collins, the Combahee River Collective, and the Asian American Feminist Collective. You will also learn about how feminisms influence each other, and affect or are affected by other movements. The most important takeaway of this chapter is that while there are many different types of feminisms that develop and operate separately, at the same time, they are all interconnected. Feminism is made up of different streams that are flowing side-by-side, currents that are moving in many ways harmoniously with common goals, but sometimes not, yet always being subjected to external forces.

DOI: 10.4324/9781003310990-3

Key terms presented in this chapter:

- Feminist emergence: when and how particular feminist movements arise, and what factors contribute to their successes and challenges
- Feminist coalitions: groups that form as a result of having common complaints or grievances
- Whitewashing: Painting the feminist movement as a majority white movement, excluding the contributions of feminists of color

## Women of Color Feminisms

Women of Color feminisms in the US is an umbrella term encompassing Black, Asian American, Chicana and Indigenous women, and anyone who identifies as non-white. The key unifying theme of Women of Color feminisms is fighting against the wide-ranging consequences of white supremacist capitalist patriarchy (hooks 2000, p. 109). While Women of Color is an identity category, feminist scholars also consider Women of Color to be a unifying entity or ethos that centers the connections between women of different races and ethnicities and the intersectional inequalities that bind them together (Taylor, 2020; Sandoval, 2000; Mohanty, 2003). Although there is certainly vast variation of experiences among Women of Color, owing to the common experiences of living in a white supremacist society, Women of Color experience similarities that generate solidarity, coalitions, and overlapping organizing. This has been true for at least 50 years of contemporary feminist activism. While the term Women of Color feminism accurately reflects, for many women, the connections between Women of Color in a heteropatriarchal society, others might find it too universal a term, not allowing for a recognition of the uniqueness of each group's experiences.

Feminist coalitions occur when feminists of different organizations, backgrounds, or approaches to social action, come together to make change either for a limited campaign or more prolonged organizing. Women of Color are primed to be coalitional in nature because of the wide spectrum of women under the Women of Color umbrella, the political nature of the term, and also "because they belong to multiple oppressed communities" (Cole & Luna, 2010, p.

74; Taylor, 2022). The Third World Women's Alliance (TWWA), for example, was a US-based feminist coalition of many feminist organizations, who fought for the liberation of all Women of Color from 1968 until 1980.

Recognizing the oppressive nature of colonialism, capitalism, imperialism, and the ways in which they disproportionately affect Women of Color, the TWWA identified these patterns of inequalities and, while primarily US-based, joined with feminists in Latin America, Asia, Africa, and the Middle East (Fujiwara, 2022). They were nothing if not intersectional. For example, in the archives of its Bay Area Chapter, founded in 1971, organizing themes included: "solidarity with working class people" (Sophia Smith Collection, 1974–75), labor, and immigration (Sophia Smith Collection, n.d.).

In the US, one of the defining texts of Women of Color feminism is *This Bridge Called my Back: Writing by Radical Women of Color* edited by Cherríe Moraga and Gloria Anzaldúa. This book was groundbreaking, and continues to be powerful. It was the first anthology written exclusively by Women of Color published in the US, and its emphasis on feminisms' role in dismantling broad structural forces redirected and forever impacted the trajectory of the feminist movement writ large. Moraga calls Women of Color feminism "a political practice that is shaped first from the specific economic conditions and the cultural context of our own land-base…" (Moraga and Anzaldúa, 1983, p. xx). *This Bridge Called my Back* got its title from a poem called "Bridge" included in the anthology, in which Black queer poet Donna Kate Rushin outlines the numerous ways in which she is asked to be a bridge between multiple communities, a bridge that requires explaining her experiences and perspectives, and even educating white feminists and others about oppression. This is the "bridge" work that feminists of color are pressured to do by white feminists and by the world at large, which inevitably leads to frustration and anger. Much of the anthology *This Bridge Called my Back* draws on the experiences of Women of Color feminists in their own ethnic and racial communities, as well as within white feminist communities.

*This Bridge Called my Back* was one of the earliest tangible applications of intersectionality. Through poetry and writing, Women of Color shared political views, personal experiences with feminism and inequalities, and visions for the future. The entire anthology of *This Bridge* explicitly addresses the racism within the feminist movement, and the consequences for interlocking experiences of oppression to Women of Color.

Following in this collaborative tradition, one recent intersectional and grassroots organization that convenes Women of Color is Sister Diaspora for Liberation, which creates community and solidarity among Women of Color predominantly in the New York City area. As a collective, they focus on political liberation and holistic health, and provide opportunities for community-building through art and writing. One way they do this is to support a reading group that features books by Black, Indigenous, and Women of Color authors. They organize to realize their goals both in-person and online.

## The Emergence of Black, Indigenous, Asian American, and Chicana Feminisms

Black, Indigenous, Asian American and Chicana feminisms have all accomplished substantive feminist change. Their origins have been analyzed to shed light on how feminisms have developed differently and similarly in varying contexts.

In her book *Separate Roads to Feminism* (2004), Benita Roth examines Black, Chicana and white feminisms in the 1970s in the US. Each emerged separately and had its own sources of grievances and mobilization, with different relationships with the larger movements (Chicano movement, Civil Rights movement, white left movement). Each of these feminisms had different priorities, with complex negotiations and relationships around fighting for the advancement of their larger movement goals, and for the advancement of women in their communities. Thus, this resulted in three organizationally distinct feminisms. Through these cases, we can see the tensions as well as harmonies between anti-racist and feminist work, and between different forms of feminisms.

While there are significant differences between strands of feminists, scholars have also written about the similarities. For example, García (1989) stated that:

> "Chicana, Black, and Asian American feminists were all confronted with the issue of engaging in a feminist struggle to end

sexist oppression within a broader nationalist struggle to end racist oppression. All experienced male domination in their own communities as well as in the larger society."

(p. 220)

As a result, feminists were in many ways unified by experiencing and challenging sexism and racism. However, exactly how to advance feminist goals within their own communities was dependent on the unique interplay between racial and gender dynamics in that context.

While the fine points of this debate are interesting pertaining to intra-movement dynamics, we do know without a doubt that these different forms of feminisms influenced each other, pushed the movement forward, and experienced setbacks and success in both separate and united ways. One of the most important takeaways related to the emergence and sustaining of all forms of feminism is the plurality of the movement.

Studies of 1960s and 1970s feminism reveal the strongest attribute of the movement: the multiplicity of feminisms. Writes Benita Roth (2004):

"When the second wave of feminism is seen as feminisms, the audacity of all feminists who challenged the status quo from wherever they were situated is recaptured and highlighted, and we are forced to recognize the power of feminist visions."

(p. 215)

Much has been written about the sexism in large mixed-gender movements. Women faced gender inequality in civil rights movements (Robnett, 2000), Chicana nationalist movements, environmental movements, peace movements, and others. More recent scholarship has found that movements such as Occupy Wall Street and #BlackLivesMatter have also marginalized women (Hurwitz, 2020; Brown et al., 2017). This has removed gender equality from the agenda of many social movements, with arguments made that there are bigger fights to be had, that gender equality is unimportant, or that issues of gender inequality are just not a priority in the overall arc of social justice.

While this was certainly infuriating to activists, any social movement working to upend the status quo will expect resistance from all angles. Engrained inequalities in their larger communities certainly challenged their efforts. Nonetheless, it is surprising that social movements and movements for social justice are themselves sites for inequalities. It is important to understand, then, the ways in which women were confronting inequalities on a number of different fronts as they organized as feminists.

## Black Feminism

Black feminism centers Black people, with an emphasis on women and those of marginalized genders. In its efforts to dismantle the white supremacist, capitalist, patriarchy (hooks, 1981), Black feminism is intersectional. Black feminism drives many different forms of social justice work and social change activities, and also informs intellectual endeavors, art, and creative pursuits (Brown, 2022). When, in the 1960s and 1970s, Black women were marginalized in civil rights and Black power movement organizing, along with historic and ongoing exclusion from white feminist communities, Black feminism proliferated and thrived.

One of the most well-known Black feminists organizations is the Combahee River Collective, founded in 1974 in Boston, Massachusetts by Barbara Smith, Beverly Smith, Demita Frazier, Cheryl Clarke, Akasha Hull, Margo Okazawa-Rey, Chirlane McCray, and Audre Lorde. They were among the first to theorize intersectionality, pointing out how intersecting inequalities shape Black women's experiences. In 1977 they wrote: "We are actively committed to struggling against racial, sexual, heterosexual, and class oppression, and see as our particular task the development of integrated analysis and practice based upon the fact that the major systems of oppression are interlocking" (p. 15). The Combahee River Collective was founded as a "radical alternative" to the National Black Feminist Organization (NBFO) (Taylor, 2017, p. 4). The NBFO was founded in August 1973 "because of sexism in the Black Power movement and racism in the women's liberation movement" (Taylor, 1998, p. 19).

Black feminists faced challenges similar to many feminists of color. They had to work to carve out spaces of their own within a broader feminist movement, as they dealt with "[t]he problem of balancing the genuine concerns of black women against continual pressures to absorb and recast such interests within white feminist frameworks" (Collins, 1996, p. 14). Other challenges to Black feminist organizing identified by the Combahee River Collective include navigating the boundary between supporting/investing in one's community and racial group, and desiring to change the gendered power structure, while coming to grips with some Black men's negative reaction to feminism (Combahee River Collective, 1977). As Patricia Hill Collins writes (1996), even naming Black feminism calls attention to the racism in the feminist movement and to the significance of Black women in feminism.

When Black feminism first emerged, primary grievances were: "Sterilization, abuse, abortion rights, battered women, rape and health care" (Combahee River Collective, 1977). The practice of forced sterilization of Women of Color and disabled women ravaged and traumatized Women of Color at the time, particularly in prisons and welfare systems, and was linked to the lack of bodily autonomy that has long plagued them (Roberts, 1998). Echoing the Combahee's statement, at the first NBFO conference in 1973, feminists discussed "employment, childcare, lesbianism, welfare, sexuality, media image, incarceration, addiction, and the relation of black women to one another and to the women's rights movement" (Taylor, 1998, p. 20). Many of these remain priorities today and continue to be defining features of Black feminism, although the grievances have expanded to meet the changing nature of our communities.

Although Black feminism has evolved over time, there have been some overarching topics that activists have addressed. Because of the intersection of racism and sexism in the healthcare field, Black feminists have always focused on improving Black women's health and healthcare, particularly around reproductive justice (Ross, 2006). For over 40 years the National Black Women's Health Project (now known as the Black Women's Health Imperative) has worked to destigmatize many health topics, including birth control and abortion. It provides health care services to Black women, even training doulas, professionals who care for and guide persons giving birth. The organization was an early advocate of HIV prevention. It now emphasizes the full spectrum of women's mental, reproductive, and general physical health. Black women's health organizations abound, including Sisters Network (for Black women experiencing breast cancer) and Sad Girls Club (for Black women's and girls' mental health).

## Spotlight on an Organization

Black Mamas Matter Alliance is an organization that seeks to change policy, drive research, and foster collaborative conversations about Black motherhood and maternal health. Informed by many principles of Black feminism, this organization addresses the white supremacy of the healthcare field. It also celebrates and honors the dignity and humanity of Black women. Their tactics include social media toolkits and in-person and virtual gatherings.

Much of Black feminism of the 1970s and beyond has included if not centered queer and trans Black women, girls, and gender non-conforming individuals. As Dr. Treva Lindsey said: "One truth, especially within the context of black feminisms, is that queer black feminism has always been part of this. That queer black women, queer black folks have always been in these spaces" (Lindsey, 2019). People like Barbara Smith, Audre Lorde, and groups like the Combahee River Collective emphasized the importance of sexuality and inclusion in their Black lesbian feminist intersectional practices. More recently, building on this intersectional history, the term "Black queer feminism" has been used by activists and scholars such as Mecca Jamilah Sullivan (2019).

Black feminists have played a central role in Black resistance movements. However, in many cases their contributions and leadership have been dismissed. For example, while the Black Power movement is historically thought of as a masculine and man-led movement, historian Ashley Farmer (2017) finds an abundance of ways that Black women contributed to the successes and advancement of the Black Power movement. #Blacklivesmatter was founded by radical Black women Patrisse Cullors, Ayọ Tometi, and Alicia Garza, yet in many ways it was more attentive to the experiences of Black men and overlooked Black women who were also victims of police violence. These examples show how Black women have successfully organized for Black resistance, but have been eliminated from some of its histories and organizing.

In the past ten years, discrimination and violence against Black women, trans, and gender non-conforming individuals have escalated and drawn more attention and advocacy. To provide an example, Incite! is an organization of radical Women of Color working to "end state violence and violence in our homes and communities." Their work focuses on violence against trans people of color, as well as intersecting inequalities such as transphobia, racism, sexism, ableism, ageism, heterosexism, and colonialism. One approach they use is providing resources for organizers, which include guidance and frameworks for approaching intersectional issues like police violence, gender violence and race, and militarism.

While Black feminism is the main mode of feminist activism for Black women, other neighbors to Black feminists include Womanism (Brewer 2020). Womanism was initially coined by Alice Walker (1983), the author of *The Color Purple*, and it can be considered a sister to Black feminism. Layli Phillips (2006) defines womanism as: "a social change perspective rooted in Black women's and other women of color's everyday experiences and everyday methods of problem solving in everyday spaces, extended to the problem of ending all forms of oppression for all people..." (p. xx). Many Black feminist organizations, such as the Womanist Working Collective, use the word womanist to signal their orientation. The Black Women Radicals (n.d.) describe their work as "Rooted in intersectional and transnational feminisms and Womanisms." The term womanist does resonate with many women and its introduction was a decisive movement in the development of intersectionality and feminism. However, there is no consensus about the term and its relationship to feminism. Womanism may appropriately describe a person who resists the term feminist, owing to its association with whiteness, but still wants to embrace or connect with other women (Taylor, 2015). Research indicates that some Black women use the terms womanist and feminist interchangeably, while some prefer one or the other (Boisnier, 2003; White, 2006).

In the last twenty years, online feminism has been a major factor in the proliferation and development of Black feminist perspectives (see also Chapter 5 for a discussion about online feminisms). Online feminism has spread Black feminist thought far and wide. In many cases Black women and feminist commentary have been folded into mainstream news sources such as *The New York Times* (Roxane Gay, Tressie McMillan Cottom) or *Slate* (Jamilah Lemieux). Black feminists' intellectual production and activism has continued the tradition of Black women innovating digital and activist tools (Steele, 2021). Leading the conversations about digital technologies, intersectionality, and social change, Black feminists have also resisted online "misogynoir" (or, pernicious racism and sexism) (Bailey, 2021).

**Misogynoir:** refers to the discrimination directed specifically at Black women. Coined by scholar Moya Bailey (2021), the term combines "misogyny," which is the prejudice and oppression of women, with "noir," the French word for "black." This concept underscores the importance of recognizing that the oppression Black women experience is a result of sexism and racism.

The Crunk Feminist Collective blog was founded in 2010 by Women of Color. Crunk feminism, named after a Southern style of hip hop music, is an iteration of Joan Morgan's hip hop feminism (1999). The Collective's mission is to "create a space of support and camaraderie for hip hop generation feminists of color, queer and straight, in the academy and without, by building a rhetorical community, in which we can discuss our ideas, express our crunk feminist selves, fellowship with one another, debate and challenge one another, and support each other."

The collective was formed because as scholar-activists, its members felt that much was missing from their day-to-day academic conversations about topics of current interest, particularly pertaining to communities of color. They also wanted to elevate the voices and writing of Women of Color using feminist perspectives. In their mission statement on their website page (n.d.), they define their crunk feminism: "what others may call audacious and crazy, we call CRUNK because we are drunk off the heady theory of feminism that proclaims that another world is possible. We resist others' attempts to stifle our voices, acting belligerent when necessary and getting back when we have to. Crunk feminists don't take no mess from nobody!"

Members of the collective have published two books. One, by Brittney C. Cooper, Susana M. Morris, and Robin M. Boylorn, is an anthology of Crunk's writing (2017). More recently, Crunk Feminists Brittney Cooper, Chanel Craft Tanner, and Susana M. Morris wrote a book for younger feminists called *Feminist AF: A Guide to Crushing Girlhood* (2021).

For generations, Black feminist artists and writers have made waves if not tsunamis in many different settings (Thorsson, 2023). Writers like Audre Lorde, June Jordan, and Roxane Gay have transformed their fields by sharing their own personal experiences as Black lesbian feminists, and also provided critical perspectives on current events relevant to all people. Angela Davis, Kimberlé Crenshaw, and bell hooks are in similar camps as Black feminist intellectuals who have revolutionized how we understand not only Black women's experiences but also the multifold nature of oppression. Black feminist musicians have reigned for generations and influenced the development of jazz and popular music in exciting ways, in particular, the trajectory of the Blues (Davis, 1998). Black musicians whose music has shaped feminisms include Aretha Franklin, Queen Latifah, Beyoncé, Megan Thee Stallion, and Janelle Monáe.

**Amanda Gorman** made history as the first National Youth Poet Laureate. Informed by Black feminism, Gorman's work addresses issues of social justice, race and gender. In a 2021 interview, she revealed that one of the questions she asks prospective friends is "are you an intersectional feminist?"

**Research Prompt:** Watch her recite "The Hill We Climb" at President Joe Biden's 2021 inauguration and read one additional poem by Gorman. How does her poetry reflect intersectional feminism and Black feminism? Compare her work to another woman of color poet such as June Jordan or Chrystos. How does their poetry seem similar or different?

The cultural messages and music created by these Black women put Black women at the forefront of public consciousness and illuminates Black women's experiences, all critical to advancing justice and equality. Relatedly, Black feminist organizations also remain powerful agents for change. Groups like Black Women Radicals, dedicated to supporting and advancing Black feminist leaders, and the School for Black Feminist Politics continue the traditions of Black feminism. They organize online with alliances and coalitions, and look to a strong Black feminist future. Much of these groups' work is also providing historical context and raising up the Black feminists who have paved the way for today's Black feminism, such as June Jordan and the original National Black Feminist Organization members.

## Asian American Feminism

Asian American feminism includes a broad range of US feminists under the Asian American and Pacific Islander (AAPI) umbrella. From Americans with East Asian to South East Asian heritage and beyond, these feminists have been organizing from the 1950s and 1960s. According to the Asian American Feminist Collective on their website (n.d.), Asian American feminism is: "an ever-evolving practice that seeks to address the multi-dimensional ways Asian/American people confront systems of power at the intersections of race, gender, class, sexuality, religion, disability, migration history, citizenship and immigration status."

As is the case with all contemporary US feminisms, the Asian American feminist movement first emerged in the US out of the broader social movement energy of the 1960s and 1970s, including anti-war and Civil Rights movements. Initially, in the 1960s, Asian American women mobilized with Asian American men to address racism and classism in their communities and in society at large (Chow, 1987). As is common in all mixed-gender organizing (Hurwitz, 2020), the women experienced sexism and exclusion from the men in the movement (Chow, 1987).

Although Asian American feminism flourished and was successful in many respects, there were several notable barriers, such as being overlooked in much of the literature on feminism and social movements. Learning about this and other barriers helps us understand the trajectory of Asian American feminism and the feminist movement writ large.

First and foremost, Asian American women were marginalized in white-women dominated feminist organizations (Chow, 1987;

Yamada, 1983), and since they did not immediately find a connection to these white feminist women, they organized within their own ethnic groups. At the same time, there was a lack of understanding at best or an insensitivity at worst to the specific issues facing Asian American women, in both feminist communities and in broader white-dominated society. Second, the overall labor exploitation of Asian American women prevented many of them from joining movements, which are energy and time intensive (Chow, 1987). Finally, there was also a fear that embracing feminism, which was associated with white and Western women, would compromise their allegiances to their own ethnic identities and heritage (Suzuki et al., 2012), or would cause, as Chow (1987) states, "setbacks for the Asian American cause, co-optation into the larger society, and eventual loss of ethnic identity for Asian Americans as a whole" (p. 288). However, as Yamada (1983) writes, "it should not be difficult to see that Asian Pacific women need to affirm our own culture while working within it to change it" (p.73) and the two do not need to be mutually exclusive. Indeed many other feminists faced similar challenges with desiring to affirm their own cultures or families while also desiring change. These factors together, as well as the geographically diffuse nature of the Asian American community, have meant that Asian American feminism has been less visible than many feminisms (Fujiwara, 2022).

> **Colonization** is defined as one country taking over or controlling another, physically, through stealing land and property. **Imperialism** is commonly understood to be one country's political and/or economic (industry, trade) control over another. Colonization and imperialism are deeply related to both gender and racial domination.

Asian American feminists seek to raise their visibility and have their voices valued, and to create change that will better the lives of all Women of Color. In *This Bridge Called My Back* (1983), Yamada writes:

"Asian American women still remain in the background and we are heard but not really listened to. Like Muzak, they think we are piped into the airwaves by someone else. We must remember that one of the most insidious ways of keeping women and minorities powerless is to let them only talk about harmless and inconsequential subjects, or let them speak freely and not listen to them with serious intent. We need to raise our voices a little more, even as they say to us 'This is so uncharacteristic of you.' To finally recognize our own invisibility is to finally be on the path toward visibility. Invisibility is not a natural state for anyone."

(p. 35)

It should be noted that relative to other types of feminisms, there was and still is comparatively little research and information available about Asian American feminisms. Despite this, beginning with gusto in the 1970s, both formally and informally, Asian American feminists successfully addressed a variety of injustices. They made major strides in feminist organizing in the areas of economic equality and representation in education, celebrating ethnic heritage, and the visibility of AAPI people generally in media (Suzuki et al., 2012). What first began as grassroots and casual community groups often became more formal organizations (Suzuki et al., 2012).

One important unifying grievance of Asian American feminists in the 1970s was the war in Vietnam, led by Asian American feminists and student organizers. The themes were the intersecting injustices encapsulated by the Vietnam war, and included anti-militarization, anti-imperialism, and anti-war activism. Asian American feminists led much of the activism. Discussion of the anti-Vietnam war movement appeared in *Asian Women*, a 1971 publication by University of California, Berkeley feminists, that is reportedly one of the first Asian American feminist publications presenting anti-imperialist and anti-racist perspectives. It set the tone and momentum for Asian American feminist organizing and brought attention to the community-based activism and unequivocal feminist writing central to the Asian American feminist movement. (Fujiwara, 2022)

This legacy is perpetuated in many Asian American feminist groups, such as the Asian American Feminist Collective (AAFC). A collective, by definition, is non-hierarchical and makes decisions by consensus, which follows many feminist traditions. Founded in 2017, the AAFC is deeply intersectional and builds upon the leadership of feminists of color who have come before them: "We are indebted to ways Black feminist thought and Third World feminist movements enable us to think and act critically through our own positionalities to address systems of anti-Black racism, settler colonialism, and xenophobia" (Asian American Feminist Collective, n. d.). The AAFC prioritizes helping AAPI communities by convening the members and producing feminist media and storytelling. Events they have held include discussions of forming solidarities across Asian American and Black feminist communities and an Asian American feminist history workshop.

Community-based organizations advocating for Asian American feminists have abounded over the last five decades, including those focusing on domestic violence and sexual assault, immigrant rights, and housing (Fujiwara, 2022).

An example of a more formalized organization (meaning staff, chapter offices, funding streams) serving Asian American women and girls is the National Asian Pacific American Women's Forum, founded in 1996. While they address many social justice issues, they have most recently concentrated on reproductive justice and abortion, anti-Asian harassment and violence, economic justice, and immigrant rights. They follow in the rich Asian American feminist tradition of uplifting AAPI women and their visions and concerns, using intersectional perspectives to address complex social issues, and conducting research that centers Asian American women.

Do you know who was the first Woman of Color elected to the US House of Representatives? Or who was the first Asian American woman to serve in Congress? Or who was the first Asian American to run for US President?
    *ANSWER*: all of the above, Patsy Mink (Alexander, n.d.)

In addition to the community-based and formal organizing, intellectual production, writing, and research have also been crucial to Asian American feminists. They used literature and art to affirm their experiences and focus on the unique complexities of being an Asian American woman. The work of writer Maxine Hong Kingston illustrates this. The incorporation of Asian American studies programs and departments in universities and colleges around the country, providing space for research and teaching about Asian American women and feminisms also continued the Asian American intellectual traditions. In addition, these institutional spaces also established networks and communities for Asian American feminist students to mobilize for social change, especially around issues such as domestic violence, immigrant rights, and housing and labor rights (Fujiwara, 2022).

Although Asian American communities have always been targets of racism and xenophobia, hate crimes against these communities skyrocketed during the COVID-19 pandemic. A study by the Center for the Study of Hate and Extremism found that Anti-Asian hate crimes reported to police in the 16 largest cities increased by 164 percent between the first quarter of 2020 and the first quarter of 2021 (Levin, 2021). Since it is common for these crimes to go unreported, it is probably worse than this. This crisis came to a head in Atlanta in March of 2021, when a white man killed eight people at massage spas; six of the victims were Asian women spa workers.

Asian American feminist organization Red Canary Song stepped up in response to these murders. They held a vigil, released a statement, gathered their communities, and raised funds for the victims' families. In a clear indicator of the connections between movements, at Red Canary Song's vigil, speakers not only asserted that the Atlanta spa shootings were targeting Asian women, but also stated that more police is not the solution. (Attention to defunding police organizations was heightened at this time.) Another speaker pointed out the ongoing concurrent prevalence of anti-Black racism.

**Reflection:** Identify one Asian American feminist writer, musician, comedian or public figure. In what ways do their experiences reflect the discussions posed in this section?

## Indigenous Feminism

Indigenous feminisms are heterogenous, perhaps more than others. Activists stress connections between colonialism, human rights, racism and sexism, with a clear emphasis on intersectionality and bodily autonomy. Those who include themselves under the Native/ Indigenous feminisms' umbrella are multifaceted and diverse. Indigenous feminists reside on Turtle Island (commonly referred to as North America outside of Indigenous communities) and are from the Indigenous homelands known as the United States, including Alaska, Hawai'i, and other territories.

Gearon (2021) defines Indigenous feminism as "an intersectional theory and practice of feminism that focuses on decolonization, Indigenous sovereignty, and human rights for Indigenous women and their families." While Goeman and Denetdale (2009) argue that there is no singular definition of Native feminism, they write:

> "as Native feminists, our dreams and goals overlap; we desire to open up spaces where generations of colonialism have silenced Native peoples about the status of their women and about the intersections of power and domination that have also shaped Native nations and gender relations."

> (p. 10)

Indigenous feminisms are particularly nuanced, owing to the historical and ongoing colonization in the US. Because of the brutalization against Native communities and the importance of sovereignty to Native people, Indigenous communities have a distinct set of attributes that shape their feminisms and approaches to justice/social change.

Many Indigenous communities employ matriarchal perspectives, where women-identified people are revered and upheld as leaders and even spiritual figures. Indigenous communities embrace and venerate two-spirited people, a term first used in the 1990s referencing those individuals holding both male and female spirits (although it reflected the ongoing nature of phenomenon honored in some earlier Indigenous communities) (Thurston, n.d.). As such, their concept of gender egalitarian community is very different from that of other feminisms. Because these perspectives are so central to Indigenous cultures and spirituality, their communities are in some ways primed for feminist ideologies (Allen, 1986, as cited in Ross, 2009, p. 41).

The **gender binary** is the system that classifies all people as one of two genders, man or woman. For many people, gender is more of a spectrum than a binary, and throughout history there have been individuals who identify outside of the binary.

Indigenous feminists argue that the gender structures and hierarchies that white colonizers forced upon Native communities have indelibly shaped gender relations in Indigenous communities.

In the essay "Not Murdered, Not Missing: Rebelling Against Colonial Gendered Violence" by Indigenous feminist writer and activist Leanne Betasamosake Simpson (2014), she writes:

"I think it's in all of our best interests to take on gender violence as a core resurgence project, a core decolonization project, a core of any Indigenous mobilization. And by gender violence I don't just mean violence against women, I mean all gender violence. This begins for me by looking at how gender is conceptualized and actualized within Indigenous thought because it is colonialism that has imposed an artificial gender binary in my nation."

As Simpson argues, one tool of colonization is the imposing of heteropatriarchy and the gender binary on Indigenous communities. Colonizers forced Indigenous communities to assimilate to their own ways and eroded the matriarchal lineages of many Indigenous communities. Colonizers enforced rigid gender binaries of male domination, challenging both the matriarchal and two spirit traditions. Generations of gender scholars have found that sexism and rigid gender binaries so central to US social life also create cultures of sexual violence against women. The dynamics brought to Indigenous communities by colonizers likely drove gender-based violence in these communities. Thus, a critical issue to Indigenous feminists is the sexual abuse, disappearances, and murder of Indigenous women.

**Heteropatriarchy:** Combining "heterosexual" and "patriarchy," this term signals a system of power in which heterosexual men dominate. It also highlights how heterosexuality and patriarchy reinforce and bolster each other.

Native scholar and activist Sarah Deer (2017) finds: "Native women experience the highest rates of sexual assault in the nation" (p. 775). One in three Native women will be raped in their lifetime, and over half of Native people have experienced some sort of sexual violence (ibid). Over 70 percent of rape assailants of Indigenous women are white, in contrast to gender-based violence in other racial groups which are primarily intra-racial (Smith, 1999). The disappearance and/or murder of Indigenous women and girls is often related to gender-based violence. In 2020 alone more than 2,300 Indigenous women and girls were missing across the country (Ortiz, 2020). While these are relatively recent figures and robust historical data are not available, we know for certain that Indigenous women have been victims of violence since the earliest colonizers in what we now know as the US. These experiences frame feminist activism of Indigenous communities, and drive Native feminist organizing to change the culture of sexual abuse and rape of Native women and children. In her book *The Beginning and End of Rape: Confronting Sexual Violence in Native America* Sarah Deer (2015) argues: "rape should be the number one priority for tribal nations. All other challenges faced by tribal nations are linked to the history and trauma of rape" (p. xx), connecting the history of colonizers' cruelties with the broad health of Indigenous peoples. There are also complex legal dimensions between US law and tribal law. To provide a few examples, tribal nations have scant resources for law enforcement and investigation of crimes; and there is often lack of knowledge about tribal jurisdiction (Deer, 2015; National Alliance to End Sexual Violence, n.d.).

Manifestations and ramifications of colonization continue today. See campaigns specifically focused on missing Indigenous women: Missing and Murdered Indigenous Women (#MMIW or #MMIWG)

In many ways, organizing by Indigenous feminists has successfully transformed patterns of gender-based violence that have arisen with the colonization of their communities. Scholar and activist Luana Ross (2009) traces the development of Native and Indigenous feminisms since the 1960s. She writes of the impacts of Native feminisms:

> "For one, domestic violence programs are now in Native communities. These institutions are a result of Native feminist struggles. People dialogue more about issues of violence, which was difficult to do in the past. Moreover, I think feminist efforts contributed to the resurrection of various Native women's societies. As well, we are beginning to hear the stories of brave women from our communities. Partially because of feminism, women's stories and songs from my community are returning."
>
> (p. 46)

Yet another example: Native women Tillie Black Bear (Sicangu Lakota) and Lenora Hootch (Yup'ik) started shelter programs that provide services and community for women who have suffered from domestic violence and sexual assault (Deer, 2015). Indeed, women's solidarity combined with the interrogation of the gendered dimensions of colonization are powerful engines that propel Indigenous feminists.

Environmental justice, protection of the environment, and intersecting issues of the harms of colonization and assimilation are other important feminist issues that are specific to Indigenous populations. Indigenous feminists view land and life as interconnected and interdependent, not as separate entities. Indigenous environmentalist Winona LaDuke writes about the destruction of Indigenous land and life in her book *All Our Relations: Native Struggles for Land and Life*. She notes: "While Native peoples have been massacred and fought, cheated, and robbed of their historical lands, today their lands are subject to some of the most invasive industrial interventions imaginable" (p. 3), including being marked for nuclear and toxic waste dumps, and the desecration of sacred sites. The pollution of Indigenous lands specifically affects reproduction, and maternal and child health in the form of birth defects, infertility, disease, and chronic illness. A UN report (2012) concluded "The severe and ongoing harm caused by environmental toxins to Indigenous women, girls, unborn generations and Indigenous Peoples as a whole, requires immediate attention."

Liddell and Kington's study (2021), which analyzes the relationship between environmental toxins and the health of Indigenous children, quoted an Indigenous woman recalling her motivation to become an activist:

> "Well, in my community we had an oil-field waste site...I was living in a toxic town...still do.... We got together, kids at the bus stop and parents would say their kids were sick with asthma and every month it's the same thing. And then we realized they had dumped toxic waste inside of our community. So I became an environmentalist, not by choice but.... we fought for seven years against the oil and gas company...I was fighting for the rights of my community and my kids to live a normal, happy life as we knew it in a small town....we watched kids with no asthma become asthmatic. We watched kids would grow up with...severe diarrhea, nausea, dizziness, vertigo. It's different effects from all these chemicals, from the oil and gas industry."

(p. 9)

Here, we see her path to activism, and we see the connections between land sovereignty and health and the disproportional effects of land desecration on women and children. Many women activists are also leaders of intersectional movements of sovereignty and nationalism. One example of this activism is the late Hawaiian Haunani-Kay Trask, who long advocated for sovereignty of Hawai'i and for its independence from the violence and colonization of Americans. As a professor of Hawaiian studies, as well as an activist in the Hawaiian sovereignty movement, she analyzed and mobilized against the interlocking systems of racism, sexism, and colonization.

One of the largest Indigenous movements in recent history was the fight against the Dakota Access Pipeline (#NODAPL). The Dakota Access oil pipeline spans four states (North Dakota, South Dakota, Iowa, Illinois). By installing a pipeline on or near the Standing Rock Sioux reservation, the Indigenous people and their allies objected on many counts. The construction destroyed lands sacred to the Standing Rock Sioux, and as oil pipelines always leak, they would certainly affect their land and main water supplies.

Building on the history of Indigenous people defending their land, autonomy, and the sacred nature of water, the protests were large, intentionally peaceful, yet met with violence, intimidation, falsehoods about the activists, and years of legal action. Leading the battle were Indigenous women.

**Joye Braun (Cheyenne River Sioux)** was an activist and water protector (1969–2022). With the Indigenous Environmental Network, she fought against fracked gas pipelines, and dedicated her life to environmental justice. Braun's lodge was the first to be set up at Standing Rock to oppose the Keystone XL pipeline. President Biden revoked the permit of The Keystone XL on January 20, 2021, which was Braun's birthday. In her honor, it became a day of environmental activism.

"Women, we're life-givers," she said in a Jezebel article. "Whether it's about the Keystone XL pipeline, [proposed Canadian pipeline] Energy East, uranium mining, mountaintop removal, it all affects water. We start life in water, in the womb." Braun describes the visions of her daughter, who suffers from seizures: "In our culture, those who have epilepsy can see things that no one sees," she explains. "She was telling me that the snakes were coming." Her daughter saw "the water on fire, and the earth on fire," and a line of people marching against the snakes. "The women were standing in front," she says. "And then behind the women were the men and behind the men was the nachan [chiefs] and behind them were the children. And behind the children were the animals. Four legged and winged and swimming things that don't have a voice." ... "'Lots of people had dreams and visions out there where the women are in front,' she said, quietly, from her yurt, as the snow continued to fall. 'It has always been the women.' ..." (Merlan, 2016).

Indigenous feminist and Indigenous women-led mobilizing is vast, much of it involving decolonization and the honoring of sacred Native ways and lore. One example of successful mobilization is the Indigenous Feminist Organizing School, which brought together Indigenous feminists from around the world to discuss their priorities and create solidarity. The Gearon (2021) priorities came out of that meeting. Other organizing priorities are: issues of women's health and bodily autonomy, finding missing Indigenous women, climate justice, policy, education, interpersonal violence, women and children's safety, #LandBack, and many others.

Cultural production such as art, poetry, and writing has also impacted the evolution of the Indigenous feminist movement. Beth Brant, for example, wrote extensively on Indigenous feminisms, sexuality, and organizing, and supported and amplified other Indigenous women writers. Chrystos is a two-spirited, lesbian, Indigenous writer and poet, featured in *This Bridge Called My Back: Writings by Radical Women of Color*. In the poem "I Walk in the History of My People," Chrystos (2015) highlights the indignities experienced by Indigenous women and communities, owing to colonization, such as hunger, lack of access to water, and appropriation of the sacred. She describes how she feels trauma deep in her "marrow" as a result of the marginalization of and brutality towards her people (p. 53).

Perhaps more so than any other type of feminism, Indigenous communities have a complex relationship to both the broader feminist movement and white feminists. Research shows that many Indigenous women and women-serving organizations are apprehensive about embracing feminist identities. One reason for this, familiar to Women of Color feminists, in that they wish to distance themselves from white feminists (Gearon, 2021). In many ways, however, Indigenous communities have fundamentally different struggles than other feminists because of colonization and the erasure of Indigenous communities by white people. Of the tensions in Indigenous feminisms, Jihan Gearon (2021) wrote:

> "Indigenous feminism can change our world, if given the chance. The particular words aren't the important thing, and if others would rather call themselves 'matriarch' or 'matriarch-in-training', or a word in their Indigenous language that means more to them, I say go for it. My goal is not to debate words or force everyone to use the same ones, but to insist that Indigenous feminism, like all solutions to problems in Indian Country, is about decolonizing."

**LaDonna Brave Bull Allard**, who passed away in 2020, was an Indigenous leader and visionary who led the #NODAPL (No Dakota Access Pipeline) movement. As a citizen of the Standing Rock Sioux Tribe, she founded the Standing Rock Camp which gave space and resources for the thousands of activists united in the preservation of her community's land and water. Integral in the success of the #NODAPL movement, LaDonna Brave Bull Allard also acknowledged that the fight for Indigenous land rights and respect of the earth would be a fight of generations, as quoted in Todrys's book *Black Snake Standing Rock, the Dakota Access Pipeline, and Environmental Justice* (2021):

> "It is my home," she declared. "I will not back down. And when I am gone, my daughter will be standing there, and my granddaughter, and all the generations after."

(p. 225)

*Figure 2.1* LaDonna Brave Bull Allard (Jens Schwarz/laif/Redux)

**Research prompt:** Conduct research about Indigenous land back campaigns on your campus, or in your community, state, or region. Browse the resource section of the Sogorea Te' Land Trust's website: sogoreate-landtrust.org. Also see their resource "How to Come Correct." What are their recommendations and best practices for allies?

## Chicana Feminism

Chicana feminism emerged in the 1960s and 1970s. It is a rich and varied movement of Mexican-American women advocating for their rights and advancement within their families and communities, and with a clear understanding that liberation must be an intersectional project (Suárez, 2018). Chicana feminists emphasize community, solidarity with other Women of Color, and writing, poetry, art, and other creative pursuits.

**Gloria Anzaldúa** shaped the Chicana feminist movement through her writing, including co-editing *This Bridge Called My Back* with Cherríe Moraga and authoring the seminal Chicana feminist text *Borderlands/ La Frontera: The New Mestiza* (1987). Born in Harlingen, Texas in 1942, Anzaldúa theorized the lived experiences that propelled Chicana women's activism the decade before, and built and sustained communities of feminists through her writing (Keating and González-López, 2011). As a lesbian Chicana, Anzaldúa theorized the complexities of physical and metaphorical borders for Chicanas, a theme that has continued to be influential in Chicana literature (Torres, 2003). When reflecting on Anzaldúa's contributions, Cherríe Moraga stated "She created this metaphor about outsiderhood that really impacted generations of students and activists," and "To all of us, she was a source of profound inspiration in the way she made writing her life's warrior work" (Nakao, 2004).

Chicana feminism can really only be understood within the larger framework of Chicano organizing. Chicana feminism sought to add women's issues to the slate of grievances of the mixed-gender Chicano Nationalist Movement, which fought for the rights, visibility, and dignity of all Chicano people. As the Chicano Nationalist movement of the 1960s progressed, the sexism in that movement was untenable for many of its women activists. Thus, Chicana feminisms initially prioritized involving more women in Chicana organizing generally (Blackwell, 2011; Roth, 2003).

Alma García (1997) wrote: "Throughout the 1970s, this initial generation of self-proclaimed Chicana feminists viewed the struggle against sexism within the Chicano movement and the struggle against racism in the larger society as central ideological components of their feminist thought" (p. 5).

The development and history of Chicana activism is also intimately tied up with the numerous Chicana feminist Conferences, many of them led by youth and students. Around 1968, within the Chicano Youth Liberation Movement, young women who were part of the broader Chicano Nationalist Movement began to find a voice and argue for feminist needs. Students and youth participants began to take feminist concerns to their own local mobilized communities. In 1971, a major moment in Chicana feminist history occurred in Houston, Texas at the First National Chicana Conference, or "Conferencia de Mujeres Por La Raza": "They were coming together in Houston to discuss their experience as women in the movement and how to mobilize together. They did not see themselves as dividing the movement; they were strengthening it," writes Maylei Blackwell (2011, p. 188). More than 600 Chicanas attended to connect with each other and establish goals and priority issues for the Chicana movement, including abortion, education access, and childcare centers.

Mirta Vidal (1971) outlines the main concerns of the Chicana feminist movement:

> "Chicanas are beginning to challenge every social institution which contributes to and is responsible for their oppression, from inequality on the job to their role in the home. They are questioning 'machismo,' discrimination in education, the double standard, the role of the Catholic Church, and all the backward ideology designed to keep women subjugated."
>
> (p. 3)

While the ethnic and racial dimensions of women's rights are not at all uniform, you will note that many of the above listed grievances run parallel to the women's rights movement's concerns on the whole, mostly irrespective of the racial and ethnic background of the feminist. In fact, Chicanas identified the similarities in all women's activism.

In many movements women and feminists were often told that their concerns would be attended to eventually, and/or that there were larger problems that needed to be addressed before women's issues, and/or that women were betraying the men in their ethnic and racial communities by organizing as women. Chicana women were subsequently accused of being traitors and sell-outs to white feminists for wanting to address gender and sexism (Garcia, 1997; Roth, 2003). While it is impossible to know how much this sentiment stifled organizing, it is an ongoing conflict between feminists and non-feminists, independent of their race and ethnicity. Although perennially frustrating to activists that women's issues were sidelined, the situation motivated them and provided energy to the Chicana movement generally.

Elma Barrara (1971), a leader in the Chicana movement, wrote about the similarities of Chicana and white women's dissent:

> "I have been told that the Chicana's struggle is not the same as the white woman's struggle. I've been told that the problems are different and that... the Chicana's energies are needed in the barrio and that being a feminist and fighting for our rights as women and as human beings is anti-Chicano and anti-male. But let me tell you what being a Chicana means in Houston, Texas. It means learning how to best please the men in the Church and the men at home, not in that order."
>
> (p. 12)

Barrara's comments illustrate not uncommon tension between feminists and many adjacent groups, such as larger movement organizing. Feminism carried the reputation within the Chicano National Movement as individualist and something that "detracted from the Chicano movement's 'real' issues, such as racism" (García, 1989, p. 225). This conflict around individual versus community was also present in many other strands of feminism.

Many Chicana feminist leaders identified as lesbian, and built solidarity with other Chicana feminists in their resistance and community-building. In Chicano communities, as in most communities, lesbianism stands in opposition to traditional modes of heterosexuality that uphold women's virtues as wives, mothers, and their capacity to serve men. As such, feminists who challenge those priorities or who wish to dismantle these dominant norms of femininity are met with resistance. Chicana lesbian feminists such as Cherríe Moraga, Gloria Anzaldúa, and others carved out important Chicana feminist voices that objected to the norms of femininity, despite being treated with hostility. In *This Bridge Called My Back*, Cherríe Moraga writes "My Lesbianism is the avenue through which I have learned the most about silence and oppression, and it continues to be the most tactile reminder that we are not free human beings" (p. 22).

Chicana feminist organizing occurs in many different ways. They have worked and continue to work through community gatherings, feminist publishing (Kitchen Table Press was founded by several feminists of color, including Chicana women), consciousness-raising groups, academic outlets, and in artistic and creative ventures. Chicana feminists organize on their own, within their specific communities, as well as form coalitions with other Women of Color feminists.

Chicana feminist newspapers, such as one published by the group Las Hijas de Cuauhtémoc in Long Beach, California, were both signs of feminist consciousness in the Chicana world, and instruments for its preservation (Vidal, 1997). Many feminist periodicals were by and for Women of Color broadly, such as the Third World Women's alliance newspaper called *Triple Jeopardy*. Through these periodicals, Chicana and Women of Color feminists were able to create a collective identity, define feminism and their relationship to the feminist movement, outline options and avenues for liberation, discuss challenges they faced together, and share images and text that normalized their experiences and world views (Beins, 2015). In terms of writing, literature, and poetry, Chicana feminist leaders include: Sandra Cisneros, Ana Castillo, Denise Chávez, Lorna Dee Cervantes, Cherríe Moraga, and Gloria Anzaldúa.

Feminism was in large part a working-class movement, in opposition to the dominant middle-class nature of many white feminists in the movement (García, 1989). While Chicana feminists regularly advocated for the inclusion of women's grievances in the Chicano Nationalist Movement, they were also focused on addressing intersecting oppressions related to poverty, gender, and race. Throughout history, Chicana feminists and women have successfully fought and organized against a variety of injustices that benefit all Chicana and Chicano people, such as organizing for farmworker rights or to protest police brutality (Vidal, 1997).

As the movement has advanced over time, and Chicanas continue to experience marginalization, Chicana feminists have resolved to continue their fight against the interlocking oppressions of racism, capitalism, and patriarchy, which are unique to Chicana feminists as well as common in some ways with other Women of Color (García, 1989; Segura, 1984). Moreover, Chicana feminist issues have in the last few decades broadened to include grievances related to Latina communities more generally, reflecting the growth in migrants from Central and South America. Issues that face those populations include immigration and related grievances, such as the rising attention to women's fertility in anti-immigrant discourse (García, 2017).

Recent examples of Chicana feminism include the Mujeristas Collective, whose intersectional feminism is expressed largely on Instagram (@mujeristasco). They describe their work as an art collective for Latina and Women of Color creators based in New York, and their feminist activism includes publishing and distributing zines and hosting community events. They write: "Using zines and community events as our medium, our goal is to document and present a diverse collection of work from a global, feminist perspective. We believe this work, of pushing for social change and equity through art and community outreach, is an important aspect in the worldwide struggle for liberation." A new generation of Chicana and Latina feminist authors has also emerged, building upon and inspired by Chicana intellectual traditions. These include Estella González, Elizabeth Acevedo, Erika Sánchez, and Isabel Quintero.

**Research Reflection:** Conduct research about the life of a Chicana feminist artist or writer. Consider: Cherríe Moraga, Gloria Anzaldúa, Favianna Rodriguez, Melanie Cervantes, Alma López, Ester Hernández, or Amalia Mesa-Bains. How did they come to their Chicana feminism? What are the main themes in their writing and art, and how do they address the intersectional Chicana feminist experience?

## Whitewashed Feminisms

When we think of the mainstream feminist movement, many people think of feminisms dominated by white women. Indeed, much of the early feminist organizing, especially at the national level, struggled with racial diversity and was often not intersectional in nature (see Chapter 3 for an in-depth discussion). As illustrated in this chapter, many feminists also organized primarily within their own racial and ethnic groups, particularly because they had their own complex dynamics to tend to when it came to dismantling sexism.

However, since the 1970s, the feminist movement has been whitewashed (Roth, 2003). Whitewashing, echoing the construction term that means slapping white paint all over a structure, is a condition that highlights how feminism and commentary about feminism oftentimes only features the whiteness and white feminists in the movement. That is, the movement sometimes has been presented as whiter than it is. This is for two primary reasons, one coming from within the feminist movement itself and the other from external sources.

First, many white-led feminist organizations did not acknowledge variations in experiences based on race, class, gender, or sexuality. In a white supremacist society, much of this was and is manifested principally in racism perpetuated within social movements, including feminism. Even though progressive and radical social movement groups try to advance justice and equity, they are not harmonious utopias, and indeed many also replicate racist, sexist, classist, transphobic or homophobic environments.

Racial tension in feminism was felt by many Women of Color. For example, white feminists were seen to confront gendered structures of power and inequality, but often lacked analysis of class and race (Chow, 1987; García, 1989). At the same time, there were certainly some feminists who successfully mobilized across racial/ethnic and other identity lines, particularly those who organized for specific campaigns like reproductive justice or one-off events like the 1970 Strike for Women's Equity Day (Valk, 2008).

Second, for generations, when the mainstream media needed commentary about feminism, they would turn to a small handful of feminists who eventually became unofficial spokespeople for the movement. These feminists were nearly always white and highly educated. Thus, a complex and racially diverse movement was whitewashed by this skewed coverage in the media. Even though the white women spokespeople could be commenting on the activities of a racially and ethnically diverse movement, their photos and experiences became, to readers and viewers of huge media outlets, synonymous with feminism. That then shaped how the general public saw the movement and who fit in the movement (or not). These media opportunities for a limited number of white feminists beget other media and speaking opportunities for them, repeating throughout popular culture and mediascapes the message that feminism is for white women.

With the rise of social media, especially X, formerly known as Twitter (RIP), anyone with access to the internet and a device, could share their thoughts on feminism. Journalists started to follow the folks on social media with impressive followings, especially Black women and other Women of Color, many who wouldn't have previously been seen as spokespeople for the movement. While this was sometimes perilous because it meant that ideas and thoughts were easily lifted from tweets or co-opted, it did mean that with rising opportunities for dissemination of online feminism, the stage for feminism became larger and more inclusive.

## Lesbian, Queer, and Trans Feminisms

Feminisms have always been entwined with lesbian and queer individuals and communities. Lesbians, for the most part, have historically been key bearers of feminist culture, leading feminist organizations, questioning the normativity of the heterosexual nuclear family, drawing attention to the ramifications of the patriarchy, and modeling coalition building and inclusion (Taylor and Whittier, 1992). Many of the most famous feminist activists, intellectuals, and leaders over the course of history have been lesbians, including Audre Lorde, Cherríe Moraga, Leslie Feinberg, and Barbara Smith. Given intersectional feminisms' critique of the power structures of institutions such as family, work, school and government, feminism in many ways goes hand in hand with lesbian and queer movements that draw attention to inequality in these same institutions.

In the lesbian manifesto "The Woman-Identified Woman" by the Radicalesbians (1970), the authors write against rigid sex roles, heteronormativity, and male supremacy in their radical vision of feminism:

"It is the primacy of women relating to women, of women creating a new consciousness of and with each other, which is at the heart of women's liberation, and the basis for the cultural revolution. Together we must find, reinforce, and validate our authentic selves."

(Fahls, 2020, p. 84)

This was a major moment in the development of the feminist movement and feminist solidarity: the Radicalesbians were advocating for women to band together regardless of their sexuality, as well as to recognize that gender oppression occurred not only by men centering themselves in the world, but by men creating gender roles that maintained a gender hierarchy with women at the bottom (Stryker, 2017, p. 125).

In the 1960s, the connections between feminism and LGBTQ activism became pronounced as LGBTQ communities were being attacked by police and others through laws outlawing cross-dressing and same-sex relationships. While first stirrings of what would become the gay rights movement in the US started almost immediately post-World War II, the collective energy to push back against homophobia reached a peak with the civil rights and feminist movements of the 1960s and 1970s. In 1969, police raided popular New York City gay bar The Stonewall Inn, and the patrons resisted. This Stonewall Uprising, which included many days of protests, was considered the genesis of the modern-day LGBTQ movement. It also joined lesbians, drag queens, and gender non-conforming individuals together in LGBTQ mobilization.

A few years prior to Stonewall, across the country in San Francisco, transgender individuals, drag queens, and gay men resisted arrest and demanded their rights at Compton Cafeteria. One night in 1966, having been pushed to their limits after being harassed by homophobes at the cafeteria, they rioted in the restaurant and streets. Despite occurring nearly sixty years ago, many of the protestors' grievances remain germane to today's LGBTQIA and queer feminists. The eminent trans historian Susan Stryker notes in her book:

"The circumstances that created the conditions for the riot continue to be relevant in trans movements today: discriminatory policing practices that target members of minority communities, urban land-use policies that benefit cultural elites and displace poor people, the unsettling domestic consequences of US foreign wars, access to health care, civil rights activism aiming to expand individual liberties and social tolerances on matters of sexuality and gender, and political coalition building around the structural injustices that affect many different communities."

(Stryker, p. 152)

Stryker's quote illustrates how many of the grievances driving LGBTQ activism in the 1960s were consistent with feminist concerns.

While not monolithic, lesbian feminist communities, culture, and movement-building was an important part of the feminist movement in the 1960s and 1970s. Lesbian separatist organizations, businesses, newspapers, and communities proliferated in the 1960s and 1970s, such as the Furies and Olivia Records, with an ethos that emphasized women's communities and networks as a way forward to a more radical and egalitarian future. That said, there were many feminists, including the Combahee River Collective, who wholeheartedly disavowed separatism (Enszer, 2016).

The impulse for separatism is related in part to ongoing homophobia and tension within feminist communities about the inclusion of queer, lesbian, and trans individuals. Part of this emerged when many heterosexual feminists in the 1970s worked to make their movement attractive to heterosexuals outside the movement, in order to broaden its mass and mainstream appeal. Many non-lesbian feminists of the time were driven by the fear that feminism and lesbianism together were too much for some mainstream communities to support. For example, writes Alma García (1989):

"In a political climate that already viewed feminist ideology with suspicion, lesbianism as a sexual lifestyle and political ideology came under even more attack. Clearly, a cultural nationalist ideology that perpetuated such stereotypical images of Chicanas as 'good wives and good mothers' found it difficult to accept a Chicana feminist lesbian movement."

(p. 226)

To provide another example, some leaders of the National Organization for Women (NOW), one of the largest national feminist organizations of the time, were resistant to the inclusion of lesbians (Echols, 1989). Betty Friedan, co-founder of NOW, made homophobic and anti-lesbian comments and argued that lesbians were a "lavender menace," posed to derail if not destroy the women's movement (Rosen, 2000). This caused a schism in the organization and which led to the founding of the Radicalesbians, initially called "the Lavender Menace" (Stryker, 2017, p. 125).

Another part of the tension in feminism, particularly in queer communities, was that many feminists themselves did not support trans individuals, believing that, as Stryker (2017) writes, "They [feminists] often considered such practices to be 'personal solutions' to the inner experience of distress about experiencing gender-based oppression" (p. 3). All of this together shows that there was homophobia and/or transphobia in the feminist movement. One widely cited example of trans exclusive feminism is the case of the Michigan Womyn's Music Festival, which prohibited trans women, and eventually shut down (Currans, 2020). Some of this transphobia continues today, particularly in subpopulations such as "gender critical feminists" or TERFS/trans exclusive radical feminists (see Chapter 1) (Thurlow, 2022; Butler, 2024). That said, over time and continuing today, most feminists have widely supported queer and trans populations, and vice versa.

While lesbian feminists have not disappeared, beginning in the 1990s, heightened attention has been paid to queer feminisms. Queer feminists saw gender differently from many earlier iterations of feminism. While previous forms of feminism viewed gender (and sometimes race and class) as rigid categories and primary modes of oppression, queer feminists viewed gender more as a system of power that is socially constructed and constantly enacted and reenacted, or even an opportunity for expression and self-understanding (Stryker, 2017, p. 156–157).

Many queer feminist movements are intersectional in practice and emphasize solidarity, community, social change, and coalition. Queer feminists prioritize issues of sexuality, gender, race, and intersectional related issues and work to dismantle heteronormative practices and institutions, and gender binaries (Sullivan, 2019). In some ways, queer feminisms are less uniform and have murkier boundaries than the other forms of feminisms in this chapter, owing to the vast number of people and groups under the queer feminisms' umbrella, the integration of queer feminism into a variety of progressive movements, and the somewhat blurry/shifting terminology. Current and recent examples of social justice movements that incorporate queer feminisms and coalitions abound. Occupy Wall Street had queer feminist caucuses for transgender and queer rights, using traditional feminist tactics (Hurwitz, 2020). Black Lives Matter was founded by Black queer feminists.

**Heteronormative:** a social norm that assumes and reinforces the idea that heterosexuality is the standard or default sexual orientation. Heteronormativity places high value on heterosexual relationships and family structures while marginalizing or stigmatizing others.

Around 2022–23 there were rapid shifts in technology, economy, and politics in the US, as well as a backlash against #MeToo, Black Lives Matter, and social justice organizing. With this as the backdrop, transgender individuals have become targets of attack (Gill-Peterson, 2024), and to many conservatives, are representative of progressive social movements that have gone too far. The lives and experiences of transgender individuals entered public discussion at unprecedented levels, making trans communities and individuals experience increasing levels of violence, hostility, and surveillance. Many have been targeted by so-called Bathroom bills, anti-drag legislation, parental rights laws, fights against trans athletes, and a host of laws to limit the rights and humanity of members of the queer and trans communities. Feminists and other social justice groups argue that the war on trans individuals is also a war against progressive views of gender, and part of a larger backlash-driven effort to return to and maintain traditional gender roles and control over women's bodies (Bassi and LaFleur, 2022). As such, many feminists have underscored their dedication to trans inclusion as part of the overall goals of intersectional feminism.

In an article called "How We Talk About Trans Inclusion Matters," trans woman writer Aly E. outlines three primary reasons trans women need to be included in feminism:

"Trans women ought to be included in the feminist coalition because we share some experiences of misogyny with cis women, because we share liberatory goals with feminism, and because our exclusion makes feminism weaker" (2018).

**Research Reflection:** Conduct research on drag bans in the United States. Where are they happening? What are the goals of the drag bans? Who is being targeted and why? What are the impacts of this legislation?

**Sylvia Rivera** (1951–2002) was a trans woman of color activist who transformed LGBTQIA+ activism (La Fountain-Stokes, 2021). She began her activism at the watershed 1969 Stonewall Riots in New York City, about which she was famously quoted: "For six nights, the 17-year-old Rivera refused to go home or to sleep, saying 'I'm not missing a minute of this—it's the revolution!',", stated Emma Rothberg (2021) in an article for The National Women's History Museum. Throughout her life, Rivera was a fierce advocate for the inclusion of trans people in gay liberation and progressive activism. She understood the interlocking nature of oppression that trans individuals faced and sought to support them materially as well as in mobilization for social change broadly. In 1970, she and Marsha P. Johnson founded the Street Transvestite Action Revolutionaries (STAR), an organization that supported and housed trans youth, primarily, in lower Manhattan (Stryker, 2017, p. 110). A radical organization, it was a model for progressive organizations and, in many ways, ahead of its time (Shepard, 2013). In 1973, at the Christopher Street Liberation Rally, Rivera gave a now-celebrated speech called "Y'all better quiet down," which was one of her major moments. In the speech she called out gay liberation activists for ignoring and turning their backs on trans individuals, who were being beaten, raped, and thrown into jail. It was Rivera's group STAR who aided these individuals, not the middle-class white activists involved in gay liberation.

Along with her close collaborator Marsha Johnson, Rivera dedicated her life to creating community and social change for trans and queer communities. She truly enacted coalitional politics and intersectional alliances. Although her life was not without its battles and challenges, Rivera shaped trans activism in innumerable ways. Her legacy lives on in the Sylvia Rivera Law Project.

## Chapter 2 Mini Toolkit: Audre Lorde and Feminist Poetry as Transformation

Audre Lorde (1934–92) described herself as a "black, lesbian, mother, warrior, poet" in her public appearances (Sehgal, 2020). A famous poet and teacher, throughout her life Lorde was dedicated to fighting sexism, racism, homophobia, and injustice. Her work has been transformative to generations of feminists, drawing attention to hope for change as well as the everyday nature of the indignities of racism, classism, and sexism. Throughout the feminist movement women's writing and creative work have drawn attention to its grievances and actions. Collaborating with feminists including Cherríe Moraga, Barbara Smith, and Hattie Gossett, Lorde founded Kitchen Table: Women of Color Press. The press published many seminal texts by Black women and Women of Color in rebuttal to the white domination of the publishing world that offered little opportunity for these women to tell their stories.

To get involved and to learn more:

- Consider how creative writing by feminists of color both reflect and influence the feminist movement:
- Find Lorde's poetry online, and consider how it reflects what you know about feminism.
- What are key themes that arise in both Lorde's writing, and in what you know of the feminist movement?
- Do you recognize any themes from Chapter 2 in Lorde's poetry?
- Pick one additional writer and compare an excerpt of her writing to Lorde's. Consider June Jordan, Adrienne Rich, Toni Morrison, or Amanda Gorman.
- Is there anyone else, a musician or artist you like, who might also be expressing feminist themes?

# Chapter 2 Dive Deeper

*Trans Studies Reader* (Susan Stryker)
*Black on Both Sides: A Racial History of Trans Identity* (C. Riley Snorton)
*Critically Sovereign* (Joanne Barker)
*Digital Archive for Documenting Chicana Artifacts*: https://chicanap ormiraza.org
*"Indigenous Feminisms" in The Oxford Handbook of Indigenous People's Politics* (Joanne Barker)
*How We Get Free: Black Feminism and the Combahee River Collective* (Keeanga-Yamahtta Taylor)
*Beyond Respectability: The Intellectual Thought of Race Women* (Brittney Cooper)
*Asian American Feminisms and Women of Color Politics* (Shireen Roshanravan & Lynn Fujiwara)
*Words of Fire: An Anthology of African-American Feminist Thought* (Beverly Guy-Sheftall)
*Sister Outsider: Essays and speeches* (Audre Lorde)
*Compulsory Heterosexuality and Lesbian Existence* (Adrienne Rich)
*I am Your Sister: Collected and Unpublished Writings of Audre Lorde* (Edited by Rudoph P. Byrd, Johnnetta Betsch Cole, and Beverly Guy-Sheftall).
Film: Screaming Queens: The Riot at Compton's Cafeteria

# References

Alexander, K.L. (n.d.) Patsy Mink. *The National Women's History Museum.* From www.womenshistory.org/education-resources/biographies/patsy-mink.
Anzaldúa, G. (1987). *Borderlands/La Frontera: The New Mestiza* (1st ed.). Aunt Lute Books.
Asian American Feminist Collective. (n.d.). *Home.* Retrieved October 28, 2023, from www.asianamfeminism.org.
Bailey, M. (2021). *Misogynoir Transformed: Black Women's Digital Resistance.* New York: New York University Press.
Barker, J. (2013). Indigenous Feminisms. In *The Oxford Handbook of Indigenous People's Politics.* Oxford Academic. doi:10.1093/oxfordhb/9780195386653.013.007.

Barker, J. (2017). Critically sovereign. In *Duke University Press eBooks*. doi:10.1215/9780822373162.

Barrara, E. (1971). Statement by Elma Barrara. In M. Vidal (Ed.), *Chicanas Speak Out - Women: New Voice of La Raza*, p. 12. Pathfinder Press.

Bassi, S. & LaFleur, G. (2022). Introduction: TERFs, Gender-Critical Movements, and Postfascist Feminisms. *TSQ: Transgender Studies Quarterly*, 9(3), 311–333. doi:10.1215/23289252-9836008.

Beins, A. (2015) Radical Others: Women of Color and Revolutionary Feminism. *Feminist Studies*.

Black Women Radicals. (n.d.). *About: Black Women Radicals*. Retrieved October 28, 2023, from www.blackwomenradicals.com/about.

Blackwell, M. (2011). *¡Chicana Power! Contested Histories of Feminism in the Chicano Movement*. Austin, TX: University of Texas Press.

Boisnier, A.D. (2003). Race and Women's Identity Development: Distinguishing Between Feminism and Womanism Among Black and White Women. *Sex Roles*, 211–218. doi:10.1023/A:1024696022407.

Breines, W. (2002). "What's Love Got to do with it?" White Women, Black Women, and Feminism in the Movement Years. *Signs*, 27(4), 1095–1133. doi:10.1086/339634.

Brewer, R. (2020). Black Feminism and Womanism. In N. Naples (Ed.), *The Companion to Feminist Studies*.

Brown, M. (2022). Black Feminism. In D.A. Snow, D. Della Porta, B. Klandermans, & D. McAdam (Eds), *The Wiley-Blackwell Encyclopedia of Social and Political Movements*. doi:10.1002/9780470674871.wbespm628.

Brown, M. (2022). #SayHerName. In D.A. Snow, D. Della Porta, B. Klandermans, & D. McAdam (Eds), *The Wiley-Blackwell Encyclopedia of Social and Political Movements*. doi:10.1002/9780470674871.wbespm628.

Brown, M., Ray, R., Summers, E., & Fraistat, N. (2017). #SayHerName: A case study of intersectional social media activism. *Ethnic and Racial Studies*, 40(11), 1831–1846.

Butler, J. (2024). *Who's Afraid of Gender?* Macmillan.

Carmen, A. & Wahuiyi, V. (2012). Indigenous Women and Environmental Violence [Report]. *United Nations*. Retrieved November 9, 2023, from www.un.org/esa/socdev/unpfii/documents/EGM12_carmen_waghiyi.pdf.

Chow, E.N.-L. (1987). The Development of Feminist Consciousness among Asian American Women. *Gender and Society*, 1(3), 284–299. www.jstor.org/stable/189565.

Chrystos. (2015). I Walk in the History of My People. In *This Bridge Called My Back: Writings by Radical Women of Color* (4th ed.). State University of New York Press.

Cole, E.R. & Luna, Z.T. (2010). Making Coalitions Work: Solidarity across Difference within US Feminism. *Feminist Studies*, 36(1), 71–98. www.jstor.org/stable/40608000.

Collins, P.H. (1996). WHAT'S IN A NAME? Womanism, Black Feminism, and Beyond. *The Black Scholar*, 26(1), 9–17. www.jstor.org/stable/41068619.

Combahee River Collective. (1977). The Combahee River Collective Statement. Retrieved November 8, 2023, from https://www.loc.gov/item/lcwaN0028151/.

Cooper, B.C., Morris, S.M., & Boylorn, R.M. (Eds). (2017). *The Crunk Feminist Collection*. The Feminist Press.

Cooper, B.C. (2017c). *Beyond Respectability: The Intellectual Thought of Race Women*. University of Illinois Press. doi:10.5406/illinois/9780252040993.001.0001.

Cooper, B., Tanner, C.C., & Morris, S. (2021). *Feminist AF: A Guide to Crushing Girlhood*. Norton Young Readers.

Crenshaw, K. & African American Policy Forum. (2023). *#SayHerName: Black Women's Stories of Police Violence and Public Silence*. Haymarket.

Crunk Feminist Collective. (n.d.). Mission Statement. Retrieved November 5, 2023, from www.crunkfeministcollective.com/about.

Currans, E. (2020). Transgender Women Belong Here: Competing Feminist Visions at the Michigan Womyn's Music Festival. *Feminist Studies*, 46(2), 459–488.

Davis, A. 1998. *Blues Legacy and Black Feminism*. Penguin Random House.

Deer, S. (2015). *The Beginning and End of Rape: Confronting Sexual Violence in Native America*. University of Minnesota Press. www.jstor.org/stable/10.5749/j.ctt17w8gfr.

Deer, S. (2017). Bystander No More? Improving the Federal Response to Sexual Violence in Indian Country. *Utah Law Review*, 2017(4), article 7. https://dc.law.utah.edu/ulr/vol2017/iss4/7.

E, A. (2018, May 2). How We Talk About Trans Inclusion Matters. *Medium*. Retrieved November 14, 2023, from https://alyesque.medium.com/how-we-talk-about-trans-inclusion-matters-75e1c6fce5dc.

Echols, A. (1989). *Daring to be bad: Radical feminism in America 1967–1975*. Minneapolis: University of Minnesota Press.

Enszer, J.R. (2016) "How to stop choking to death": Rethinking lesbian separatism as a vibrant political theory and feminist practice. *Journal of Lesbian Studies*, 20(2), 180–196, doi:10.1080/10894160.2015.1083815.

Fahs, B. (2020). *Burn it Down: Feminist Manifestos for the Revolution*. Verso.

Farmer, D.A. (2017). *Remaking Black Power How Black Women Transformed an Era*. The University of North Carolina Press.

Félix, D. (2021, April 7). The Rise and Rise of Amanda Gorman. *Vogue.* www.vogue.com/article/amanda-gorman-cover-may-2021.

Fujiwara, L. (2022). Asian American Feminism. In D.A. Snow, D. Della Porta, B. Klandermans, & D. McAdam (Eds), *The Wiley Blackwell Encyclopedia of Social and Political Movements*, (2nd ed.), pp. 231–234. Wiley Blackwell.

Fujiwara, L. & Roshanravan, S. (Eds). (2018). *Asian American Feminisms and Women of Color Politics*. University of Washington Press. www.jstor.org/stable/j.ctvcwnmk1.

García, A.M. (1989). The Development of Chicana Feminist Discourse, 1970–1980. *Gender and Society*, 3(2), 217–238. www.jstor.org/stable/189983.

García, A. M. (1997). *Chicana feminist Thought: The Basic Historical Writings*. Routledge.

García, S.J. (2017). Racializing "Illegality": An Intersectional Approach to Understanding How Mexican-origin Women Navigate an Anti-immigrant Climate. *Sociology of Race and Ethnicity*, 3(4), 474–490. doi:10.1177/2332649217713315.

Gearon, J. (2021, February 11). Indigenous Feminism Is Our Culture. *Stanford Social Innovation Review.* https://ssir.org/articles/entry/indigenous_feminism_is_our_culture#.

Gill-Peterson, J. (2024). *A Short History of Trans Misogyny*. Verso.

Goeman, M.R. & Denetdale, J.N. (2009). Native Feminisms: Legacies, Interventions, and Indigenous Sovereignties. *Wicazo Sa Review* 24(2), 9–13. doi:10.1353/wic.0.0035.

Greenfeld, L. & Smith, S. (1999). American Indians and Crime. Bureau of Justice Statistics. https://bjs.ojp.gov/content/pub/pdf/aic.pdf.

Guy-Sheftall, B. (1995). *Words of fire: an anthology of African-American feminist thought*. New Press.

hooks, b. (1981). *Ain't I a Woman: Black Women and Feminism*. New York: Routledge.

hooks, b, (2000). *Feminist theory: From margin to center*. Pluto Press.

Hurwitz, M.H. (2020). *Are We the 99%?: The Occupy Movement, Feminism, and Intersectionality*. Temple University Press.

Keating, A. & González-López, G. (2011). *Bridging: How Gloria Anzaldúa's Life and Work Transformed Our Own*. Austin, TX: University of Texas Press.

LaDuke, W. (1999). *All our relations: native struggles for land and life*. South End Press.

La Fountain-Stokes, L. (2021). The life and times of trans activist Sylvia Rivera. *Critical dialogues in Latinx studies: A reader*, 241.

Levin, B. (2021). Report to the Nation: Anti-Asian Prejudice & Hate Crime. Center for the Study of Hate and Extremism.

Liddell, J.L. & Kington, S.G. (2021). "Something Was Attacking Them and Their Reproductive Organs": Environmental Reproductive Justice in an Indigenous Tribe in the United States Gulf Coast. *International Journal of Environmental Research and Public Health*, 18(2), 666. doi:10.3390/ ijerph18020666.

Lindsey, T. (2019, November 2). Is Womanist to Feminists as Purple is to Lavender?: African American Women Writers and Scholars Discuss Feminism. National Museum of African American History and Culture. Retrieved November 8, 2023 from https://nmaahc.si.edu/explore/stories/ revolutionary-practice-black-feminisms.

Lorde, A. (1981, Fall). The Uses of Anger . *Women's Studies Quarterly*, 9(3).

Lorde, A. (1984). *Sister Outsider: Essays and speeches*. Crossing Press.

Merlan, A. (2016). *Meet the Brave, Audacious, Astonishing Women Who Built the Standing Rock Movement*. Jezebel, December 8.

Mohanty, C. (2003). *Feminism Without Borders: Decolonizing Theory, Practicing Solidarity*. Durham, NC: Duke University Press.

Moraga, C. & Anzaldúa, G. (1983). *This Bridge Called My Back: Writings By Radical Women of Color*. New York: Kitchen Table Press.

Morgan, J. (1999). *When Chickenheads Come Home To Roost: My Life as a Hip Hop Feminist*. Simon & Schuster.

Mujeristas Collective. (n.d.) About. Retrieved November 9, 2023, from http s://mujeristascollective.com/about.

Nakao, A. (2004, May 20). Gloria Anzaldúa—writer. SFGATE. Retrieved November 8, 2023, from www.sfgate.com/bayarea/article/Gloria-Anza ld-a-writer-2776125.php.

National Alliance to End Sexual Violence. (n.d.). Tribal Sovereignty. Retrieved November 5, 2023, from https://endsexualviolence.org/where_ we_stand/tribal-sovereignty.

North, A. (2018, August 17). The political and cultural impact of Aretha Franklin's "Respect," explained. *Vox*. www.vox.com/2018/8/17/17699170/a retha-franklin-2018-respect-song-otis-redding-feminism-civil-rights.

Ortiz, E. (2020, July 30). Lack of awareness, data hinders cases of missing and murdered Native American women, study finds. *U.S. News*. www. nbcnews.com/news/us-news/lack-awareness-data-hinders-cases-missing-m urdered-native-american-women-n1235233.

Phillips, L. (2007). *The Womanist Reader: The First Quarter Century of Womanist Thought*. Routledge.

Rich, A. (1980). Compulsory Heterosexuality and Lesbian Existence. *Signs*, 5(4), 631–660. www.jstor.org/stable/3173834.

Roberts, D. (1998). *Killing the Black Body*. Penguin Random House.

Robnett, B. (2000). *How Long, How Long?: African American Women in the Struggle for Civil Rights*. Oxford University Press.

Rosen, R. (2000). *The World Split Open: How the Modern Women's Movement Changed America*. Penguin.

Ross, L. (2006). Understanding Reproductive Justice: Transforming the Pro-Choice Movement. *Off Our Backs*, 36, 14–19. doi:10.2307/20838711.

Ross, L. (2009). From the "F" Word to Indigenous/Feminisms. *Wicazo Sa Review*, 24(2), 39–52. www.jstor.org/stable/40587780.

Roth, B. (1999). The Making of the Vanguard Center:Black Feminist Emergence in the1960s and 1970s. In K. Springer (Ed.), *Still Lifting, Still Climbing: African American Women's Contemporary Activism*, pp. 70–90. NewYork: New York University Press.

Roth, B. (2004). *Separate Roads to Feminism: Black, Chicana, and White Feminist Movements in America's Second Wave*. Cambridge University Press. doi:10.1017/CBO9780511815201.

Rothberg, E. (2021, March). Sylvia Rivera. The National Women's History Museum. Retrieved November 14, 2023, from www.womenshistory.org/education-resources/biographies/sylvia-rivera.

Sandoval, C. (2000). *Methodology of the Oppressed*. Minneapolis: University of Minnesota Press.

Segura, D. (1984). *Chicanas and Triple Oppression in the Labor Force*. National Association for Chicana and Chicano Studies Annual Conference. 12th Annual: Chicana Voices, Austin, Texas, pp. 47–65. https://scholarworks.sjsu.edu/naccs/1984/Proceedings/9?utm_source=schola rworks.sjsu.edu%2Fnaccs%2F1984%2FProceedings%2F9&utm_m edium=PDF&utm_campaign=PDFCoverPages.

Sehgal, P. (2020, September 15). A Timely Collection of Vital Writing by Audre Lorde. *The New York Times*. Retrieved November 15, 2023, from www.nytimes.com/2020/09/15/books/review-audre-lorde-selected-works.html.

Schwarz, J. (2017). *No Title*.

Shepard, B. (2013). From Community Organization to Direct Services: The Street Trans Action Revolutionaries to Sylvia Rivera Law Project. *Journal of Social Service Research*, 39(1), 95–114. doi:10.1080/01488376.2012.727669.

Simpson, L. (2014, March 17). Not murdered and not Missing: Rebelling against Colonial Gender Violence. https://nbmediacoop.org/2014/03/17/not-murdered-and-not-missing/.

Smith, B. (1979). Letter to Sojourner. *Sojourner*, September, 2.

*Sophia Smith Collection, Ad Hoc. (1974–75). smith_ssc_m-s00697_as139088_001*. Sophia Smith Collection of Women's History. From https://findingaids.smith.edu/repositories/2/digital_objects/5266. Accessed April 1, 2024.

*Sophia Smith Collection. Asian women's history, undated, smith_ssc_m-s00697_as139145_001*. Sophia Smith Collection of Women's History. From https://findingaids.smith.edu/repositories/2/digital_objects/5995. Accessed April 1, 2024.

Springer, K. (2005). *Living for the revolution*. Duke University Press. doi:10.1215/9780822386858.

Steele, C.K. (2021). *Digital Black Feminism*. New York: NYU Press.

Stryker, S. (2008). Transgender History, Homonormativity, and Disciplinarity. *Radical History Review (100)*, 145–157. doi:10.1215/01636545-2007-026.

Stryker, S. (2017). *Transgender History: The Roots of Today's Revolution*. Seal Press.

Suárez, F. (2018). Identifying with Inclusivity: Intersectional Chicana Feminisms. In J. Reger (Ed.), *Nevertheless, They Persisted*, pp. 25–42. Routledge.

Sullivan, M. (2019, May 31). Black Queer Feminism. *Oxford African American Studies Center*. From https://oxfordaasc.com/view/10.1093/acref/9780195301731.001.0001/acref-9780195301731-e-78530.

Suzuki, L.A., Ahluwalia, M.K., & Alimchandani, A. (2012). 183 Asian American Women's Feminism: Sociopolitical History and Clinical Considerations. In E.N. Williams & C.Z. Enns (Eds), *The Oxford Handbook of Feminist Multicultural Counseling Psychology*. Oxford University Press. doi:10.1093/oxfordhb/9780199744220.013.0010.

Taylor, K.-Y. (2017). *How We Get Free: Black Feminism and the Combahee River Collective*. Haymarket.

Taylor, L. (2020). *Feminism in Coalition: Thinking with US Women of Color Feminism*. Durham, NC: Duke University Press.

Taylor, U.Y. (1998). Making Waves: The Theory and Practice of Black Feminism. *The Black Scholar*, 28(2), 18–28. doi:10.1080/00064246.1998.11430912.

Taylor, V. & Whittier, N.E. (1992). Collective identity in social movement communities: Lesbian feminist mobilization. In A.D. Morris & C.M. Mueller (Eds), *Frontiers in social movement theory* (pp. 104–129). Yale University Press.

The Womanist Working Collective. (n.d.). *Womanist Praxis*. Retrieved October 28, 2023, from www.womanistworkingcollective.org/womanist.

Third World Women's Alliance. (n.d.) Bay Area chapter records. *Sophia Smith Collection, SSC-MS-00697 Smith College Special Collections*. https://findingaids.smith.edu/repositories/2/resources/931.

Thorsson, C. (2023). *The Sisterhood: How a Network of Black Women Writers Changed American Culture*. New York: Columbia University Press.

Thurlow, C. (2022). From TERF to gender critical: A telling genealogy? *Sexualities*, 0(0). doi:10.1177/13634607221107827.

Thurston, I. (n.d.). The History of Two-Spirit Folks. *The Indigenous Foundation.* Retrieved November 13, 2023, from www.theindigen ousfoundation.org/articles/the-history-of-two-spirit-folks.

Todrys, K. (2021). *Black Snake Standing Rock, the Dakota Access Pipeline, and Environmental Justice.* Bison Books.

Torres, E.E. (2003). *Chicana Without Apology: The New Chicana Cultural Studies.* Routledge.

University of California, Berkeley. (1971). Asian Women. In *Feminist Resources Collection, SPC-2018–2014,* California State University Dominguez Hills, Gerth Archives and Special Collections.

Valk, A. (2008). *Radical Sisters.* University of Illinois Press.

Vidal, M. (1971). *Chicanas Speak Out—Women: New Voice of La Raza.* Pathfinder Press.

Vidal, M. (1997). "New Voice of La Raza: Chicanas Speak Out" in A. Garcia (Ed.) *Chicana Feminist Thought: The Basic Historical Writings.* Routledge.

Walker, A. (1983). *In Search of Our Mothers' Gardens: Womanist Prose.* Harcourt Brace Jovanovich.

White, A.M. (2006). Racial and Gender Attitudes as Predictors of Feminist Activism Among Self-Identified African American Feminists. *Journal of Black Psychology,* 32(4), 455–478. doi:10.1177/0095798406292469.

Yamada, M. (1983). Asian Pacific American Women and Feminism. In C. Moraga & G. Anzaldúa (Eds), *This Bridge Called My Back: Writings by Radical Women of Color,* pp. 68–72. State University of New York Press.

# 3  Waveless Feminism and Movement Persistence

In chapter two, you learned about how a wide variety of feminists have created and advanced the movement. But how exactly has the feminist movement persisted for so long and been meaningful to so many people? This chapter takes a close look at the dynamics that allow the movement to ebb and flow, surge and retreat, and yet continue to be relevant over generations, even during times when feminism is declared dead and finished. You will learn about the problematic nature of the feminist wave framework (first wave, second wave, and third wave feminisms), which is the primary way in which feminist history is taught and colloquially understood. Alternatively, the theoretical frameworks of abeyance and waveless feminism are presented to more accurately reflect the complexities of the movement over time. Then you will read about several examples of feminism's demise even when it was alive and well, and the trend of feminism's "premature burial" (Hawkesworth, 2004). One of the primary takeaways from this chapter is that feminist communities and networks are critical to the sustenance of a movement over time, highlighted in the concluding toolkit that examines a local feminist organization.

Key terms presented in this chapter:

- Political opportunity
- Social movement community
- Resource mobilization
- Abeyance theory
- Waveless feminism
- Feminist wave framework

DOI: 10.4324/9781003310990-4

- False feminist death syndrome
- Feminist backlash
- Online activism/Social media

## The Persistence of Feminism

Feminism has been called the longest-lasting movement in modern history. Throughout time, all around the world, feminism has been practiced in divergent ways. It ebbs and flows according to community and geographic location. Feminism might be flourishing in one community and struggling in another.

All movements surge– go up and down–especially long-standing movements. Think about some social movements you know or have read about. At some times they are very active and you hear a lot about them, read about them in the news, and see activists posting on social media. At other times, a movement and its activists are quieter or not in the public limelight.

While gender and intersectional inequalities are ever-present/ever-green, and some feminists are always pursuing justice, there are periods of time when a specific event will galvanize a large surge of activism, suddenly drawing in more people and eliciting more attention (Ferree and Hess, 2000). Surges are common, oftentimes related to a motivating political or community grievance. You might think of #BlackLivesMatter, #SayHerName, #MeToo, or the Women's March as large surges of activism. These surges are heterogeneous–sometimes geographically specific and in-person, or online.

So why is this the case, and why does feminism emerge and peak when it does? Three interrelated reasons help us understand:

1   Political opportunities
2   Resources
3   Social movement communities

At different times in our cultural and political spheres, there are varying levels of openness to, interest in, and energy for massive social movement mobilization such as feminism. Activists often organize when there is increased political opportunity to create change. When Barack Obama was president, for example, he and Vice President Biden focused attention on Title IX and the problem of sexual assault on college campuses. This established the tone that these issues matter, and that activists involved with these issues could expect support or progress. This time period was rife with political opportunity, thus increasing chances for movement success, and emboldening feminists to advocate for change at the local and national levels. With a perspective of political opportunity, activists are strategic and pointed rather than wild or unmeasured (McCammon et al., 2001).

Another related engine for the emergence of heightened social movement activity is when egregious injustice has occurred or been revealed, and public outcry opens opportunity for change. When the extent of Harvey Weinstein's sexual assault history and the degree to which he was protected by others was reported in the New York Times, it injected furor into anti-gender-based violence organizing. The resulting #MeToo continued to present the opportunity for women who had been victims of gender-based violence to come forward, to demand support and respect, and to change our culture of sexual assault. Masses of women could only speak out after it became clear through high-profile cases that there was a potential for change in this arena. While prior to #MeToo, survivors were silenced and could expect blame and stigmatization, #MeToo allowed survivors to experience community and commiseration. Indeed, new laws and policies were implemented, and knowledge about and sensitivity to the issue of gender-based violence expanded.

The second interrelated element that drives movement emergence and surges are resources (Van Dyke, 2017). Feminism, as does any movement, needs resources to achieve its goals and the movement likely will not advance without them. Resources can be understood broadly, such as funding and money; leaders, people and networks; activist expertise; organizations; ideas and creativity. At different points in time, different resources might be available or needed. Sometimes funding is needed to send activists to a national protest. At other times, there might be a need for a robust local organizational structure with strong leaders to address a grievance and push a movement forward.

But opportunity and resources only tell part of the story of how and why feminist movements surge at some points and ebb at other points. The third reason relates to communities and networks. Social movement communities and networks keep the movement going across time periods and geographical locations (Staggenborg, 1998). Surges of feminist activism can only occur when a core level of feminists is available. The 2017 Women's March wouldn't have happened without the strong solidarity of national and community-based networks of feminists already in existence. A large protest does not rise up out of nowhere.

A clear example of a surge with a solid base of feminists supporting the activism is when Elliot Rodger, a violent, misogynist, "incel," went on a shooting rampage in Isla Vista, California, near the University of California, Santa Barbara (UCSB) campus. Many people were instantly motivated by Rodger's stated hatred of women. The killings sent shock waves around the world, resulting in millions of #Yesallwomen tweets revealing how all women are victims of discrimination. Think how this horrific tragedy that disrupted the peaceful beachside UCSB could have motivated a gun control movement, but it was actually the feminists who jumped up to draw attention to the fact that for generations women have experienced violence at the hands of men.

One view of that surge, owing to the hateful acts of Elliot Rodger, might be that with #Yesallwomen feminists spontaneously appeared.

That would be incorrect.

The galvanization of feminists in the wake of the Isla Vista murders happened because, not only was there strong public sentiment against the murders, but, even more importantly, there existed a solidarity of online and offline feminist networks and communities. Feminist organizations and feminist studies students at UCSB had been confronting topics of assault and violence against women prior to the Rodger's murders and were positioned, in the aftermath of the tragedy, to march down the streets of Isla Vista. They convened discussion groups to support each other through the trauma of the events. They took leadership in online coverage that viewed Rodger was not operating in a vacuum; that his sexism was in many ways propped up by sexist structures and practices of which we are all part. This, put together, was the engine for the global #Yesallwomen movement. If these longstanding and pre-existing networks and feminist communities were not ready when the shootings happened, such a surge would not have happened. (Crossley, 2017)

*Figure 3.1* UCSB students marching in Isla Vista, CA protesting gender-based violence after the May 2014 shootings (MONICA ALMEIDA/The New York Times/Redux)

**Research Reflection:** Investigate the #Yesallwomen campaign. What were its most important themes and concerns? How was information about #Yesallwomen disseminated? What were some ways in which #Yesallwomen connected with the broader feminism movement?

**Research Reflection:** What surges of feminism come to mind? Have there been moments of heightened feminist activity in your school, community, state, or online networks? Why did they arise? Were there events that led to them?

## Between the Surges: The Abeyance Theory

That the feminist movement has continued for so long is remarkable and should not be taken for granted. Certainly, part of its persistence is due to the fact that gender inequality is so durable and difficult to dismantle, making feminism continually relevant. Let us take a closer look at what sustains a movement for so long and what happens between the surges.

Theoretical frameworks help us make sense of a complex movement such as feminism. They help us understand the connections between important moments of history and the response of movement participants, and a movement's dynamics and evolution.

Social movement abeyance is the theoretical framework we apply to movements like feminism that persist over a long period of time. Abeyance incorporates an analysis of the peaks and valleys in movement organizing: "The term 'abeyance' depicts a holding process by which movements sustain themselves in nonreceptive political environments and provide continuity from one stage of mobilization to another" (Taylor 1989, p. 761).

The abeyance theory outlines how when a social movement is not at its highest amount of activity, such as before #Yesallwomen or before #MeToo, there are structures, networks, organizations, and communities of solidarity carrying the feminist movement along. Abeyance theory shows us that between the surges of activism, there might seem to be little happening when, in reality, there is. Abeyance challenges the notion that feminism is born and then dies, as a phenomenon that occurs over and over again.

> The abeyance framework has been used to understand the evolution of a wide variety of social movements. Sociologist Verta Taylor, who developed the abeyance framework, wrote:
>
> > "Most movements have thresholds or turning points in mobilization which scholars have taken for 'births' and 'deaths.' This research suggests that movements do not die, but scale down and retrench to adapt to changes in the political climate. Perhaps movements are never really born anew. Rather, they contract and hibernate, sustaining the totally dedicated and devising strategies appropriate to the external environment."
> >
> > (1989, p. 772)

In addition to the birth and death myth of movements belied by the abeyance theory, abeyance also helps us interpret the success and failure of movements and their organizations. For example, the National Black Feminist Organization (NBFO) was relatively short-lived, but incredibly important in the history and development of Black feminism. Of NBFO, Black feminist scholar Dr. Kimberly Springer said in an interview for the Black Women Radicals: "just because these organizations don't exist anymore doesn't mean they weren't successful. And if we think about them as planting, not only harvesting the seeds of their predecessors but planting more seeds, I think they were incredibly inspiring" (n.d.). The example of planting seeds is illustrative of abeyance, in that while seeds are underground for a time, they eventually break ground, blossom, and continue the cycle of seed to blossom.

There are many different examples of abeyance structures that keep a movement going when its visibility is diminished. Online abeyance structures (Crossley, 2017) ensure feminisms' continuity regardless of how supported it is by broader society. Feminist communities and relationships form on social media, such as with groups of people who are interested in the same feminist topic, or who comment on the same feminist news outlets. Jezebel.com, founded in 2007, shuttered in late 2023 and then opened again under new ownership, is one example of a news outlet that has continued despite ups and downs in the feminist movement. Jezebel covered politics, celebrity, and pop culture in both serious and light articles, all with a feminist lens.

Online abeyance structures are critical to the perpetuation of the feminist movement. A popular and long-lasting website like Jezebel, for example, which at one count was getting 37 million page views a month (Mascia, 2010), serves to normalize feminist views. Jezebel created a community as well as a mindset that feminist perspectives were valuable, insightful, necessary, and yes, popular. It generated a positive view of feminists as being cutting-edge and humorous. While Jezebel stood the test of time, other blogs such as Feministing or Racialicious were influential while they lasted. After the heyday of the feminist blog, social media has provided a forum for feminists with a new set of hot takes. For example, Feminista Jones and Tressie McMillan Cottom have large followings online, and they frequently comment on current events from a feminist point of view. All of these online feminists educate a new generation of feminists, and build community that keeps a movement afloat.

Another form of abeyance structure is institutional abeyance (Crossley, 2017). That is, when feminist practices and perspectives become embedded in institutions such as colleges and universities, or health care systems, elements of the movement remain viable over time and generations. So ethnic and gender studies programs and departments bring the perspectives of historically marginalized groups to higher education. Campus activities such as Take Back the Night and Sexual Assault Awareness Month integrate feminist issues within the academic calendar as annual occurrences. To provide another example of institutional abeyance structures, community clinics serve low-income women, oftentimes focusing on reproductive care issues that may be guided by feminist principles of health care. While clinics' services may be altered by the changing landscape of reproductive justice, they continue to provide for the community and be guided by goals of equality and justice.

Perhaps the most important thing to remember about the abeyance theory is that it helps us understand that the feminist movement does not die. As long as there are gender and intersectional inequalities, there will be feminist movements to fight against them. Research has found that feminism is a robust, ever present movement.

## Waveless vs. Wave Feminism

In this section, we will explore two different metaphors to understand the persistence of feminism over time– the "wave" framework and "waveless feminism." The metaphors shape how we think about feminism, and they are shorthands to conceptualize and streamline the dynamics of a complex movement.

This section builds on our understanding of movement emergence and surges and the long-lasting dynamics of social movements. They complicate the common narrative of feminist "waves." (You may have heard most about second wave feminism which is part of the "wave" framework through which feminism is usually interpreted). Scholars have thought about feminists' persistence and feminist opposition using other metaphors, for example Chela Sandoval (1991), who proposes a "topography" of feminist consciousness. However, the feminist wave framework has dominated our thinking about contemporary feminism. This section explores the two different metaphors, "waveless" vs. "wave" feminism.

# Waveless Feminism

As you have learned, feminism is an ongoing movement that pushes forward through changes, challenges, and successes. It is important that as we analyze feminism, we see the full and complex picture of the movement. In order to have accurate measurements, and not be reductive or homogenizing, an understanding of feminism that acknowledges the complexities is necessary and useful.

A particularly helpful metaphor to think about feminism and all its complexities is that it is "waveless" (Crossley, 2017). The progression of feminism is akin to a river. Sometimes the movement flows rapidly and loud, such as during protests against sexual assault of #MeToo, or against police brutality of #SayHerName. During these periods of time, there is mass support of a movement, many activists and allies, and significant attention to feminism. Like a large river at its most robust, it is flowing, loud, robust, deep, and wide. In any large river, sometimes there are offshoots and tributaries from the main body of water. Those offshoots might represent feminists who are more focused on very specific targeted audiences, such as feminists who are organizing to change particular workplaces, industries, or neighborhoods. An example of one of these feminisms would be The Guerrilla Girls, who are working to diversify the art world (see Chapter 5 toolkit); or another example would be the neighborhood or community group that is providing support to transgender residents. In these examples, the feminists are part of the main feminist movement in the sense that they share water and are moving in the same direction as the river itself. However, they are not necessarily part of the main river of mass mobilization. It is these tributaries and forks in the river that help us understand why we refer to the feminist movement as plural feminisms, because there are many different streams of feminism that are flowing at the same time.

To continue with the waveless metaphor, also as a river, there can be rapids caused by a rocky bottom or sediment build-up. This might be understood as what happens when there is conflict in the feminist movement, such as around the organizing of the national Women's March, or when there are other external obstacles, such as when Russia was promulgating false information online about Women's March leaders in an effort to sow discontent in feminist organizing

(Barry, 2022). Yet, at other moments, the river is shallow, dry, or merely trickles, during times when there is not a lot of support for the movement. One period of time in the feminist movement that could represent this part of the river is during the 1980s, when feminism experienced a backlash after its previous successes, and mass attention to the movement fell out of fashion (Crossley, 2017).

"Waveless" feminism also helps us conceptualize how a movement is shaped by external events, such as how a river and its flow are shaped by the weather. A river, as you know, experiences rising and falling levels as a result of the climate. If it is a dry season or year, the river might be shallow. If it is a particularly rainy season or year, the river might be very high, running rapidly, or even spilling over its banks. To translate that to feminist terms, such a time period is that in which feminists are regenerated and experience an expansion in support, resources, and numbers of activists and allies.

The metaphor of waveless feminism is useful because it highlights how the movement is in motion, dynamic, and complex. It shows that even though the movement has different iterations, different moments of time in which it is especially vigorous or not, it still has some forward motion as does a river. Like water, the feminist movement is essential to the sustenance of our communities and society, and feminists are working for justice and equality that will ultimately benefit all.

Waveless feminism does not mean that the movement is in complete harmony or that there are no controversies facing feminists. It does mean, however, that it is moving, generally speaking in a similar direction and that it will, regardless of the conditions, continue, as long as gender inequality and related inequalities persist (Crossley, 2017).

The "waveless" imagery helps us understand the motion and complexity of feminism. It helps us see the movement all around us, as continually flowing. It trains us to think of feminism in intersectional and inclusive ways, which are changing, but ever-present. Waveless feminism doesn't privilege one mode of feminism over another, rather, it has room for all modes of feminism.

## Feminist Wave Framework

While waveless feminism is the most effective metaphor to examine feminism, it is important for readers to know that another frame of reference has dominated much of teaching and thinking of feminism. It is commonly called the feminist wave framework, as you may have heard, first, second, and third wave feminism. While it remains a popular shorthand in academic and broader settings, many scholars and activists alike criticize it for being inaccurate.

In contrast to waveless feminism, a wave of feminism is uniform and clearly has very fast and active peaks and then troughs. It is singular, with all the water coming together in one area as a wave, and then, poof, all of a sudden, disappearing. There may be sets of waves, with many waves coming to shore in rapid succession, but typically a wave is uniform. There are no offshoots, and all the water is going in one direction.

The feminist wave framework is shorthand to describe heightened periods of feminism on a national scale. While popular and continually cited, the feminist wave framework creates an inaccurate narrative of the feminist movement. Based on the information presented in this chapter, we know that feminism is more continuous and complex than a wave. Nonetheless, it is useful for readers to understand the feminist wave framework and to be able to compare and contrast wave vs. waveless feminism.

The feminist wave framework has been commonly thought of in three parts. The first wave was in the mid 19th to early 20th centuries, and focused on political and legal rights such as the right to vote. It is important to note that these rights benefited primarily white women, as there were still many women, mainly Black women and other Women of Color, who did not secure these rights until later.

The second wave was in the 1960s and 1970s when there was a massive spread of protest across progressive movements, including feminism, civil rights and peace movements. This is considered the classic time when women's movements from across the racial and ethnic spectrum were organizing, and when women secured reproductive and workplace rights.

The third wave of feminism has different origin stories. Some attribute it, as does Kimberly Springer (2002), to the late 1980s when Women of Color conceptualized feminism to be Women of Color-led and racially diverse. Others point to Black feminist author Rebecca Walker, who, in 1997, coined the term third wave in her edited anthology *To Be Real: Telling the Truth and*

*Changing the Face of Feminism.* The third wave of feminism is less clear than the first two waves but it was generally thought of as a feminism that is more racially diverse than the previous versions of feminism, and a feminism that is specifically engaged in by young people and queer people.

After the third wave, there have been several claims that a fourth wave or fifth wave has arrived. However, any claim of a wave beyond the 1990s, has basically fallen apart or at the very least, lacks the "stickiness" of the first three waves.

The feminist wave framework does correctly identify mass, general surges, and major milestones in feminist advancements. However, it gives an inaccurate picture of feminism that is either in a huge massive surge or nothing. It discounts the really vital work done between surges and mistakes one community's surge for everyone's surge. In fact, what is one community's feminist surge might be another's most challenging or least successful moment.

The feminist wave framework paints in very broad brushstrokes, reducing a variegated movement to singular dimensions. More than just making it simple, it focuses mostly on the feminism of white women who are generally privileged. As such, it is a whitewashing of a movement that is in actuality not exclusively white, making it seem more harmonious, more homogenous than it really is. So our very histories, our very framework of understanding have actually generated a false and problematic image of a movement.

Black feminist Kimberly Springer (2002) writes about the wave model: it "obscures the historical role of race in feminist organizing" and:

> "If we consider the first wave as that moment of organizing encompassing woman suffrage and the second wave as the women's liberation/women's rights activism of the late 1960s, we effectively disregard the race-based movements before them that served as precursors, or windows of political opportunity, for gender activism."
>
> (p. 1061)

Historians and other scholars have debated the utility of the feminist wave framework, with many of them arguing that the metaphor flattens a complex movement (Hewitt, 2012). So why do some people still use it? For some historians, the feminist wave framework allows them to generalize feminist activism during discrete periods of time, easily leading to comparisons and, owing to its simplicity, ensuring the inclusion of feminist and women's issues in textbooks that oftentimes ignore or gloss over women's issues (Laughlin et al., 2010, p. 84). Not inconsequentially, the wave metaphor is easy to grasp, so even someone without much knowledge of the movement might think they know what a "second wave feminist" is like (Laughlin et al., 2010). It is very hard to start fresh from that.

It is important to underscore how the feminist wave framework has misrepresented feminism and its history. It's not just that it is shorthand as feminist, but that it shapes how we understand the movement's history. It also may confine our future imagination of the movement. Instead, it is better to relinquish the desire to figure out a framework when feminism is just too complex to have one.

**Research Reflection:** Research one recent reference to second, third, or fourth wave feminism in the news media and/or in social media content. How is the feminist wave framework used or how is the feminist wave described? What is it shorthand for? Do you see evidence of waveless feminism in this reference?

## Analyses of Feminisms' Ancillary Trends

Understandings of the feminist movement have been shaped by news, media, and popular culture. Here are three different examples of narratives trying to make sense of feminisms' evolution.

### False Feminist Death Syndrome

The term False Feminist Death Syndrome was first used by media critic Jennifer Pozner (2003) as a way to analyze the peculiar way that feminism is constantly called dead, or its existence questioned, when actually the movement is alive and thriving.

One consequence of the feminist wave framework is that it is easy for us to see feminism as all-or-nothing, at the peak of a wave or dead in the trough of the wave. Part of it might be that waves have a "death" built into them also oftentimes a conservative US President or a shift in gender and racial dynamics can encourage belief in feminism's death.

So what? Why does this matter, you may ask. Who cares whether people think feminism is dead or not? Perceptions of social movements are significant. Public views on who is involved in a movement, and the overall image of a movement is critical to its survival. When a movement is constantly declared dead or irrelevant, then it makes a movement and its activists invisible. It becomes hard to attract new supporters, raise funds, or draw attention to the persistence of inequalities.

A major moment for feminism occurred in 1998 in *Time*, one of the world's largest circulating magazines and known historically to be a significant commentator on politics, culture, and the economy. That year, the July issue made a huge splash with the cover depicting four white feminists (Susan B. Anthony, Betty Friedan, Gloria Steinem, and, curiously "Ally McBeal" who is really actor Calista Flockhart), and the large red font asking: "Is Feminism Dead?"

This article showed thousands of readers that (white) feminism is essentially meaningless and diluted, with "its days of flat shoes and fiery protest behind it" (Bellafante, 1998, p. 54). When feminism is pronounced dead, the public may be convinced that any remaining feminists must be wrong or stupid to continue organizing, and that a reader might not have to make the annual donation to a feminist organization. It makes those people who remain in the movement fight an uphill battle. Feminism has been called dead and alive, over and over again. While in some ways social movement activists who are intent on changing the status quo will always experience pushback, feminism has explicitly had to manage the "death narrative" more so than other movements. Despite the consistency and perseverance of gender and other interrelated inequalities, feminists are compelled to argue for their relevance.

The ramifications of this narrative show that it is all the more important to propagate accurate perceptions of the feminist movement and its history, to recognize that a shift in its goals, ideas, or support structures does not mean that it is gone, and that it is okay for a massive movement like feminism to be heterogeneous, flourishing (or not) in unexpected places at unpredictable times. Despite this, as long as gender and interrelated inequalities persist, so will feminists.

**Research Reflection:** Research Jennifer Pozner's False Feminist Death Syndrome. What are its three key themes according to Pozner? Find one example of the syndrome in your social media feed or recent media coverage of feminism.

## *Feminist Backlash and Postfeminism*

After a period of feminist successes, in the cycle of social movement activity there is typically backlash (Mansbridge and Shames 2008). We can think of backlash as resistance to progressive change. Journalist Susan Faludi made the term famous in her book *Backlash: The Undeclared War Against American Women* (1991). She argues that in the 1980s there was a conservative backlash against the successes of feminism in the 1960s and 1970s. From her analysis of politics, media, and public opinion, Faludi demonstrated that there was an overall sentiment that feminists had gone too far. Themes of backlash have been exhibited in the perpetuation of stereotypes or scare tactics in public discourse, such as the narrative that the feminist movement is responsible for the demise of the family, for the unhappiness of men, or for any host of societal ills specifically involving family, marriage, and children. None of this was supported by research, in fact, most of it is totally fabricated. Nonetheless, these stereotypes still stand.

We can also see in the 2020s, after the height of #MeToo, a period of intense backlash against feminists (Grady, 2023). This took the form of politicians supporting laws taking basic fundamental rights away from pregnant people and women, such as the repeal of Roe vs. Wade, and the ongoing restrictions on bodily autonomy. Additionally, there is increasing popularity of public discourse romanticizing the traditional white nuclear heterosexual family. One of the major moments of the backlash against the successes of #MeToo occurred during the Johnny Depp and Amber Heard trial. Heard and her supporters were subjected to intense online harassment, and domestic violence was minimized and survivors vilified. According to Aja Romano in *Vox* (2022), Depp paid for "an army of bots" to spread lies about Heard and build his support and the far right "manosphere" "seems to have decided discrediting Amber Heard is the key to destroying every woman who accuses men of abuse or domestic violence." In tandem with the trial, there was a resurgence of acceptability in attacking women with misogynist threats, justification of domestic violence, and glorification of physically domineering white masculinity: not that the latter had disappeared at any point in time, but that during #MeToo there was more sympathy towards gender-based violence survivors. Many have labeled this trial as a clear time of backlash, and a consequence of the success of #MeToo.

**Moira Donegan** is a journalist and leading expert on feminism, gender, politics and the law. In a June 2022 *Guardian* article Donegan described the current moment of backlash with the backdrop of the Depp/Heard trial:

"While most of the vitriol is nominally directed at Heard, it is hard to shake the feeling that really, it is directed at all women – and in particular, at those of us who spoke out about gendered abuse and sexual violence during the height of the #MeToo movement. We are in a moment of virulent antifeminist backlash, and the modest gains that were made in that era are being retracted with a gleeful display of victim-blaming at a massive scale. One woman has been made into a symbol of a movement that many view with fear and hatred, and she's being punished for that movement."

The undertone for much of these backlash situations is that feminism is unnecessary, gender and intersectional inequalities are invented, and that whatever gains feminists have previously made have caused irreparable damage to our society.

Backlash supposes that there has been progress, and believes it needs to be reversed. British cultural studies theorist Angela McRobbie complicated the aftermath of a progressive feminist surge, and instead of focusing on the conservative responses to feminism, she focused on the savvy young women for whom feminism was typically relevant. In her article "Post-feminism and popular culture" (2007), McRobbie identifies a "postfeminist" period of time in which the recent gains of feminism are accepted and enjoyed by women. However, because the progress is taken for granted, there is a sense that feminism is no longer needed and that previously fought against modes of sexism were not actually that bad. Feminism is seen as done, over, and perhaps fuddy duddy, while its advancements are still appreciated. These women, often seen as "cool girls," are progressive and forward thinking, although McRobbie and others assert they are actually contributing to the "undoing" of feminism. Emerging from this phenomenon, sociologist Pamela Aronson (2003) labels some feminists "fence-sitters," women who won't categorize themselves as either feminists or nonfeminists and who concentrate on "evaluating the ideologies and stereotypes associated with feminism" (p. 916). These controversies about feminism illuminate the complexities in feminisms' ongoing nature, and the different approaches to what happens between surges of activism.

Evaluating postfeminism from a waveless feminism perspective is revealing. Given waveless feminisms' assurances that feminism is ongoing despite its peaks and valleys, there is never really a post, or *after* feminism, because the movement continues and each phase is in some ways preparing for the next. In contrast, in its very name, postfeminism supposes the false feminist death syndrome, or a time in which the movement is finished. At the same time, however, postfeminisms' analysis of the reaction to feminisms' success and women's navigation of shifting gender dynamics is useful.

## Case Study, Girl Boss Era

At some points in time, feminism has become very popular and garnered significant media attention. Such media attention can get feminism wrong or applies the feminist label to something that is not quite accurate (Zeisler, 2016). One example of this was the heyday of the Girl Boss era, beginning in approximately 2014 and declining rapidly around 2020. You may have heard of the star of Girl Bosses, *Nasty Gal's* Sophia Amoruso, who also wrote a book called "#Girl-Boss" and whose story was made into a Netflix series. Other well-known Girl Bosses include cosmetic company *Glossier's* Emily Weiss, women-clubhouse *The Wing's* Audrey Gelman, suitcase giant *Away's* Steph Korey, clothing company *Reformation's* Yael Aflalo, and athleisure purveyor *Outdoor Voices'* Tyler Haney. These Girl Bosses, many if not most of whom were young, white, and from affluent backgrounds, were ambitious and successful women entrepreneurs. Part and parcel of the Girl Boss era was the feminist ethos of women's empowerment and advancement. They also garnered substantial media attention, and Girl Bosses were widely held up as models of a new generation of feminists. They raised billions of dollars from investors (#riseandgrind). At one point Emily Weiss' *Glossier* was valued at over \$1 billion (Gupta, 2022).

However, in time, nearly all of them met their demise as entrepreneurs, because of claims of toxic work environments (Gupta, 2022), racism (Nesvig, 2020), or poor management (Kircher, 2023). Wrote Gupta for *The New York Times* (2022): "The accusations were particularly damaging precisely because most of these women climbed the ranks by proclaiming to be feminists, and implicitly, to be a new kind of boss" (note the "implicitly"). Indeed: "Wing support staff interviewed by *The New York Times* said they grew cynical about the company's version of feminism, which they said didn't include them" (Leonard, 2020). The decline of the Girl Boss was in large part also due to their being held up as models of feminism, which some extrapolated to mean they would be exceptional leaders who would challenge the status quo of the business world (Cheung, 2022b).

So how did it all collapse so rapidly? Well, the Girl Boss declined as the pandemic was raging, revealing massive and unprecedented gender, racial, and class inequalities. The Girl Boss also fell apart as tensions in corporate America increased following the murder of George Floyd. During that time, many companies, including many Girl Boss companies, released statements and gave funds to Black Lives Matter nonprofits. However, some of these very organizations were also plagued by accusations of racism, many of which were aired on social media. The combination of pandemic inequalities, Black Lives Matter, and the awareness of intersectional feminism, meant there was little patience for the Girl Boss and her faux feminism.

In a sense, the feminist Girl Boss was doomed, as Bridget Smith (2021) wrote "...the philosophy was flawed from its inception. Rather than pushing for institutional improvements, the girlboss exists within the institution. To be a girlboss is not to destroy the patriarchy but to independently conquer it. Girlboss feminism is also far from intersectional." There was the overall expectation that Girl Bosses would create a new women-forward business ethos that would transform much more than their industry. They were put on pedestals as beacons of hope in a white man-dominated business world. Samhita Mukhopadhyay told Jezebel: "It's this failed promise of, 'put these women in charge of companies and that will lead to the elevation of all people within a certain class or gender,' and we've seen that's not true" (Cheung, 2022b). But who made the promise? How did these women begin to carry all these expectations? Certainly, the Girl Bosses didn't collectively promise to elevate all people in their company or work to eradicate social ills. Rather each was (initially, at least) simply a savvy business executive who happened to be a young woman (likely white).

The Girl Boss example does teach us about the tensions in feminism, and the chasm between intersectional feminism and other feminisms more focused on individual success. Kylie Cheung wrote the following for Jezebel on International Women's Day in 2022:

> "In the US, girlboss capitalism and the rise of the She-E-O have obscured the inextricable links between capitalist, patriarchal, and white supremacist oppressions. Because of the glass-ceiling shattering successes of a few often highly privileged women... we're supposed to forget that many feminist struggles are rooted in capitalism, and many labor and economic injustices rooted in patriarchy."

A major critique of Girl Boss feminism is that it is taking the principles of women's advancement and using them to make as much money as possible while likely stepping on many people on the way up.

While the Girl Bosses deserve much of the criticism directed their way, it is also important to examine its gendered nature. As one commentator wrote: "a male girlboss is just a boss" (Jones, 2023). In fact, some men have been bad managers, racist, sexist, and have driven their businesses into the ground with unsustainable business practices. And yet, their stories are often unexceptional. High-profile cases of men who have lied to their investors and swindled billions of dollars from their corporations certainly make the nightly news. But the everyday garden variety of man start-up king who fails does not receive the kind of attention that the Girl Boss did– in fact a *New York Times* article in the fall of 2023 (Kircher, 2023), was still discussing the decline of the Girl Boss, and a last Girl Boss business to close.

## Chapter 3 Mini Toolkit: Feminist Community and Black Joy Farm

Feminist resistance has occurred over generations. Perhaps because of its continuous and varied nature, there have been many theories about the dynamics of feminisms during periods before and after surges. We do know that even when feminists are not drawing national attention to the movement, intersectional feminists are still organizing and working on change in their communities.

Women's movement scholar Jo Reger has dedicated much of her work to analyzing the persistence of feminism through community-level organizing. She writes (2012) "When we conceptualize feminism, or any social movement activism, as occurring in waves, we create a rise and decline that does not necessarily capture the community-level mobilization of a movement" (p. 193). In this toolkit, you will learn about the importance of community in feminist change- making through the Black Joy Farm, which is part of the Black Feminist Project. The Black Joy Farm, "a radical food-growing green space in the South Bronx" (Black Feminist Project, n.d.) provides community-building space and fresh food to people particularly affected by poverty, the intersections of racism and sexism, and homophobia. They especially serve what they call MaGes, or individuals with marginalized genders, such as those who are gender queer or transgender. This organization, while a valuable community group, is not necessarily exceptional. Rather, it is representative of an organization practicing intersectional and everyday feminism, taking care of its neighbors and some of the neediest populations.

Black Joy Farm's community-building is feminist activism because it creates a space for individuals who are particularly harmed by society's inequalities related to gender and race. It allows them to share their experiences, to make connections with others who hold similar views, to learn that their own individual challenges are in all likelihood not unique to them but are symptomatic of larger structural inequalities, to build friendships, and last but not least, to experience joy. Providing basic sustenance (food) to a community is feminist activism because we all need food to live, and helping ourselves and others experience healthy and full lives is a revolutionary act. In a society in which women and people of color are disproportionately living in poverty and concentrated in low paying jobs, providing them with nutritious food grown by other community members for little to no cost is a radical idea. Put together, strong and resilient individuals and feminist communities are created, a clear and powerful resistance to a world that is so often working against these individuals.

This type of community activism would not be reflected in the feminist wave framework. It is neither huge nor dramatic, so is easily overlooked by narrow definitions of feminism. Instead, if we use a wide lens to view feminism, we can see how small-scale, local groups can have a tremendous impact.

To get involved and to learn more:

- Research Black Joy Farm. What is their mission, and how do they employ intersectionality in their work?
- Research an organization in your area or state that is building community among feminists, women, girls, and/or gender non-conforming individuals. Compare its goals and approaches to those of Black Joy Farm.
- Through an online search, find another local or community-based organization that is creating feminist change through community-building. How does this organization fit into waveless feminism and the evolution of feminism described in this chapter?

## Chapter 3 Dive Deeper

*Badass Feminist Politics* (Edited by Sarah Jane Blithe and Janell C. Bauer)
*Is It Time to Jump Ship? Historians Rethink the Waves Metaphor* (Kathleen A. Laughlin, Julie Gallagher, Dorothy Sue Cobble, Eileen Boris, Premilla Nadasen, Stephanie Gilmore, Leandra Zarnow)
*Third Wave Black Feminism?* (Kimberly Springer)
*Trick Mirror* (Jia Tolentino)
*Burn It Down!: Feminist Manifestos for the Revolution* (Breanne Fahs)

## References

Almeida, M. 2014. [No title].

Aronson, P. (2003). Feminists or "Postfeminists"?: Young Women's Attitudes toward Feminism and Gender Relations. *Gender and Society*, 17(6), 903–922. www.jstor.org/stable/3594676.

Bellafante, G. (1998, June 29). Feminism: It's All About Me! *Time*. Retrieved November 21, 2023, from https://content.time.com/time/subscriber/article/0,33009,988616-1,00.html.

Barry, E. (2022, September 18). How Russian Trolls Helped Keep the Women's March out of Lock Step. *The New York Times*. From https://www.nytimes.com/2022/09/18/us/womens-march-russia-trump.html.

Black Feminist Project. (n.d.) Black Joy Farm. Retrieved November 21, 2023, from www.theblackfeministproject.org/blackjoyfarm.

Cheung, K. (2022a, March 8). International Women's Day Isn't A Corporate Holiday You Ghouls . *Jezebel*. Retrieved November 29, 2023, from https://jezebel.com/international-women-s-day-isn-t-a-corporate-holiday-yo-1848622410.

Cheung, K. (2022b, April 8). Hollywood's Best Punchline Is the 'Girlboss'. *Jezebel*. Retrieved November 21, 2023, from https://jezebel.com/hollywoods-best-punchline-is-the-girlboss-1848767485.

Crossley, A.D. (2017). *Finding Feminism: Millennial Activists and the Unfinished Gender Revolution*. NYU Press. doi:10.2307/j.ctt1ggjjdg.

Davis, A. (2009, November 12). *Difficult Dialogues* [Lecture]. National Women's Studies Association Conference, Atlanta, United States of America.

Donegan, M. (June 1, 2022). The Amber Heard-Johnny Depp trial was an orgy of misogyny. *The Guardian*. Retrieved November 21, 2023, from www.theguardian.com/commentisfree/2022/jun/01/amber-heard-johnny-depp-trial-metoo-backlash.

Faludi, S. (1991). *Backlash: the undeclared war against American women*. Anchor Books.

Ferree, M.M & B.B. Hess. (2000). *Controversy and Coalition: The New Feminist Movement Across Four Decades of Change*. Routledge.

Grady, C. (2023, February 3). The mounting, undeniable Me Too backlash. *Vox*. Retrieved November 21, 2023, from www.vox.com/culture/23581859/me-too-backlash-susan-faludi-weinstein-roe-dobbs-depp-heard.

Gupta, A. (2022, May 31). The Sunsetting of the Girlboss Is Nearly Complete. *The New York Times*. Retrieved November 21, 2023, from www.nytimes.com/2022/05/26/style/glossier-emily-weiss.html.

Hawkesworth, M. (2004). The semiotics of premature burial: Feminism in a postfeminist age. *Signs: Journal of Women in Culture and Society*, 29(4), 961–985.

Hewitt, N.A. (2012). Feminist Frequencies: Regenerating the Wave Metaphor. *Feminist Studies*, 38(3), 658–680. www.jstor.org/stable/23720198.

Jones, D. (2023, August 10). Yes, the Girlboss is dead—But Her Replacement Isn't So Great, Either. *Vogue*. Retrieved November 21, 2023, from www.vogue.com/article/girlboss-is-dead-but-her-replacement-isnt-so-great-either.

Jones, F. (2019). *Reclaiming Our Space: How Black Feminists Are Changing the World from the Tweets to the Streets*. Beacon Press.

Kircher, M. (2023, October 3). What Happened to Shen Beauty?. *The New York Times*. Retrieved November 21, 2023, from www.nytimes.com/2023/10/03/style/shen-beauty-brooklyn.html?searchResultPosition=1.

Laughlin, K.A., Gallagher, J., Cobble, D.S., Boris, E., Nadasen, P., Gilmore, S., & Zarnow, L. (2010). Is It Time to Jump Ship? Historians Rethink the Waves Metaphor. *Feminist Formations*, 22(1), 76–135. www.jstor.org/stable/40835345.

Leonard, S. (2020, May 5). Socialist Feminism: What Is It and How Can It Replace Corporate 'Girl Boss' Feminism? *Teen Vogue*. Retrieved November 21, 2023, from www.teenvogue.com/story/what-is-socialist-feminism.

Mansbridge, J. & Shames, S. (2008). Toward a Theory of Backlash: Dynamic Resistance and the Central Role of Power. *Politics & Gender*, 4 (4), 623–634. doi:10.1017/S1743923X08000500.

Mascia, J. (2010, July 11). A Web Site That's Not Afraid to Pick a Fight. *The New York Times*. Retrieved November 20, 2023, from www.nytimes.com/2010/07/12/business/media/12jezebel.html.

McCammon, H.J., Campbell, K.E., Granberg, E.M., & Mowery, C. (2001). How Movements Win: Gendered Opportunity Structures and U.S. Women's Suffrage Movements, 1866 to 1919. *American Sociological Review*, 66(1), 49–70. doi:10.2307/2657393.

McRobbie, A. (2004). Post-feminism and popular culture. *Feminist media studies*, 4(3), 255–264. doi:10.1080/14660970.2023.2211535.

Mendez, K. (n.d.). Honoring 50 years of the National Black Feminist Organization: an interview with Dr. Kimberly Springer. *Black Women Radicals*. Retrieved November 20, 2023, from www.blackwomenradicals.com/blog-feed/kimberly-springer.

Nesvig, K. (2020, June 14). Reformation Founder Yael Aflalo Resigns After Allegations of Racism. *Teen Vogue*. Retrieved November 21, 2023, from www.teenvogue.com/story/reformation-founder-yael-aflalo-apologizes-for-past-racist-behavior.

Ohlheiser, A. (2017, October 19). The woman behind 'Me Too' knew the power of the phrase when she created it—10 years ago. *The Washington Post*. Retrieved November 19, 2023, from www.washingtonpost.com/

news/the-intersect/wp/2017/10/19/the-woman-behind-me-too-knew-the-p
ower-of-the-phrase-when-she-created-it-10-years-ago.

Pozner, J.L. (2003). "The 'big lie': False feminist death syndrome, profit, and
the media." In *Catching a wave: Reclaiming feminism for the 21st century*,
R. Dicker & A. Piepmeier (Eds). Boston: Northeastern University.

Reger, J. (2012). *Everywhere and Nowhere: Contemporary Feminism in the
United States*. Oxford University Press.

Romano, A. (2022, May 20). Why the Depp-Heard trial is so much worse
than you realize. *Vox*. Retrieved November 21, 2023, from www.vox.
com/culture/23131538/johnny-depp-amber-heard-tiktok-snl-extremism.

Sandoval C. (1991). U.S. third world feminism: the theory and method of
oppositional consciousness in the postmodern world. *Genders*, (10), 1–24.

Smith, B. (2021, October 15). *The Fall of the #GirlBoss*. The Women's
Network. Retrieved November 21, 2023, from www.thewomens.net
work/blog/the-fall-of-the-girlboss.

Springer, K. (2002). Third Wave Black Feminism? *Signs*, 27(4), 1059–1082.
doi:10.1086/339636.

Staggenborg, S. (1998). Social Movement Communities and Cycles of Protest: The Emergence and Maintenance of a Local Women's Movement.
*Social Problems*, 45(2), 180–204. doi:10.2307/3097243.

Taylor, V. (1989). Social Movement Continuity: The Women's Movement in
Abeyance. *American Sociological Review*, 54(5), 761–775. doi:10.2307/
2117752.

Van Dyke, N. (2017). Movement Emergence and Resource Mobilization:
Organizations, Leaders, and Coalition Work. In H.J. McCammon, V.
Taylor, J. Reger, & R.L. Einwohner (Eds), *The Oxford Handbook of U.
S. Women's Social Movement Activism*, pp. 354–375. Oxford University
Press. doi:10.1093/oxfordhb/9780190204204.013.18.

Zeisler, A. (2016). *We Were Feminists Once: From Riot Grrrl to Covergirl,
the Buying and Selling of a Political Movement*. New York: Public
Affairs.

# 4  What do Feminists Care About?

This chapter is all about the inequalities that drive feminists to create change and organize. In order to fully understand feminists and feminisms, it is important to comprehend the vast spectrum of inequalities that affect women's lives which in turn generate feminist movements. You will learn that feminists have a variety of concerns that drive their organizing, depending on their communities and experiences. You will also learn that the inequalities feminists care about are deeply connected with the work of other social movements, both feminist and non-feminist.

Key themes throughout this chapter include inequalities in the workplace, in the home, and in the family. All of these inequalities are interconnected and related to our society and community's expectations of women, what women should prioritize, and how women should act in the world, in both public and private spheres. Interwoven throughout this chapter are themes of power and domination. Note that these are but subsets of all the feminist issues that determine feminist action.

The inequalities that mobilize feminists are related to the intersections of gender, race, class, sexuality, and other categories of identity. Women from different backgrounds and with different life circumstances will not have the same concerns and will be motivated to organize for different causes. However, there are many across-the-board issues that unequivocally affect most women, which is where we start this chapter.

Key terms presented in this chapter:

- Wage gap
- Gender-based violence

DOI: 10.4324/9781003310990-5

- Healthcare inequalities
- Reproductive health care
- Prison industrial complex
- Climate change and environmental inequalities
- Childcare insecurity
- Inequality in technology and Online Harassment
- Media inequality
- Political representation

## Wages and the Wage Gap

Women have been working for wages as long as there have been wages. While many more women worked for pay in the 1970s than previously, owing to socioeconomic conditions many women (and particularly Women of Color) have always had to work. According to a 2023 Pew study, only 23 percent of US heterosexual married households consist of men being the sole breadwinner, and women's economic contributions to the household have continued to grow steadily (Pew Research Center, 2023). Nevertheless, there is a dramatic wage gap between men and women. The wage gap is the difference between the "median weekly full-time earnings for all women compared to all men," across industry and occupation (Institute for Women's Policy Research, 2022). More women are living in poverty than any other group because they make less money. If there was ever an issue affecting all women, this is it.

The wage gap varies slightly from year to year but has not improved significantly in recent history. In fact, a state-by-state study found that women's economic well-being was stagnant or declining in most US states (The Institute for Women's Policy Research, 2018).

In a 2021 study by the Institute for Women's Policy Research (IWPR), "Compared to the median weekly earnings of White men working full-time, Hispanic women's full-time earnings were just 58.4 percent, Black women's 63.1 percent, and White women's 79.6 percent" (p. 1). In other words, for every approximately 58 cents that a Hispanic woman makes, a non-Hispanic white man makes a dollar. In 2022 the wage gap cost women $1.6 trillion over all types of employment (National Partnership for Women & Families, 2023).

Although women are now surpassing men in college education, their wages have not risen concurrently. 36 percent of millennial women have college degrees, compared to 28 percent of men millennials, yet they continue to be paid less (Institute for Women's Policy Research, 2015).

The wage gap is a commonly cited statistic and phenomenon. Perhaps this is one reason why the existence of this extreme and persistent inequality fails to shock. Jocelyn Frye, the president of the National Partnership of Women & Families said to CNBC in 2023: "We've had the pay gap for so long, people have become desensitized to it and think it's normal…But it's not anything that we should consider normal, and we ought not to normalize disparities that ought not to exist."

There are three primary factors that contribute to the wage gap (Pew Research Center, 2016). Note that much of this research is based on heterosexual marriages and nuclear families. First, in the same occupation and job, men will be paid more than women. Women are paid less for the same work. Women are not promoted, or are not seen as fit as men for management and high-pay positions (Pew Research Center, 2016). One research study (Hodges and Budig, 2010) found fathers are rewarded with greater pay in the assumption that they need to provide financially for their families, and men who are white, college-educated, and professional receive the largest "fatherhood bonus." In contrast, research by Correll, Benard, and Paik (2007) showed that job candidates who are mothers are penalized with less pay and judged less competent and committed to their work than fathers, with African American and white women experiencing this "motherhood penalty" to similar degrees.

The second perspective from which the wage gap can be understood is that women of all races and ethnicities are disproportionately concentrated in low-paying jobs and industries, such as care work, retail, or other positions in the service industry. This phenomenon is known as occupational segregation. Despite the fact that women on the whole are becoming more educated, they are increasingly overrepresented in low-wage work (National

Women's Law Center, 2017). Sarah Jane Glynn, a senior advisor at the Labor Department's Women's Bureau, said to CNBC in 2022:

> "These jobs in these sectors are devalued because of the folks who are doing the work... It's the fact that it's women — and often what color who are doing this labor — that has been shown to directly lead to its devaluation. And this is part of the reason why occupational segregation contributes to the wage gap."

"Women's professions," or any field in which women are concentrated, are devalued. However, when men enter a field, it gains status. For example, computer programming was historically a low-status occupation dominated by women. As men became programmers the profession's importance and pay increased (Ensmenger, 2012). Research by Christine L. Williams (1992) shows when men enter employment spheres dominated by women, such as elementary school teaching, nursing, social work, and librarianship, they will ride the "glass escalator;" meaning they are rapidly promoted and experience many advantages that benefit their careers, independent of ability or experience. This is not the case when a woman enters an occupation dominated by men. There are limits to the jobs and professions that women can enter, and at the same time, whatever fields they enter will be devalued.

But the wage gap is not about what happens in the workplace alone. The third driver of the wage gap is due to the fact that women spend much more time than men on caretaking, child-rearing, and domestic duties. This holds true for all racial and ethnic groups (Hess et al., 2020). Arlie Russell Hochschild (1989) calls women's additional responsibility for caretaking and household labor "the second shift," meaning many women work one shift in the paid labor force and then come home to an additional unpaid shift. Factor in that caretaking and all domestic and household labor is time and energy-intensive (Fielding-Singh and Cooper, 2023). It requires planning, communicating, identifying needs, managing and prioritizing the desires of multiple people, and making decisions (Daminger, 2019; see also Cooper, 2014). This additional labor disproportionately falls on women and affects how many hours they can devote to paid labor- plus allows less time to advance their careers, less time to attend work functions if required outside of work hours, less time to work extra hours, less time to get additional credentials, all done with significantly less energy.

One might imagine that when a woman advances in her profession and career, her skills and talents would mitigate the wage gap. Not so. As white women and Women of Color advance in their careers, the wage gap between women and men widens. The 2023 Nobel Prize-winning economist Claudia Goldin and her collaborators (2017) write: the "gender earnings gap widens considerably during the first decade and a half after schooling ends particularly for college graduates, those in certain sectors, and those who were ever-married" (p. 113). While the gap varies a bit by industry and by whether a woman attended college or not, the overall theme holds. Reasons for the widening gap include having children, women's need for flexibility in a job to allow for caretaking and household duties, or fewer advancement opportunities in a job (Goldin et al., 2017). It should be noted that this is not necessarily what a woman desires. She may intend to prioritize her career advancement but is held back by gendered expectations, both in a job and in the home (Ely and Padavic, 2020). Researchers have identified that in dual-earner high-achieving heterosexual couples, men's careers frequently take priority, even when the women had expected egalitarian arrangements that would allow them to be similarly dedicated to their careers as their partner (Ely et al., 2014).

**Professor Claudia Goldin**, 2023 Nobel Prize winner in Economics. Goldin is on the faculty at Harvard University and is the first woman to win the Nobel Prize solo in her field. With expertise in the wage gap, Goldin's research has also identified just how significant the division of care work and household labor is for perpetuating gender inequality. She said to CNBC "Make It" in October 2023: "We are never going to have gender equality, or narrow the pay gap, until we have couple's equity."

Wage gap reverberations are felt across the country in profound ways, and in almost all races and ethnicities women have higher rates of poverty than men (Center for American Progress, 2020). Poverty rates are particularly high for Black, Latinx, and Native women, disabled women, women born out of the US, and households headed by single mothers (Sun, 2023). To provide some additional examples, almost 25% of Hispanic women and more than 20% of Black women work in services (lowest earnings) compared to just over 10% of white women, "and one in 11 white men" (IWPR).

**The feminization of poverty**: This term points out that poverty now overwhelmingly affects women. Scholars have used the term "feminized" to emphasize the gender-specific nature of poverty, and to draw attention to the social structures that contribute to the economic vulnerability of women.

The ramifications of such poverty are extreme. According to research in *The Lancet* (Bor, Cohen, & Galea, 2017) there are strong connections between an individual's socioeconomic condition and their health, and many negative health outcomes for low-income Americans. Because women are overrepresented in poor populations, many children experience these adverse outcomes as well. A report by the Institute for Women's Policy Research (2018) found: "More than four in ten households (43.1 percent) headed by single women with children live in poverty, compared with nearly one in four (23.6 percent) households headed by single men with children and fewer than one in ten (8.5 percent) married couples with children."

The COVID-19 pandemic also had a serious impact on wages and poverty in the United States, with income, food, and housing insecurity rising. Although federal support of families and children increased during the pandemic and child poverty reached its lowest rate in 2021 (Sun, 2023), according to one 2022 study from the National Women's Law Center, "Black, non-Hispanic women and Latinas were more likely than white, non-hispanic men and women to report a recent loss of household employment income" (p. 2). While the state of equality has been worsening overall, the wage gap paradoxically narrowed during the pandemic, but not because women's wages rose. The Institute for Women's Policy Research (2021) found that: "Women's average earnings increased more than men's because lowest paid women were the most likely to lose jobs during the COVID-19 shecession—and are no longer counted in the average women's weekly median earnings. As a result of the missing lowest-paid women, the gender wage gap narrowed."

A "**Shecession**" is an economic decline that disproportionately affects women, such as during and immediately following the 2019 pandemic. The term was used first by C. Nicole Mason, president of the Institute for Women's Policy Research in the context of the 2008 economic crisis. The concept highlights the importance of considering gender-specific dynamics when analyzing economic trends, and developing policies to address the uneven effects of recessions on different demographic groups.

## Case Study, Wage Gap and Trucking

The trucking industry is known to pay better than many other industries that don't require a college degree, and truckers can make a lucrative salary, particularly as they gain experience (Eavis, 2023). However, the door to this profession is largely closed to women. According to a 2023 *New York Times* report by Peter Eavis, many trucking companies have informal policies that prohibit men from training women. Women can't be hired if they can't be trained. Eavis found that some are concerned that mixed-gender training will lead to sexual harassment by the man trainer, with the close quarters during training and sleeping in the truck on long hauls. Some companies have sidestepped this by having trainees sleep in hotels, while others point out that perhaps women should not be effectively barred from an industry because of possible sexual abuse by men in that same industry. A complaint has been filed at the Equal Employment Opportunity Commission by women caught in this catch-22 situation. For more information, see the organization Real Women in Trucking.

## Gender-Based Violence

Gender-based violence is an umbrella term for violence against women and transgender people. It has been a major grievance for feminists over many generations. Gender-based violence includes intimate partner violence, between romantically or sexually involved individuals; domestic violence, against women and children living in a household together; any kind of rape or sexual assault, stalking, and sexual harassment including but not limited to workplace sexual harassment. While women can be perpetrators of gender-based violence, the overwhelming majority of violence against women is by men perpetrators (Hattery and Smith, 2019, Fleming et al., 2015).

Each of these categories has significant nuance and complexity, and is certainly intersectional in nature. It is difficult to research and gather statistics, owing to both the stigma and secrecy surrounding gender-based violence, as well as the wide spectrum of behaviors that constitute gender-based violence.

Why does gender-based violence occur and what can we learn about it? Gender-based violence is largely attributed to power, and exertion of power and control over women by men (Hattery and Smith, 2019). It is a misconception that it is about sexual desire or attraction. In settings in which the gender binary and gender hierarchies are especially pronounced, such as in the military, fraternities, and even academia, gender-based violence is seen as a heightened problem; in these settings traditional gender norms are upheld and even revered (Armstrong and Hamilton 2015; Martin, 2016). The way in which leaders convey the importance/lack of importance of sexual harassment in their organization matters to individuals and the overall climate (Hart, Correll, and Crossley, 2018). Moreover, a major study found that: "Organizational climate is, by far, the greatest predictor of the occurrence of sexual harassment, and ameliorating it can prevent people from sexually harassing others" (National Academies of Sciences, Engineering, and Medicine, 2018, p. 171).

**Toxic masculinity** refers to a set of deeply ingrained societal expectations regarding how men and boys should behave. It prescribes that they should be emotionally reserved, insensitive, and tough. Those who do not conform to these norms often face social stigmatization and criticism. The culture of toxic masculinity emphasizes dominance over women, and is also related to sexism, homophobia, and to the prevalence of gender-based violence (Harrington, 2021; Katz, Earp, and Rabinovitz, 2013).

Regardless of the causes, the statistics on gender-based violence are staggering. One alarming statistic is that one in four women undergraduates is sexually assaulted, according to a 2019 report produced by the Association of American Universities (Cantor et al., 2019). More broadly, the National Intimate Partner and Sexual Violence Survey (2016/2017) found that one in four women experienced completed or attempted rape during her lifetime, nearly one in two women experienced unwanted sexual contact over the course of their life, and "[m]ore than 2 in 5 non-Hispanic American Indian/Alaska Native (43.7%) and non-Hispanic multiracial (48.0%) women were raped in their lifetime" (Leemis et al., 2022, p. 5).

Interpersonal and domestic violence often escalates to the extreme. Of the women in the US who were victims of murder or nonnegligent manslaughter in 2021 and who were reported to the authorities, 34 percent were killed by an intimate partner (Smith, 2022). The gender-based killing of women is termed femicide. The US has very high rates of femicide in comparison to other high-income countries. In fact, statistics show that everyday in the US, three women are killed at the hands of an intimate partner (Sanctuary for Families, 2023).

These statistics shift with considerations of race/ethnicity, class, and other identity categories. Men kill Black women and girls at rates three times higher than white women, and kill Indigenous women and girls at rates six times higher than white women (Sanctuary for Families, 2023). According to research from the US Department of Justice (2004), of all races, Native American/Indigenous women are the most likely to experience rape or sexual assault, primarily by non-Native and non-Indigenous perpetrators (Rosay, 2016). Transgender individuals experience much more interpersonal violence than cisgender people (Peitzmeier et al., 2020).

Are you interested in learning more about the prevalence of sexual harassment in US workplaces and institutions? Kirby Dick and Amy Ziering's documentary *The Invisible War* explores the epidemic of sexual assault in the US military. It has won or been nominated for many prestigious awards. It has motivated survivors to come out, instigated lawsuits revealing the culture of sexual assault in the military, and led to policy change.

After watching the documentary, reflect on the main points of the film. What was surprising to you? How is the military similar to or different from other contexts? What changes occurred as a result of the film?

Another form of gender-based violence is sexual harassment. Sexual harassment in the workplace has been an important feminist issue for generations, with spikes of attention to the issue at various periods of time, such as during Anita Hill's testimony in 1991 and the events of #MeToo in 2017. Much of the awareness was devoted to high-profile cases of perpetrators who held elite and powerful positions, i.e. Clarence Thomas, Harvey Weinstein, and Matt Lauer. However, it is important to note that sexual harassment is rampant on all levels and in all industries, although the consequences of coming forward may be more severe and pronounced in hourly and low-wage jobs (frequently dominated by Women of Color). In low-wage jobs, power asymmetries are more extreme than in high-wage jobs (think service sector and customer-facing jobs, where workers must constantly meet customer needs) (Semuels, 2017).

Accommodation and food service are the industries with the most sexual harassment reports filed (Semuels, 2017). In one survey, two-thirds of women fast food workers reported experiencing sexual harassment from restaurant management, and nearly 80 percent of women experienced sexual harassment from customers (Center for American Progress, 2017). Other low-wage work that has garnered attention for sexual harassment is farming (Ramchandani, 2018; Sexsmith et al., 2023; Waugh, 2010).

What about reporting sexual harassment? There are many barriers, including the fear of retaliation and workplace cultures that vilify survivors (Bergman et al., 2002). Those on lower socio-economic brackets might have a more extreme fear of reporting sexual harassment if they are living paycheck to paycheck. Speaking to financial consequences, one study by McLaughlin et al. (2017) found that workplace sexual harassment causes financial difficulties when survivors need to change jobs, severely disrupting or limiting career advancement (see also Loya, 2015).

A study by Peitzmeier et al. (2022) stated that during the COVID-19 pandemic abused women experienced greater intensity of domestic violence, and those who had not previously experienced violence in the home began experiencing it. New or more intense cases of interpersonal violence in this study were found to be more concentrated in marginalized communities, highlighting the importance of an intersectional lens.

**Anita Hill** is a professor at Brandeis University. On October 11, 1991, Professor Hill testified in a Senate Judiciary Committee hearing that Supreme Court nominee Clarence Thomas had sexually harassed her when they both worked at the Equal Employment Opportunity Commission. She sat before a committee of 14 white men, answering their questions in a televised hearing, sharing her experiences of ongoing sexual harassment by Thomas in excruciating detail. Other witnesses were prepared to corroborate Hill's testimony, but were not called. Sukari Hardnett was one of them.

In an interview for NPR in 2018, Hardnett said:

> "Well, I worked in the same position that Anita Hill worked in as a special assistant to the chairman in the chairman's office. And oftentimes, I saw people come in and out of the chairman's office... And I knew that what she was saying was true because I'd observed some of those very same situations myself."

On October 15, 1991, the Senate voted to confirm Thomas' nomination.

In an interview on NPR in 2021, Hill reflects on her testimony: "Thirty years later, I'm here to say that even though Clarence Thomas was confirmed, I do believe that what I did was effective because it opened the conversation publicly in a way that had never been done before... I've heard from people whose lives have been changed because that conversation was open."

**Christine Blasey Ford** is a professor at Palo Alto University. On September 27, 2018, Dr. Ford testified in a Senate Judiciary Committee hearing that Supreme Court nominee Brett

Kavanaugh had sexually assaulted her while they were both in high school (Ford, 2024). Ford described Kavanaugh's sexual violence in detail. Deborah Ramirez and other witnesses who had also come forward with accusations against Kavanaugh were ignored (Mayer and Farrow, 2018). Ford's testimony ignited solidarity and protest of women and gender-based violence survivors. The hashtag "WhyIdidntReport" blew up. Women across the world declared "I believe Christine Blasey Ford."

A *Time* magazine cover article (Edwards, 2018) described the reaction to Dr. Ford's testimony:

> "Republican Senator Chuck Grassley, the chairman of the Judiciary Committee, congratulated Ford on her bravery. President Trump, rarely one to give credence to the claims of female accusers, called Ford 'a very fine woman' and a 'credible witness,' and deemed her testimony 'compelling.' Within hours, three Republican governors and the American Bar Association had called for a delay on Kavanaugh's confirmation vote until there could be a thorough investigation. The prominent Catholic magazine America withdrew its support for the nominee. An NPR/PBS NewsHour/Marist poll released Oct. 3 found that 45 percent of respondents thought Ford was telling the truth, compared to 33 percent who believed Kavanaugh."

On October 6, 2018, the senate voted to confirm Kavanaugh's nomination.

## Health Disparities

Feminists have historically drawn attention to gender and intersectional inequalities in healthcare. Inequalities are found in all areas, including clinical trials, diagnosis, treatment, funding to research different diseases, and medical education (Klein et al. 2019; Altieri et al. 2019). The tradition of historical travesties and medical research is well documented, such as the case of Marion Sims, a physician and leader in the development of the field of obstetrics and gynecology, who in the 1840s experimented on awake Black women (Wailoo, 2018).

Across many conditions and diagnoses, marginalized patients have worse outcomes, invalidation of their symptoms, and underdiagnosis of their health problems (Moyer, 2022; Kirkland, Talesh, and Perone, 2021; Washington, 2008). One study found that health care providers overlooked severe symptoms of neck pain in young people, women, and people of color, but ordered lab tests for men who reported the same symptoms (Hamberg et al., 2002). Another study found that misdiagnosis of stroke is more likely among women, Medicare/Medicaid recipients, and non-white patients (Newman-Toker et al., 2014). There are also major gender and racial disparities in the treatment of heart disease (Mensah and Fuster, 2022). One study found that women admitted to the emergency department with a heart attack are more likely to die than men, if cared for by a male physician (Greenwood et al., 2018). Finally, from the medical education standpoint, white medical residents were found to hold scientifically false beliefs about biological differences between Black and white patients (such as the incorrect belief that Black patients experience less pain and have thicker skin than white patients) that could perpetuate racial biases in treatment (Hoffman et al. 2015).

There are also documented inequalities related to health events such as menstruation, pregnancy, childbirth, and menopause. Menstruation remains stigmatized and misunderstood, despite its common nature. In fact, it was not until August 2023 that period products' absorption was tested with actual blood rather than saline (DeLoughery et al., 2023). "Period poverty" or "lack of access to menstrual products, hygiene facilities, waste management, and education" (Michel et al., 2022, p. 1) disproportionately affects people of color and those of low socioeconomic status (Rapp and Kilpatrick, 2020). Researchers and medical professionals have called period poverty a "public health crisis" (Davies, 2021), and have found that those living in period poverty are restricted in their school or work attendance, civic participation, and overall activity.

The tampon tax is a tax on period products. Many groups have organized against it. In early 2023, CVS announced that it was reducing the price of its CVS brand period products by 25 percent as well as covering the state sales tax of those products.

Does your state have a tampon tax? Why is this so important? See allianceforperiodsupplies.org.

Intersectional perspectives on fertility and pregnancy reveal layers of inequalities. Although there is an increasing trend of Assisted Reproductive Technologies (ART) being covered in workplace health insurance, disparities remain, queer and Black individuals still find it largely inaccessible (Tam, 2021; Seifer et al., 2020).

Variations in the experiences of pregnant people highlight multiple facets of intersectional inequalities. Pregnant people in rural areas, often with inadequate healthcare, are more likely than urban women to experience pregnancy complications and possible death (Committee on Health Care for Underserved Women, 2014). Black and pregnant poor women experience high rates of surveillance (monitoring) related to their pregnancies resulting in criminalization of miscarriages and stillbirths (Goodwin, 2020). Robust research by Hill et al. (2022) indicates that Black pregnant women have extremely high rates of death, owing to pregnancy and childbearing complications, as well as high infant mortality rates, attributed to economic dynamics related to health insurance and also the overlooking or non-diagnosis of pain and other symptoms by health care providers. It is important to note that research finds this directly tied to systematic racism: "disparities in maternal and infant health persist even when controlling for certain underlying social and economic factors, such as education and income, pointing to the roles racism and discrimination play in driving disparities" (Hill et al., 2022). Research on other populations finds that "Native Hawaiian or Other Pacific Islander" populations and "American Indians" also have very high rates of infant mortality, with the non-Hispanic White and Asian populations having the lowest rates (Jang and Lee, 2022). Rates of maternal mortality in the US are nearly three times higher than other high income countries (Petrullo, 2023). Strikingly, a study of 1.8 million hospital births found that when Black newborns are cared for by Black doctors (representing a phenomenon called racial concordance) infant mortality is reduced by half (Greenwood et al., 2020).

Postpartum depression (PPD) affects people after they have given birth. It is described as a "foggy unreality" (Kennedy et al., 2002, p.

318) in which a person has feelings of depression and anxiety, problems sleeping and eating, and thoughts of harming oneself or one's child. It can have major effects on their life long after the birth of the baby, and might also affect the infant later in life (Beck, 2006). Recent research by Getahun et al. (2023) has found that rates of postpartum depression have risen dramatically, with rates of PPD in California increasing by 105 percent between 2010 and 2021. This could possibly be connected to the stresses of the COVID-19 pandemic and increased socioeconomic inequality. As Verta Taylor discusses in her book *Rock-a-by Baby: Feminism, Self-Help and Postpartum Depression*, one challenge with treating and understanding PPD is the social stigma. New motherhood is glorified, and those who have just given birth are expected to feel elated and instantly in love with their baby—the stereotype that women naturally nourish and cherish. This belies the complex physical and mental experience of childbirth and motherhood. This stigma, embarrassment, and fear of being separated from their baby or even institutionalized, means that new moms with PPD are hesitant to tell their family and even their partner about their feelings, or their health care providers for that matter (Zauderer, 2009). Another obstacle is the paucity of knowledge and research about the disorder (Kennedy et al., 2002).

Menopause most often occurs between the ages of 45–55. Data from the Mayo Clinic Health System (2021) finds that approximately 2 million women every year go through menopause, which is often accompanied by hot flashes, sleep disruption, or depression. There is a general lack of understanding of menopause among health care providers and patients, likely owing to limited research. The National Institutes of Health (NIH) has an online reporting system where users can look up investment in research by condition:

"Even though 100% of women living into late life will experience menopause, it is not one of the 292 listed topics.... A search of NIH grants funded in 2019 revealed only 28 project titles that included the term 'menopause' or some variation, compared to more than 300 that included 'pregnancy' in the title."

(Aninye et al., 2021, p. 1187)

Relative to medical education, a 2019 Mayo Clinic survey found that, of medical residents, "58 percent had received one lecture on menopause in their training and 20 percent had received no training on it whatsoever" (Gupta, 2023). In 2022 women were 53.8 percent of all enrolled US medical students, according to the Association of American Medical Colleges (Boyle, 2022). Racial disparities have also been disclosed in both the experience and treatment of menopause, with Black and Hispanic women experiencing menopause symptoms much longer than white women (Gupta, 2023), and Black women reporting more intense symptoms but receiving less treatment than white women (Blanken et al., 2022). Endometriosis is another health condition that is misunderstood, with patients experiencing up to 11 years of delay in diagnosis, attributed in part to lack of knowledge and training of health care providers and stigmatization of periods (Davenport et al., 2023).

A major health inequity of concern to feminists is weight stigma. Research shows that weight stigma negatively affects women's health care outcomes. Body Mass Index (BMI), relied on significantly by health care professionals, is seen by many as a limited indicator based on a white European man's bodily composition. Being wedded to the BMI leads to numerous inequalities, even though studies have found that healthy BMIs vary widely by individual (Jackson-Gibson, 2021). Women who are classified as having obesity using the BMI are less likely to have cancer screenings, yet are more likely than women without obesity to be diagnosed with and die from cancer, a circumstance potentially related to weight bias (i.e. embarrassment about weight, anxiety about their body) (Friedman et al., 2012). The racial dimension of weight bias has historical roots. Sociologist Sabrina Strings (2019) investigated its origins and found that, at least for 200 years, fatness was linked to immoral behavior and Blackness.

## Reproductive Health Care

### A note on gendered language and reproductive justice

There has recently been more consideration of the healthcare experience of trans and non-binary individuals in general, and in particular as it relates to pregnancy and childbirth. In an article published in 2020, a group of scholars, medical practitioners, and advocates wrote of the exclusion of transgender and nonbinary individuals in sexual and reproductive health (Moseson et al. 2020): "This exclusion prevents the advancement of science and clinical care for people of all genders, including cisgender women" (p. 1060). Many healthcare systems and providers are now working to become more inclusive and to recognize the nuances of gendered assumptions in healthcare. Some have discontinued use of "pregnant women" or "breast feeding" and instead use "pregnant person" or "chest feeding," to acknowledge that trans and nonbinary individuals also become pregnant.

One challenge of increasing inclusion in the medical field is related to medical research. Sexual Orientation and Gender Identity data are often missing from medical research. Findings may, therefore, lack nuance of gender and sexuality that is consistent with a trans or non-binary individual's experiences. For example, decades of studies of pregnancy, childbirth, and the postpartum period are based on cisgender women. Thus, to accurately discuss and cite this research requires use of the gender binary.

There are also activist and social change components to the conversation about trans-inclusive language in healthcare. While some argue that gender neutral language in all settings is the way to ensure inclusive communities, others argue that gender is inherently political, and that gender neutral language erases the gender inequality driving some policies and laws. For example, abortion bans are commonly viewed as a war on women's bodies and an effort to control women. Thus, gender neutral language has the potential to erase the gendered nature of abortion bans. Carrie N. Baker, a professor at Smith College and Carly Thomson, a professor at Middlebury College, write (2022): "While inclusive language is important because gender diverse people experience pregnancy and need abortion, using sex-neutral language risks obscuring the sexism underlying anti-abortion laws and policies—sexism that harms not only pregnant women, but also pregnant trans men and nonbinary people." Thus, some may believe that universally using gender neutral language in discussing health care, particularly abortion, is not necessarily the right approach. Reflecting the complexities of this discussion, this book vacillates between gender neutral language and non-gender neutral language depending on the research cited and context.

A major part of health care disparities in the US is reproductive health and bodily autonomy.

A person who has control and agency over their own body and health care decisions has bodily autonomy. Women's bodily autonomy has been a central goal of the feminist movement for generations. Throughout US history, women's bodily autonomy has differed among women with different abilities, and from different racial, ethnic, and class backgrounds, with many Black women and Women of color lacking bodily autonomy for generations (Roberts, 1998).

The passing of Roe vs. Wade in 1973 was a major milestone in US and feminist history. It gave women the right to control their own bodies, and decide whether they would bear children or not. Decisions about forming a family, as well as the health matters of pregnancy, became reserved for private conversations between a patient and doctor.

However, even when abortion was legal on a national scale, reproductive healthcare was unavailable to most poor women and Women of Color for reasons that include the high cost of health care/insurance or inaccessibility of a healthcare facility. One recent study found that these obstacles to receiving reproductive health care services increased between 2017 and 2020, especially for women from marginalized or disadvantaged communities (Adler et al., 2023). In a 2021 study of abortion medication availability for public college students in Massachusetts, researchers found significant barriers, including cost (averaging $680), travel time (population-weighted travel time of 103 minutes of public transportation), and scheduling (many clinics not open on weekends) (Baker and Mathis, 2021).

Advocating for abortion within the law-focused "reproductive rights" framework omits the structural inequalities involved. As a result, the phrase "reproductive justice" began to be used in an effort to recognize the social justice dimensions of reproductive health care and reproduction, and the intersectional inequalities that hinder access to a range of reproductive health care including birth control and abortion (Luna and Luker, 2013; Ross, 2006).

Many of these barriers were exacerbated when Roe vs. Wade was repealed in June 2022. Some states had anti-abortion laws already on the books, known as "trigger laws," some states resurrected pre-Roe bans, and other states passed new bans. Six months after the repeal of Roe v. Wade, 24 states had either banned abortion already or were poised to ban abortion (Nash and Guarnieri, 2023).

The state-by-state landscape for abortion policies is changing rapidly. See the following for up to date information:
*Interactive Map: US Abortion Policies and Access After Roe*, from Guttmacher Institute
*Tracking Abortion Bans Across the Country*, from *The New York Times*

When someone is denied an abortion there are many documented negative outcomes for individuals, families, health care systems, and our broader society. So-called "medical exceptions" to abortion bans (allowing a pregnant person to have an abortion in a state in which it is illegal) are confusing, unevenly applied, and with murky criteria (Fox, 2023), leading to cases such as Texas woman Kate Cox who was denied an abortion despite an extreme medical need (Donley, 2023). Abortion bans and the resulting forced pregnancies and births cause significant strain on hospitals and medical staff and trauma to parents and families. One 2023 Stanford University study by Miller et al. examining fetuses diagnosed with heart abnormalities found that with an abortion ban, hundreds of fetuses would be born with little to no chance of survival, resulting in significant increases in need for complex medical care. This strain not only affects health care providers, but also traumatizes pregnant people and their families. Moreover, in the state of Texas, reports indicate that neonatal mortality rose over 10 percent after its abortion restrictions went into effect, owing to women being forced to carry non-viable pregnancies (Knutson, 2023).

**Research Reflection:** Read about "The Turnaway Study" by Diana Greene Foster (2020) and her collaborators at *Advancing New Standards in Reproductive Health*. What are the most important consequences of being denied an abortion, according to their research?

## Spotlight: The Jane Collective

The Jane Collective was a feminist group that provided thousands of illegal abortions in 1969–73, prior to Roe vs. Wade, when abortion was illegal. Organizers reflected that they did not worry about legal prosecution. Why? Because the wives and girlfriends of so many men in power, including law enforcement officers themselves, used the Collective's services. In fact, sometimes police officers would direct individuals to the illegal collective (Bart, 1987).

## Prison Industrial Complex

There have been long lasting tensions among feminists about prisons and policing systems. Many feminists believed and continue to believe that prison or jail is the necessary punishment for perpetrators of gender-based violence, or that state intervention is necessary. However, as the injustices of the criminal justice system have been laid bare in the last few decades, intersectional feminists have generated communities of anti-carceral or abolitionist feminists (Crenshaw, 1991; Davis et al., 2022). They draw attention to the ways in which the carceral system overall is actually both a byproduct of inequality and an engine that drives more inequality.

**Research Reflection:** For more information concerning the debate between feminists about prisons and jails, research the case of the "Women's Center for Justice" in Harlem. What are the arguments for and against the so-called "feminist jail"? Can a jail be feminist, in your opinion?

While many experts agree that our current prison systems are too expensive to maintain, and are also ineffective given very high recidivism rates (Alper et al., 2018; Michalsen, 2019), a clearer picture of their problems emerge when the racial and gender inequalities of prisons are examined. For example, Black and Brown women and men are more likely than white women and men to be incarcerated, and are in jail longer (The Pew Charitable Trusts, 2023). Instead of viewing this as a social response to increased or changing crime statistics, feminists argue that it is part of a larger system of inequality.

"Activists and scholars who have tried to develop more nuanced understandings of the punishment process- and especially racism's role- have deployed the concept of the 'prison industrial complex' to point out that the proliferation of prisons and prisoners is more clearly linked to larger economic and political structures and ideologies than to individual criminal conduct and efforts to curb 'crime.'"

(Davis & Shaylor, 2001, p. 2)

In many states, research shows that rates of women's incarceration have grown significantly (mostly in local jails) (Kajstura and Sawyer, 2023). Furthermore, a high rate of incarcerated women are also survivors of gender-based violence. Scholars find that many survivors, in coping with their traumatic abuse, will run away from home or resort to drug use, ending up in the legal system (Michalsen, 2019). The link is so strong that one expert called this a "sexual violence to prison pipeline" (Kaba, 2017). Moreover, once incarcerated, rates of sexual violence against women are high (Wolff et al., 2006). Unfortunately, there is a dearth of research on the experience of transgender prisoners; a 2019 study by Brömdal et al. suggests they experience high rates of sexual violence.

There has been significant energy expended by feminists and others on addressing overall problems of the carceral state, for example to move away from cash bail and to revisit policies that send people to jail. However, Michelle Alexander (2018) argues that we must move carefully, as the replacement systems could likely replicate similar inequalities. In California, New Jersey, and New York, for example, Alexander notes that "risk assessment" algorithms are now being used to recommend to a judge whether someone who has been arrested should be released. Such algorithms are believed to be steeped in racial and gender biases, although there has been much debate (Chohlas-Wood, 2020) about the benefits and drawbacks of risk assessment tools, and an identified need for more research (Desmarais et al., 2022).

Black women and Women of Color are disproportionately affected by police violence. Attention to police brutality after the Ferguson protests and George Floyd's murder has often centered men victims of police violence. However, research related to women victims has been shining a light on their experiences (Brown et al., 2017; Ritchie, 2017; see Chapter 1 for a profile of #SayHerName).

In March 2020 **Breonna Taylor**, a 26 year old Black woman was shot and killed in her apartment during a police raid gone wrong. As one report said, the raid was "compromised by poor planning and reckless execution" (Oppel et al., 2023). A Report by the US Department of Justice (2023) found that the Louisville police department, responsible for Taylor's death, had a track record of abusive and discriminatory practices. As of early 2024 there had been no convictions in her murder.

## Climate Change and Environmental Inequalities

Climate change exacerbates existing inequalities. One UN Report from 2022 concludes "The climate crisis is not 'gender neutral.' Women and girls experience the greatest impacts of climate change, which amplifies existing gender inequalities and poses unique threats to their livelihoods, health, and safety." Indeed, all of those individuals who are the most marginalized and living in the greatest precarity are also those who are most vulnerable to climate change (Benevolenza and DeRigne, 2019). These include disabled women, poor women, queer women, Women of Color, and rural women.

To provide an example of the discriminatory effects of climate change, research has shown that after natural disasters (which are exacerbated by climate change) gender-based violence increases (Sloand et al., 2015). Also, since women are disproportionately single parents and caretakers, the burden of ensuring the safety of children and/or elders during a natural disaster often falls on their shoulders (Villarreal and Meyer, 2020).

There are also gendered dimensions to mitigating climate change. On the one hand, research has found that women have a smaller carbon footprint and have more positive attitudes towards mitigating the climate crisis than men (Huddart Kennedy et al., 2015). On the other hand, marginalized individuals' perspectives are often the least considered in conversations about climate change since these people are typically not elected political officials or other leaders who set priorities and allocate funding (Gloor et al., 2022).

Climate change is related to larger discussions about the degradation of our environment more broadly, which also has a disproportionate effect on marginalized populations. Toxic waste and dumps are more likely to be placed in poor communities and in communities of color. In general, the degradation of land, water, air, and all of our natural resources has been a problem that has led to many health problems, including those of fertility, maternal and child health (see Chapter 2).

## Childcare Insecurity

Childcare is an important feminist concern. All children need care, and young children need sustained attention and oversight at all times to keep them safe. In the US, women disproportionately provide care work: For example

> "On an average day, among adults living in households with children under age 6, women spent 1.1 hours providing physical care (such as bathing or feeding a child) to household children; by contrast, men spent 31 minutes providing physical care."
> (Bureau of Labor Statistics, 2023)

This imbalance was exacerbated during the COVID-19 pandemic (Zamarro and Prados, 2021). Childcare has not historically been a priority for federal or state lawmakers, although recently it has received more attention, owing in large part to the undeniable challenges of the pandemic for women and parents. In the absence of federal support, women's careers are hugely impacted by childcare needs. A 2023 study found that among working parents, women were four times more likely to miss work for childcare than men (Haines, 2023). Single parents, who are most likely to be women, shoulder the burden (or joy?) of childcare on their own. Indeed 30 percent of children who live with a parent, live with only one parent, and about 75 percent of those are women as single parents (Haines, 2023).

Expanding women's access to the paid workforce was a high priority of feminists in the 1970s. While that was central to many women's ability to live independent, fulfilling lives, it did not mean that feminists believed that caregiving is unimportant work or that staying home with children is not an adequate life path. Indeed, many feminists believe that there is great worth to care work, and that if this work was seen as essential and valuable, it would solve many problems associated with gender inequality.

Childcare in the US is very expensive, and in many places difficult to find. This was exacerbated during and after the pandemic, when many childcare facilities closed and providers sought other jobs. One 2021 study by NPR, the Robert Wood Johnson Foundation and the Harvard T.H. Chan School of Public Health found that "34% of families with young children are facing serious problems finding child care when adults need to work" (Kamenetz and Khurana, 2021), with childcare supply particularly challenging for Hispanic/Latino, rural, and low-income families (Center for American Progress, n.d.). The cost of childcare recently increased dramatically, while wages and salaries did not rise concurrently. In all states, childcare is considered unaffordable, based on income data and cost of childcare.

The dilemma of childcare is a problem of multiple dimensions. It relates to our nation's future, because high-quality childcare aids in the language and social development of children and even contributes to positive school achievement outcomes (Shonkoff et al., 2000; Thompson, 2016). It relates to families, because the stress and financial burden of childcare can intensify already difficult situations (León-Pérez et al., 2021). And it is related to gender inequality because the lack of affordable, quality, and available childcare means that women's careers will be more encumbered, while men's not (Center for American Progress, 2019). Childcare is clearly a feminist issue.

### Spotlight on Dorothy Pitman Hughes

Dorothy Pitman Hughes was labeled a "Black Feminist Trailblazer" in her prominent New York Times obituary on December 18, 2022 (Risen, 2022). Indeed Hughes changed the landscape of feminist leadership, especially drawing attention to Black women's lives and the need for quality, affordable childcare. Her activism, especially in New York City, revolved around her childcare center (and de facto political and community center as well) that she operated for twenty years (Seidman, 2023). She co-founded the Women's Action Alliance with close friend and collaborator Gloria Steinem, among many other national contributions to social justice and Black feminism. Of Pitman Hughes, her biographer Laura L. Lovett wrote: "Dorothy defined herself as a feminist but rooted her feminism in her experience and in more fundamental needs for safety, food, shelter and childcare" (Baker, 2021).

## Inequality in Technology and Online Harassment

Technology is a rapidly growing industry that is historically, and continues to be, largely closed to women and many people of color. Despite vast investments in diversity initiatives, women's representation in tech was at its height around 1990 and has only decreased since then, with Women of Color particularly under-represented (Alegria and Branch, 2015). Researchers have identified numerous mechanisms that maintain the tech industry's inequality. Shelley J. Correll and collaborators (2020) identified how gender bias is embedded in performance reviews in a tech company, in that behaviors for men and women are valued differently according to gendered expectations. For example, women are penalized for "taking charge," because it is a gender atypical behavior (Correll et al., 2020). Wynn (2020) has found the lack of diversity in tech is due in part to tech executives' resistance to pursuing organizational change, despite research finding organizational change can reverse the "chilly climate" of tech. Alfrey's (2022) research found that tech workers themselves minimize the problems of racial and gender homogeneity. They describe their workplaces as diverse by empha-sizing other forms of difference such as age or geographic back-ground. This language serves to uphold the notion that the lack of racial and gender diversity in tech is not a problem. In the last five years, a backlash against women in tech and diversity initiatives has grown, further stymying change in the tech industry (Bowles, 2017).

**Research Reflection:** Women have been central to major developments in computing, but have been largely overlooked. Conduct biographical research on women in computing. Who is Ada Lovelace? Judith Estrin? Katherine Johnson, Dorothy Vaughan, and Mary Jackson? Why are their contributions dis-regarded? Are there any other women you know of who have been instrumental to computing?

A growing body of research has found inequality embedded into algorithms and related technological processes (Noble, 2018). One study found extreme gender bias embedded into machine learning (Bolukbasi et al. 2016). To provide additional examples: face recognition technologies, used widely in airports and by law enforcement are least accurate on Women of Color (SITNFlash, 2020). Given racial and gender bias already fixed in many organizations and institutions, this technology has the potential to worsen institutional inequalities. A case study by researchers at Gendered Innovations of Stanford University found: "Medical technology—in this case study, especially devices, diagnostics, products, and services—harms twice as many females and other patients who do not fit a typical male profile, such as gender-diverse individuals, as males. These technologies can embed ethnic biases as well. Pulse oximeters, for example, fail to correctly analyze oxygen levels in people with darker skin far more often than in people with lighter skin."

As more of us spend more time online, online harassment has become a serious problem. Online harassment can be understood as a range of behaviors, including name-calling, embarrassment, sexual harassment, threats, stalking, surveillance, nonconsensual sharing of intimate images, circulating intimate photos without consent, identity theft, doxxing (revealing someone's address and physical location), and more (Bertazzo, 2021). It can occur on social media, gaming, online dating, texting/messaging platforms, and email. Online harassment frequently occurs simultaneously on several platforms.

While men certainly experience online harassment, it is often related to gender and its intersections. Women encounter online harassment in a more severe way than men (Bertazzo, 2021). 61 percent of women in a Pew Study say that online harassment is a major problem (Vogels, 2021). In one study (Bertazzo, 2021), seven out of ten Lesbian, gay and bisexual respondents reported online harassment; 54 percent of Black and 47 percent of Hispanic individuals who experienced online harassment reported that it was due to their race.

**Manosphere:** Anywhere online in which men express that they are victims of feminism.

In part, just being a woman online is all that is needed to create the perfect conditions for harassment. However, reports have found that feminists online experience some of the worst harassment.

**Research Reflection:** One forum for online harassment is gaming. #Gamergate began in 2014 and was a big moment in both gaming and online harassment. Research #Gamergate. Construct a timeline, a list of women who were attacked and how, and key points in the harassment campaign. Who are Zoë Quinn and Anita Sarkeesian? What, if anything, has changed since #Gamergate? Note: Not for the faint of heart.

Nonconsensual sharing of intimate images, an extreme form of online abuse in which nude photos are shared/distributed without an individual's consent, has become a serious problem and has recently received attention.

"A study by the Cyber Civil Rights Initiative found that 93% of victims suffered significant emotional distress because of their victimization; 51% had suicidal thoughts; and 49% stated they had been stalked or harassed online by users who saw their material."

(Rubio, 2022)

Fortunately, some states have been addressing these crimes. In 2023 a woman was awarded $1.2 billion in a lawsuit in a Texas court related to nonconsensual image sharing. California was the first state to outlaw nonconsensual sharing of intimate images, and over the past few years has strengthened the protections for its victims. Since perpetrators repeatedly found loopholes in the law (Rubio, 2022), in 2023 a law was added that makes it illegal to distribute or publicly display intimate photos without consent.

Investigate the Cyber Civil Rights Initiative. What do they do? Is their work intersectional? What problems are they addressing? How does their work relate to research cited in this book?

## Media Inequality

In the history of media, the viewpoints and ideas of all women have been ignored, underestimated, and undervalued. This includes a disproportionate lack of representation of women's stories in film and television entertainment and in the news, in comparison to white men's stories. There is a dearth of women in media industry leadership across the board.

Women receive biased and unequal attention when they are in the news as subjects. Black women receive significantly less attention than anyone else when they are victims of fatal police shootings (Samuels, 2021). When it comes to gender-based violence and sexual assault, the picture is equally bleak (Carll, 2003). In 139 nationwide news articles about murdered transgender or transexual persons, twenty-three of 37 individuals were misidentified (Women's Media Center, 2021). According to Carll (2003), reports of women who experience violence tend to inquire why a woman was assaulted (you were out at night?), thus holding the woman accountable for her assault rather than questioning why a woman is not safe when she is out. These stories also present gender-based violence as isolated, individual incidents. Overall, research finds that when the news media does cover sexual violence, it normalizes it, as both the fault of women victims as well as divorced from any structural inequalities (Montiel, 2015).

Women are underrepresented as authors, journalists and anchors in most news media, especially in politics and sports (Montiel, 2015). For example, a report by the Women's Media Center found that men account for 62 percent of bylines and other credits in print, online, and TV and wire news, while women account for just 38 percent (Women's Media Center, 2017). White men are the overwhelming majority of anchors and moderators in all news broadcasts. The Sunday news shows are influential in the media and political landscapes, and make and set agendas in Washington DC. An article in *The Washington Post* about these shows describes their importance to national politics: "Leading political figures, hungry for the big soapbox and establishment cred the shows conveyed, clamored for bookings and sometimes made agenda-setting news" (Farhi, 2022). Of these "agenda-setting shows," a Women's Media Center report from 2021 found "women and people of color are practically invisible."

In addition to the journalists themselves, white men dominate as "experts" in all fields of reporting (Women's Media Center, 2018). Are you a podcast fan and consider the medium to be more democratic or accessible? Unfortunately it is not. "Men hosted 79% of the top podcasts," although women make up half of listeners (Women's Media Center, 2018).

As in news, all entertainment media is also dominated by white men, both in acting and non-acting roles. Research by Women's Media Center found in 2019 that 75 percent of non-acting Oscar nominees are men. In fact, for decades the gender and racial inequality in Hollywood hasn't changed.

Research from the Geena Davis Institute on Gender and Media finds:

"With such a dearth of female representation in front of and behind the camera, it's a struggle to champion female stories and voices. The Institute's research proves that female involvement in the creative process is imperative for creating greater gender balance before production even begins. There is a causal relationship between positive female portrayals and female content creators involved in production. In fact, when even one woman writer works on a film, there is a 10.4% difference in screen time for female characters. Sadly, men outnumber women in key production roles by nearly 5 to 1."

Research by the Norman Lear Center for the Study of Entertainment, Media, and Society (2018) examined representation of immigrants in television. They found that immigrants are overrepresented as criminals and as incarcerated, and women immigrants of every racial group are underrepresented.

**Amma Asante**, award winning screenwriter and director, reflects on the need for racial and gender diversity in the entertainment industry, linking it to intergenerational change:

"The number of women film directors, especially black female directors, is abysmally low in an industry that too often is insular and resistant to change. The makeup of the

Academy is only part of the problem. Most often, it's the lack of opportunity available to women, and it's especially hard if you are a woman of color. It's important to change the narrative for little girls so that they can picture themselves in the director's chair—a position of strength, power, and prestige. Through the director's lens, I have the ability to shape, create, entertain, educate, and inspire. I would only hope that my work as a screenwriter and director gives hope to young women."

(Women's Media Center, 2018)

Children's entertainment is just as biased as other forms of media. Men and boys outnumber girls in children's entertainment. According to Geena Davis, "In family rated films, for every one speaking female character there were three male characters. The research also shows that when female characters do exist, they are very often stereotyped or hyper-sexualized," and in animated G-rated films female characters "wore the same amount of revealing clothing as the female characters in R-rated movies" (Ritman, 2015).

Needless to say, as we learn and relearn what is important in the world, whose lives are valuable, whose opinions are worth listening to, whose views are the default, media and entertainment industries reinforce hierarchies that place white men and boys above all other people.

## Political Representation

Underrepresentation of all women, and particularly Women of Color, remain entrenched in much of local, state, and national politics and political leadership. Yet there is good news. The Center for American Women in Politics, which compiles statistics about gender and race in political office, indicates that while overall still relatively small in numbers in comparison to white men, women's political representation is steadily rising. Political representation by Latinas and Black women have broken numerous records since 2022, respectively (Center for American Women and Politics and Higher Heights, 2023a; Latinas Represent, 2022). Recent record holders include Kamala Harris, the first woman of color, South Asian and Black person elected to the Vice Presidency. In 2022, Ketanji Brown Jackson was confirmed as the first Black woman on the US Supreme Court. In 2021 there was a record high of women in the senate (25 percent) and in 2023 a record high of women in the house (28.7%). In 2023 a total of 31.3 percent of Statewide elective executive office holders were women, a near record high. Also in 2023, 12 state governors were women, a record high. Mayoral positions have also increased "Of the 33 women mayors in the top 100 most populous cities as of September 2023, 8 are Black women, 3 are Latina, and 4 are Asian American/Pacific Islander women" (Center for American Women and Politics and Higher Heights, 2023b).

Although these numbers are promising, why is it that we aren't closer to gender parity? Why don't women run for public office at the same rates as men? Perhaps because when they have (think Hillary Clinton, Sarah Palin, Kamala Harris), they have been treated negatively by the media and the general public, independent of their political affiliation. For example, when Nikki Haley announced she was running for president of the US, journalist Don Lemon called her past her prime. Additionally, politicians' sexism and racism is rampant and acceptable to many voters.

Indeed, biases and sexism against women candidates in political spheres is a deterring factor in women running for office. There are other familiar reasons women do not run. Women are less likely than men to have the possibility of political office suggested to them, fundraising is particularly challenging, and women have disproportionate caretaker expectations and responsibilities (Warner, 2017). A 2022 research study (Corbett et al., 2022) found a collective sense that women are less electable than men ("pragmatic bias," or, not offering support when success is judged to be difficult). When researchers conducted an experiment showing evidence that women can win as many votes as men in general elections, research subjects would vote for women, thus illustrating heightened electability.

So, you may ask, what are the ramifications of this? Most clearly, democracy is supposed to be representative of the people. Given the demographics of the US population in comparison to the demographics of political office holders, it is not. In addition, people bring their own life experiences to their politics. If a white male politician's wife stays at home to manage all childcare and home operations, he may not place support for preschool or family needs at the top of his priority list at work. Research has found that elected officials who do have lived experiences with inequality, such as housing, food, or childcare insecurity, will be more likely to pay attention to these issues. Writes Kerry L. Haynie, Professor of Political Science and African and African American Studies at Duke University:

> "The absence of women and people of color has led to policies that limit the opportunity for those folks out in the real world. Gender and race have been a negative characteristic in terms of outcomes and opportunities. Black women and Latinas share both of these characteristics. They have been at the margins of politics and our society in any number of ways. My research suggests that because of their lived experiences, they [as legislators] tend to pay more attention to issues of poverty, inequality, healthcare and education than do other legislators."
>
> (Haynie, 2021)

**Reflection:** Can you think of any other feminist issues that are not included in this chapter? What are they?

## Chapter 4 Mini Toolkit: Non-Disclosure Agreements

Inequality is baked into our institutions, organizations, and social structures. This toolkit features an example of how workplace sexual harassment and gender-based violence is preserved through acceptable and nearly universally used legal agreements. Non-disclosure agreements (NDAs) are documents that protect confidential information between two parties. Originally intended to protect trade secrets, they were used to ensure an employee would not take confidential information to a competing company. However, the use of these agreements has expanded beyond their original intent. In the aftermath of #MeToo it has become clear that NDAs are frequently used to silence sexual harassment victims and to protect perpetrators. So, for example, let's say an individual experiences sexual harassment in the workplace and reports it to her company. She may be fired or asked to resign; she may be seen as a trouble maker while the alleged perpetrator is well-liked and/or makes a lot of money for the company. On her way out, she might be given a financial settlement as she signs an NDA, requiring that she not tell anyone about her sexual harassment. Then, as she moves to another job or when is asked about her departure from her previous position, she may be legally forbidden to say anything about the circumstances. This could seem odd to subsequent hiring managers. Keep in mind that she herself was the victim of the harassment.

The overall outcomes of NDAs in sexual assault or sexual harassment situations are formidable. In silencing survivors, the perpetrators are protected. Serial perpetrators are shielded because NDAs prevent women from knowing there were other victims of the same perpetrator. Research (Chan et al., 2024) has found that women who sign NDAs have many negative consequences to their careers, financial well-being, and emotional health. To break an NDA or go against a company with deep legal and financial resources could be prohibitively costly. Also, many women may choose not to tell anyone about their harassment experiences, even their spouses and close family members. The cost of this silence takes a huge emotional toll.

Gretchen Carlson, formerly of Fox News, sued Fox News chairman and CEO Roger Ailes for sexual harassment in July 2016. A catalyst for the #MeToo movement resurgence, afterwards, many other women stepped forward alleging the same of Ailes. Carlson has been instrumental along with her organization Lift Our Voices to bring about legislation that places restrictions around the usage of NDAs, such as the bipartisan Speak Out Act, signed by President Biden in December 2022, limiting the enforcement of NDAs (and non-disparagement agreements) in cases of sexual harassment and sexual assault.

To get involved and to learn more:

- There are multiple inequalities that are manifested in the usage of NDAs. How is the fight against NDAs related to broader feminist themes covered throughout this book?
- Can you think of any intersectional dimensions of the NDA?
- Read about the Speak Out Act. How does it address themes of gender-based violence? How did the legislation come to be?

Which political parties supported it and why? What do you
think its impact will be?
- Who are the leaders in the fight against NDAs?
- Learn about Liftourvoices.org
- Extra credit: Watch the film Bombshell

## Chapter 4 Dive Deeper

*Abolition Geography: Essays Towards Liberation* (Ruth Wilson Gilmore)
*Arrested Justice: Black Women, Violence, and America's Prison Nation* (Beth E. Richie)
*Know My Name* (Chanel Miller)
*Redefining Rape: Sexual Violence in the Era of Suffrage and Segregation* (Estelle B. Freedman)
*We Believe You: Survivors of Campus Sexual Assault Speak Out* (Annie Clark and Andrea L. Pino)
*Thick* (Tressie McMillan Cottom)
*Holding It Together: How Women Became America's Social Safety Net* (Jessica Calaraco)
*Gray Areas: How the Way We Work Perpetuates Racism and What We Can Do to Fix It* (Adia Harvey Wingfield)
Film: Hunting Ground
Film: The Janes
Film: The Mask You Live In
Film: Athlete A
Film: On the Record
Film: Confirmation
Film: Tough Guise 2: Violence, Manhood, and American Culture

## References

Adler, A, Biggs M.A., Kaller, S, Schroeder, R, & Ralph, L. (2023). Changes in the Frequency and Type of Barriers to Reproductive Health Care Between 2017 and 2021. *JAMA Netw Open*, 6(4), e237461. doi:10.1001/jamanetworkopen.2023.7461.

Alegria, S.N. & Branch, E.H. (2015). Causes and Consequences of Inequality in the STEM: Diversity and its Discontents. *International Journal of Gender, Science and Technology*, 7(3), 321–342.

Alexander, M. (2018, November 9). Opinion | The Newest Jim Crow. *The New York Times*. www.nytimes.com/2018/11/08/opinion/sunday/crimina l-justice-reforms-race-technology.html.

Alfrey, L.M. (2022). Diversity, Disrupted: A Critique of Neoliberal Difference in Tech Organizations. *Sociological Perspectives*, 65(6), 1081–1098. doi:10.1177/07311214221094664.

Alper M., DuRose M.R., & Markman J. (2018). 2018 update on prisoner recidivism: A 9-year follow-up period (2005–2014). Washington, DC: Bureau of Justice Statistics. Retrieved from www.bjs.gov/content/pub/p df/18upr9yfup0514.pdf.

Altieri, M.S., Salles, A., Bevilacqua, L.A., *et al.* (2019). Perceptions of Surgery Residents About Parental Leave During Training. *JAMA Surg*, 154 (10), 952–958. doi:10.1001/jamasurg.2019.2985.

Aninye, I.O., Laitner, M.H., & Chinnappan, S. (2021). Menopause preparedness: Perspectives for patient, provider, and policymaker consideration. *Menopause*, 28(10), 1186–1191. doi:10.1097/GME.0000000000001819.

Armstrong, E.A. & Hamilton, L.E. (2015). *Paying for the Party: How College Maintains Inequality*. Cambridge: Harvard University Press.

Baker, C.N. (2021, September 9). The Story of Iconic Feminist Dorothy Pitman Hughes: "With Her Fist Raised." *Ms. Magazine*. https://msmaga zine.com/2021/09/09/dorothy-pitman-hughes-feminist-gloria-steinem -who-founded-ms-magazine.

Baker, C.N. & Mathis, J. (2021). Barriers to Medication Abortion Among Massachusetts' Public University Students: Medication Abortion Barriers. Study of Women and Gender: Faculty Publications, Smith College, Northampton, MA. https://scholarworks.smith.edu/swg_facpubs/37.

Baker, C.N. & Thomsen, C. (2022, June 23). The Importance of Talking About Women in the Fight Against Abortion Bans. *Ms. Magazine*. http s://msmagazine.com/2022/06/23/women-abortion-bans-inclusive-language-p regnant-people.

Bart, P.B. (1987). Seizing the means of reproduction: An illegal feminist abortion collective—How and why it worked. *Qualitative Sociology*, 10 (4), 339–357. doi:10.1007/BF00988383.

Beck, C.T. (2006). Postpartum Depression: It isn't just the blues. *AJN The American Journal of Nursing*, 106(5), 40.

Benevolenza, M.A. & DeRigne, L. (2019). The impact of climate change and natural disasters on vulnerable populations: A systematic review of literature. *Journal of Human Behavior in the Social Environment*, 29(2), 266–281. doi:10.1080/10911359.2018.1527739.

Bergman, M.E., Langhout, R.D., Palmieri, P.A., Cortina, L.M., & Fitzgerald, L.F. (2002). The (un)reasonableness of reporting: antecedents and consequences of reporting sexual harassment. *The Journal of applied psychology*, 87(2), 230–242. doi:10.1037/0021-9010.87.2.230.

Bertazzo, S. (2021, June 28). Online Harassment Isn't Growing—But It's Getting More Severe. *The Pew Charitable Trusts*. Retrieved December 10, 2023, from https://pew.org/3pRgMCY.

Leemis, R.W., Friar, N., Khatiwada, S., Chen, M.S., Kresnow, M.J., Smith, S.G., Caslin, S., & Basile, K.C. (2022). *The National Intimate Partner and Sexual Violence Survey (NISVS): 2016–17 Summary Report*. National Center for Injury Prevention and Control, Centers for Disease Control and Prevention.

Blanken, A., Gibson, C., Li, Y., Huang, A., Byers, A., Maguen, S., Inslicht, S., & Seal, K. (2022). Racial/ethnic disparities in the diagnosis and management of menopause symptoms among midlife women veterans. *Menopause*, 29(7), 877–882. doi:10.1097/GME.0000000000001978.

Bolukbasi, T., Chang, K., Zou, J., Saligrama, V., & Kalai, A.T. (2016). Man is to computer programmer as woman is to homemaker? debiasing word embeddings. *NIPS*, 29, 4356–4364.

Bowles, N. (2017, September 23). Push for Gender Equality in Tech? Some Men Say It's Gone Too Far. *The New York Times*. www.nytimes.com/2017/09/23/technology/silicon-valley-men-backlash-gender-scandals.html.

Boyle, P. (2022, December 13). The nation's medical schools grow more diverse. *AAMC*. Retrieved December 6, 2023, from www.aamc.org/news/nation-s-medical-schools-grow-more-diverse.

Brömdal, A., Mullens, A.B., Phillips, T.M., & Gow, J. (2019). Experiences of transgender prisoners and their knowledge, attitudes, and practices regarding sexual behaviors and HIV/STIs: A systematic review. *International Journal of Transgenderism*, 20(1), 4–20. doi:10.1080/15532739.2018.1538838.

Bonni Cohen, B. & Shenk, J. (2020). *Athlete A* [Film]. Actual Films.

Bor, J., Cohen, G.H., & Galea, S. (2017). Population health in an era of rising income inequality: USA, 1980−2015. *The Lancet*, 389, 1475–1490.

Brown, M., Ray, R., Summers, E., & Fraistat, N. (2017). #SayHerName: A case study of intersectional social media activism. *Ethnic and Racial Studies*, 40(11), 1831–1846.

Bureau of Justice Statistics. (2004). *A BJS Statistical Profile, 1992–2002 American Indians and Crime* [Report]. https://bjs.ojp.gov/content/pub/pdf/aic02.pdf.

Bureau of Labor Statistics. (2023). *American Time Use Survey Summary*. www.bls.gov/news.release/atus.nr0.htm.

Calaraco, J. (2024). *Holding It Together: How Women Became America's Social Safety Net*. Portfolio.

Cantor, D., Fisher, B., Chibnall, S., Harps, S., Townsend, R., Thomas, G., Lee, H., Kranz, V., Herbison, R., & Madden, K. (2019). Report on the AAU Campus Climate Survey on Sexual Assault and Misconduct

[Report]. www.aau.edu/sites/default/files/AAU-Files/Key-Issues/Campus-Sa fety/Revised%20Aggregate%20report%20%20and%20appendices%201-7_ (01-16-2020_FINAL).pdf.

Carll, E.K. (2003). News Portrayal of Violence and Women: Implications for Public Policy. *American Behavioral Scientist*, 46(12), 1601–1610. doi:10.1177/0002764203254616.

Center for American Progress. (2017, November 20). Not Just the Rich and Famous. From www.americanprogress.org/article/not-just-rich-famous.

Center for American Progress. (2019, March 28). The Child Care Crisis Is Keeping Women Out of the Workforce [Report]. www.americanp rogress.org/article/child-care-crisis-keeping-women-workforce.

Center for American Progress. (n.d.) Do You Live in a Child Care Desert? [Interactive Map]. Retrieved December 12, 2023, from https://childca redeserts.org/2018.

Center for American Women and Politics and Higher Heights. (2023a). Black Women in American Politics 2023 [Report]. https://cawp.rutgers. edu/sites/default/files/2023-06/Black%20Women%20in%20Politics% 202023_Final.pdf.

Center for American Women and Politics and Higher Heights. (2023b). Women in Elective Office 2023. Retrieved December 14, 2023, from http s://cawp.rutgers.edu/facts/current-numbers/women-elective-office-2023.

Chan, A.L., Nichols, B.J., Daub, A., & Crossley, A.D. (2024). *Assessing the Impact of Non-Disclosure Agreements and Forced Arbitration Clauses on Survivors of Workplace Sexual Harassment and Discrimination*. [white paper].

Chohlas-Wood, A. (2020, June 19). Understanding risk assessment instru ments in criminal justice. Brookings Institution. www.brookings.edu/a rticles/understanding-risk-assessment-instruments-in-criminal-justice.

Clark, A.E. & Pino, A.L. (2016). *We believe you: Survivors of campus sexual assault speak out* (1st ed.). Holt Paperbacks.

Committee on Health Care for Underserved Women. (2014). Health Dis parities in Rural Women [Committee Opinion]. The American College of Obstetricians and Gynecologists. www.acog.org/-/media/project/a cog/acogorg/clinical/files/committee-opinion/articles/2014/02/health-dispa rities-in-rural-women.pdf.

Cooper, M. (2014). *Cut Adrift: Families in Insecure Times* (1st ed.). Uni versity of California Press. www.jstor.org/stable/10.1525/j.ctt6wqbcb.

Corbett, C., Voelkel, J.G., Cooper, M., & Willer, R. (2022). Pragmatic bias impedes women's access to political leadership. *Proceedings of the National Academy of Sciences of the United States of America*, 119(6), e2112616119. doi:10.1073/pnas.2112616119.

Correll, S.J., Benard, S., & Paik, I. (2007). Getting a Job: Is There a Motherhood Penalty? *American Journal of Sociology*, 112(5), 1297–1338. doi:10.1086/511799.

Correll, S.J., Weisshaar, K.R., Wynn, A.T., & Wehner, J.D. (2020). Inside the Black Box of Organizational Life: The Gendered Language of Performance Assessment. *American Sociological Review*, 85(6), 1022–1050. doi:10.1177/0003122420962080.

Crenshaw, K. (1991). Mapping the Margins: Intersectionality, Identity Politics, and Violence against Women of Color. *Stanford Law Review*, 43 (6), 1241–1299. doi:10.2307/1229039.

Daminger, A. (2019). The Cognitive Dimension of Household Labor. *American Sociological Review*, 84(4), 609–633. doi:10.1177/0003122419859007.

Davenport, S., Smith, D., & Green, D.J. (2023). Barriers to a Timely Diagnosis of Endometriosis: A Qualitative Systematic Review. *Obstetrics and gynecology*, 142(3), 571–583. doi:10.1097/AOG.0000000000005255.

Davies, S. (2021, April 5). Period Poverty: The Public Health Crisis We Don't Talk About [Text]. Retrieved December 5, 2023, from https://policylab.chop.edu/blog/period-poverty-public-health-crisis-we-dont-talk-about.

Davis, A.Y. & Shaylor, C. (2001). Race, Gender, and the Prison Industrial Complex: California and Beyond. *Meridians*, 2(1), 1–25. www.jstor.org/stable/40338793.

Davis, A.Y., Dent, G., Meiners, E.R., & Richie, B.E. (2022). *Abolition. Feminism. Now*. Haymarket Books.

DeLoughery, E., Colwill, A.C, Edelman, A., *et al*. (2023). Red blood cell capacity of modern menstrual products: considerations for assessing heavy menstrual bleeding. *BMJ Sexual & Reproductive Health*. Published online August 7. doi:10.1136/bmjsrh-2023-201895.

Desmarais, S.L., Monahan, J., & Austin, J. (2022). The Empirical Case for Pretrial Risk Assessment Instruments. *Criminal Justice and Behavior*, 49 (6), 807–816. doi:10.1177/00938548211041651.

Dick, K. (2012). *The Invisible War* [Film]. Chain Camera Pictures.

Dick, K. (2015). *The Hunting Ground* [Film]. Roco Films.

Dick, K. & Ziering, A. (2020). *On the Record* [Film]. Artemis Rising Foundation.

Donley, G. (2023, December 17). What Happened to Kate Cox Is Tragic, and Completely Expected. *The New York Times*. www.nytimes.com/2023/12/17/opinion/kate-cox-abortion-texas-exceptions.html.

Eavis, P. (2023, October 5). Women Could Fill Truck Driver Jobs. Companies Won't Let Them. *The New York Times*. Retrieved November 29, 2023, from www.nytimes.com/2023/10/05/business/economy/women-truck-drivers.html.

Edwards, H. (2018, October 4). How Christine Blasey Ford's testimony changed America. *Time*. https://time.com/5415027/christine-blasey-ford-testimony.

Ely, R.J. & Padavic, I. (2020, March 1). What's Really Holding Women Back? *Harvard Business Review*. Retrieved November 28, 2023, from https://hbr.org/2020/03/whats-really-holding-women-back.

Ely, R.J., Stone, P., & Ammerman, C. (2014, December 1). Rethink What You "Know" About High-Achieving Women. *Harvard Business Review*. Retrieved November 28, 2023, from https://hbr.org/2014/12/rethink-what-you-know-about-high-achieving-women.

Ensmenger, N. (2012). *The Computer Boys Take Over Computers, Programmers, and the Politics of Technical Expertise*. MIT Press.

Famuyiwa, R. *Confirmation* [Film]. HBO Films.

Farhi, P. (2022, September 18). Can the Sunday morning talk show be saved? *Washington Post*. www.washingtonpost.com/media/2022/09/18/sunday-morning-talk-shows-washington-media-meet-the-press.

Fielding-Singh, P. & Cooper, M. (2023). The emotional management of motherhood: Foodwork, maternal guilt, and emotion work. *Journal of Marriage and Family*, 85(2), 436–457. doi:10.1111/jomf.12878.

Fleming, P.J., Gruskin, S., Rojo, F., & Dworkin, S.L. (2015). Men's violence against women and men are inter-related: Recommendations for simultaneous intervention. *Social science & medicine (1982)*, 146, 249–256. doi:10.1016/j.socscimed.2015.10.021.

Ford, C.B. (2024). *One Way Back*. St. Martins.

Foster, D.G.( 2021). *The Turnaway Study: Ten Years, a Thousand Women, and the Consequences of Having-or Being Denied-an Abortion*. Scribner.

Fox, D. (2023, June 16). The Abortion Double Bind. *American Journal of Public Health* (113, Forthcoming), San Diego Legal Studies Paper No. 23–025, Available at SSRN: https://ssrn.com/abstract=4481560.

Freedman, E.B. 2013. *Redefining Rape: Sexual Violence in the Era of Suffrage and Segregation*. Harvard University Press.

Friedman J., Valenti J., & Cho M. (2008). *Yes means yes!: visions of female sexual power & a world without rape*. Seal Press.

Friedman, A.M., Hemler, J.R., Rossetti, E., Clemow, L.P., & Ferrante, J.M. (2012). Obese Women's Barriers to Mammography and Pap Smear: The Possible Role of Personality. *Obesity*, 20(8), 1611–1617. doi:10.1038/oby.2012.50.

Geena Davis Institute. (n.d.). *Gender in Media: The Myths & Facts*. Retrieved December 14, 2023, from https://seejane.org/research-informs-empowers/gender-in-media-the-myths-facts.

Getahun, D., Oyelese, Y., Peltier, M., Yeh, M., Chiu, V.Y., Takhar, H., Khadka, N., Mensah, N., Avila, C., & Fassett, M.J. (2023). Trends in Postpartum Depression by Race/Ethnicity and Pre-pregnancy Body Mass

Index. *SMFM 43rd Annual Meeting: The Pregnancy Meeting*, 228(1, Supplement), S122–S123. doi:10.1016/j.ajog.2022.11.248.

Gendered Innovations. (n.d.). *Medical Technology: Intersectional Approaches*. Stanford University. https://genderedinnovations.stanford.edu/case-studies/medtech.html.

Gilmore, R.W., Bhandar, B., & Toscano, A. (2022). *Abolition geography: Essays towards liberation*. Verso.

Gloor, J.L., Mestre, E.B., Post, C., & Ruigrok, W. (2022, July 26). We Can't Fight Climate Change Without Fighting for Gender Equity. *Harvard Business Review*. https://hbr.org/2022/07/we-cant-fight-climate-change-without-fighting-for-gender-equity.

Goldin, C., Kerr, S.P., Olivetti, C., & Barth, E. (2017). The Expanding Gender Earnings Gap: Evidence from the LEHD-2000 Census. *The American Economic Review*, 107(5), 110–114. www.jstor.org/stable/44250371.

Goodwin, M. (Ed.). (2020). Policing the Womb. In *Policing the Womb: Invisible Women and the Criminalization of Motherhood*, pp. i–ii. Cambridge University Press; Cambridge Core. www.cambridge.org/core/product/96C131781EEB28D595B15F6216A4F72A.

Greenwood, B.N., Hardeman, R.R., Huang, L. & Sojourner, A. (2020) Physician–patient racial concordance and disparities inbirthing mortality for newborns PNAS August 17, 117 (35) 21194–21200.

Greenwood, B.N., Carnahan S., & Huang, L. (2018). Patient–physician gender concordance and increased mortality among female heart attack patients. PNAS, August 6, 2018. doi:10.1073/pnas.1800097115.

Gupta, A.H. (2023, August 23). How Menopause Affects Women of Color. *The New York Times*. www.nytimes.com/2023/08/23/well/live/menopause-symptoms-women-of-color.html.

Haines, J. (2023, May 11). Gender Reveals: Data Shows Disparities in Child Care Roles. *U.S News*. Retrieved December 12, 2023, from www.usnews.com/news/health-news/articles/2023-05-11/gender-reveals-data-shows-disparities-in-child-care-roles.

Hamberg, K., Risberg, G., Johansson, E.E., & Westman, G. (2002). Gender bias in physicians' management of neck pain: a study of the answers in a Swedish national examination. *Journal of women's health & gender-based medicine*, 11(7), 653–666. doi:10.1089/152460902760360595.

Harriet, T. (2022, March 15). Women in low-paying jobs are losing billions as U.S. gender pay gap persists, Labor Department says. *CNBC*. Retrieved November 25, 2023, from www.cnbc.com/2022/03/15/women-in-low-paying-jobs-are-losing-billions-as-us-gender-pay-gap-persists-labor-department-says.html.

Harrington, C. (2021). What is "Toxic Masculinity" and Why Does it Matter? *Men and Masculinities*, 24(2), 345–352. doi:10.1177/1097184X20943254.

Hart, C.G., Crossley, A.D., & Correll, S.J. (2018). Leader Messaging and Attitudes toward Sexual Violence. *Socius*, 4. doi:10.1177/2378023118808617.

Hattery, A. & Smith, E. (2019). *Gender, Power, and Violence: Responding to Sexual and Intimate Partner Violence in Society Today*. Lanham, MD: Rowman & Littlefield.

Haynie, K. (2021, May 4). How Race and Gender Are Shaping Politics. Duke Faculty Advancement. Retrieved December 14, 2023, from https://facultyadvancement.duke.edu/how-race-and-gender-are-shaping-politics.

Hess, C., Ahmed, T., & Hayes, J. (2020). Providing Unpaid Household and Care Work in the United States: Uncovering Inequality [Report]. Institute for Women's Policy Research. https://iwpr.org/wp-content/uploads/2020/01/IWPR-Providing-Unpaid-Household-and-Care-Work-in-the-United-States-Uncovering-Inequality.pdf.

Hill, L., Artiga, S., & Published, U.R. (2022, November 1). Racial Disparities in Maternal and Infant Health: Current Status and Efforts to Address Them. *KFF*. www.kff.org/racial-equity-and-health-policy/issue-brief/racial-disparities-in-maternal-and-infant-health-current-status-and-efforts-to-address-them.

Hochschild, A.R. & Machung, A. (1989). *The second shift: working parents and the revolution at home*. New York: Viking.

Hodges, M.J. & Budig, M.J. (2010). Who gets the daddy bonus? Organizational Hegemonic Masculinity and the Impact of Fatherhood on Earnings. *Gender and Society*, 24(6), 717–745. www.jstor.org/stable/25789904.

Hoffman, K.M., Trawalter, S., Axt, J.R., & Oliver, M.N. (2016). Racial bias in pain assessment and treatment recommendations, and false beliefs about biological differences between blacks and whites. *Proceedings of the National Academy of Sciences of the United States of America*, 113 (16), 4296–4301. doi:10.1073/pnas.1516047113.

Huddart K., E., Krahn, H., & Krogman, N.T. (2015). Are we counting what counts? A closer look at environmental concern, pro-environmental behaviour, and carbon footprint. *Local Environment*, 20(2), 220–236. doi:10.1080/13549839.2013.837039.

Institute for the Elimination of Poverty & Genocide. (2020). Re: Lack of Medical Care, Unsafe Work Practices, and Absence of Adequate Protection Against COVID-19 for Detained Immigrants and Employees Alike at the Irwin County Detention Center [Electronic Mail]. Retrieved December 6, 2023, from https://projectsouth.org/wp-content/uploads/2020/09/OIG-ICDC-Complaint-1.pdf.

Institute for Women's Policy Research. (2015). Poverty & Opportunity. Retrieved November 24, 2023, from https://statusofwomendata.org/explore-the-data/poverty-opportunity.

Institute for Women's Policy Research. (2018). New State Grades on the Economic Status of Women Show Stagnant or Declining Progress in Most States. Retrieved November 24, 2023, from https://statusofwomendata.org/press-releases/new-state-grades-economic-status-women-show-stagnant-declining-progress-states.

Institute for Women's Policy Research. (2021, March 24). Equal Pay Day 2021: The Results of a COVID-Impacted Economy. Retrieved November 29, 2023, from https://iwpr.org/equal-pay-day-2021-the-results-of-a-covid-impacted-economy.

Institute for Women's Policy Research. (2022). Gender Wage Gaps Remain Wide in Year Two of the Pandemic. https://iwpr.org/wp-content/uploads/2022/02/Gender-Wage-Gaps-in-Year-Two-of-Pandemic_FINAL.pdf.

Jackson-Gibson, A. (2021, February 23). The Racist and Problematic Origins of the Body Mass Index. *Good Housekeeping*. www.goodhousekeeping.com/health/diet-nutrition/a35047103/bmi-racist-history.

Jang, C.J. & Lee, H.C. (2022). A Review of Racial Disparities in Infant Mortality in the US. *Children*, 9(2), 257. doi:10.3390/children9020257.

Kaba, M. (2017). *Survived and punished convening*. Chicago, IL.

Kajstura, A. & Sawyer, W. (2023, March 1). *Women's Mass Incarceration: The Whole Pie 2023*. Prison Policy Initiative. Retrieved December 14, 2023, from www.prisonpolicy.org/reports/pie2023women.html.

Kamenetz, A. & Khurana, M. (2021, October 19). 1 in 3 working families is struggling to find the child care they desperately need. *NPR*. www.npr.org/2021/10/19/1047019536/families-are-struggling-to-find-the-child-care-they-desperately-need.

Katz, J., Earp, J., & Rabinovitz, D. (2013). *Tough guise 2: Violence, manhood & American culture*. Media Education Foundation.

Katz, J. & Jhally, S. (2013). *Tough Guise 2: Violence, Manhood, and American Culture* [Film]. Media Education Foundation.

Kennedy, H.P., Beck, C.T., & Driscoll, J.W. (2002). A Light in the Fog: Caring for Women with Postpartum Depression. *Journal of Midwifery & Women's Health*, 47(5), 318–330. doi:10.1016/S1526-9523(02)00272–00276.

Kirkland, A., Talesh, S., & Perone, A. (2021) Health Insurance Rights and Access to Health Care for Trans People: The Social Construction of Medical Necessity. *Law and Society Review*, 55(4), 539–562.

Klein, R., Julian, K.A., Snyder, E.D., *et al.* (2019). Gender Bias in Resident Assessment in Graduate Medical Education: Review of the Literature. *J Gen Intern Med*, 34, 712–719. doi:10.1007/s11606-019-04884-0.

Knutson, J. (2023, July 20). Report: Texas' strict abortion ban linked to over 10% spike in infant deaths. *Axios*. www.axios.com/2023/07/20/texas-abortion-ban-infant-mortality-rate.

Latinas Represent. (2022). Latinas in U.S. Politics 2022. Retrieved December 14, 2023, from https://latinasrepresent.org/reports.

Lears, R. (2019). *Knock Down the House* [Film]. Atlas Films.

León-Pérez, G., Richards, C., & Non, A.L. (2021). Precarious Work and Parenting Stress among Mexican Immigrant Women in the United States. *Journal of Marriage and Family*, 83(3), 881–897. doi:10.1111/jomf.12761.

Loya R.M. (2015). Rape as an Economic Crime: The Impact of Sexual Violence on Survivors' Employment and Economic Well-Being. *Journal of interpersonal violence*, 30(16), 2793–2813. doi:10.1177/0886260514554291.

Luna, Z. & Luker, K. (2013). Reproductive Justice. *Annual Review of Law and Social Science*, 9(1), 327–352. 10. 1146/annurev-lawsocsci-1026 12-1340 37.

Martin, P.Y. (2016). The Rape Prone Culture of Academic Contexts: Fraternities and Athletics. *Gender and Society*, 30(1), 30–43.

Mayer, J. & Farrow, R. (2018, October 3). The F.B.I. Probe Ignored Testimonies from Former Classmates of Kavanaugh. *The New Yorker*. www.newyorker.com/news/news-desk/will-the-fbi-ignore-testimonies-from-kavanaughs-former-classmates.

Mayo Clinic Health System. (2021, November 30). Learn more about menopause. Retrieved December 6, 2023, from www.mayoclinichealthsystem.org/hometown-health/speaking-of-health/too-embarrassed-to-ask-part-3.

McLaughlin, H., Uggen, C., & Blackstone, A. (2017). The Economic and Career Effects of Sexual Harassment on Working Women. *Gender & Society*, 31(3), 333–358. doi:10.1177/0891243217704631.

Melfi, T. (2016). *Hidden Figures* [Film]. Fox 2000 Pictures; Chernin Entertainment; Levantine Films.

Mensah, G. & Fuster, V. (2022). Sex and Gender Differences in Cardiovascular Health. *J Am Coll Cardiol. Apr*, 79 (14) 1385–1387. doi:10.1016/j.jacc.2022.02.008.

Michalsen, V. (2019). Abolitionist Feminism as Prisons Close: Fighting the Racist and Misogynist Surveillance "Child Welfare" System. *The Prison Journal*, 99(4), 504–511. doi:10.1177/0032885519852091.

Michel J., Mettler A., Schönenberger S., & Gunz D. (2022). Period poverty: why it should be everybody's business. *Journal of Global Health Reports (6)*. doi:10.29392/001c.32436.

Miller, H.E., Fraz, F., Zhang, J., Henkel, A., Leonard, S.A., Maskatia, S.A., El-Sayed, Y.Y., & Blumenfeld, Y.J. (2023). Abortion Bans and Resource Utilization for Congenital Heart Disease: A Decision Analysis. *Obstetrics and gynecology*, 142(3), 652–659. doi:10.1097/AOG.0000000000005291.

Miller, C. (2019). *Know My Name*. Viking (an imprint of Penguin Random House LLC).

Mon, M. (2022, August 16). There's No Such Thing As a Feminist Jail. *Teen Vogue.* www.teenvogue.com/story/feminist-jail-nyc-abolition.

Montiel, A.V. (2015). News Media Coverage of Women. *Asia Pacific Media Educator*, 25(2), 182–193. doi:10.1177/1326365X15604260.

Moseson, H., Zazanis, N., Goldberg, E., Fix, L., Durden, M., Stoeffler, A., Hastings, J., Cudlitz, L., Lesser-Lee, B., Letcher, L., Reyes, A., & Obedin-Maliver, J. (2020). The Imperative for Transgender and Gender Nonbinary Inclusion: Beyond Women's Health. *Obstetrics and gynecology*, 135(5), 1059–1068. doi:10.1097/AOG.0000000000003816.

Moyer, M.W. (2022, March 28). *Women Are Calling Out 'Medical Gaslighting.' The New York Times.* Retrieved December 4, 2023, from www.nytimes.com/2022/03/28/well/live/gaslighting-doctors-patients-health.html.

Nash, I., Guarnieri, I. (2023, January 9). Six Months Post-Roe, 24 US States Have Banned Abortion or Are Likely to Do So: A Roundup. Guttmacher Institute. www.guttmacher.org/2023/01/six-months-post-roe-24-us-states-have-banned-abortion-or-are-likely-do-so-roundup.

National Academies of Sciences, Engineering, and Medicine. (2018). Sexual Harassment of Women: Climate, Culture, and Consequences in Academic Sciences, Engineering, and Medicine. Washington, DC: The National Academies Press. doi:10.17226/24994.

National Partnership for Women & Families. (2023, September). NEW DATA: Pay Gap Costs Women $1.6 Trillion Each Year. Retrieved November 24, 2023, from https://nationalpartnership.org/news_post/new-data-pay-gap-costs-women-1-6-trillion-each-year.

National Women's Law Center. (2017, August). Low-wage jobs are women's jobs: The overrepresentation of women in low-wage work. https://nwlc.org/wp-content/uploads/2017/08/Low-Wage-Jobs-are-Womens-Jobs.pdf.

National Women's Law Center. (2022). The Wage Gap Robs Women of Economic Security as the Harsh Impact of COVID-19 Continues [Fact Sheet]. National Women's Law Center. https://nwlc.org/wp-content/uploads/2022/03/Equal-Pay-Day-Factsheet-2022.pdf.

Newman-Toker, D.E., Moy, E., Valente, E., Coffey, R., & Hines, A.L. (2014). Missed diagnosis of stroke in the emergency department: a cross-sectional analysis of a large population-based sample. *Diagnosis (Berlin, Germany)*, 1(2), 155–166. doi:10.1515/dx-2013-0038.

Newsom, J.S. (2015). *The Mask You Live In* [Film]. The Representation Project.

Noble, S. (2018). *Algorithms of Oppression: How Search Engines Reinforce Racism.* New York: NYU Press.

Norman Lear Center for the Study of Entertainment, Media, and Society. (2018). IMMIGRATION NATION: Exploring Immigrant Portrayals on

Television [Report]. www.mediaimpactproject.org/uploads/5/1/2/7/ 5127770/immigration_nation_report_final.pdf.

NPR. (2018, September 23). Anita Hill Testimony: The Witness Not Called. Retrieved December 2, 2023, from www.npr.org/2018/09/23/650956623/a nita-hill-testimony-the-witness-not-called.

NPR. (2021, September 28). Anita Hill Started A Conversation About Sexual Harassment. She's Not Done Yet. Retrieved December 2, 2023, from www.npr.org/2021/09/28/1040911313/anita-hill-belonging-sexual-ha rassment-conversation.

Oppel, R.A., Taylor, D.B., & Bogel-Burroughs, N. (2023, November 16). What to Know About Breonna Taylor's Death. *The New York Times.* www.nytimes.com/article/breonna-taylor-police.html.

Peitzmeier, S.M., Fedina, L., Ashwell, L., Herrenkohl, T. I., & Tolman, R. (2022). Increases in Intimate Partner Violence During COVID-19: Prevalence and Correlates. *Journal of interpersonal violence*, 37(21–22), NP20482–NP20512. doi:10.1177/08862605211052586.

Peitzmeier, S.M., Malik, M., Kattari, S.K., Marrow, E., Stephenson, R., Agénor, M., & Reisner, S.L. (2020). Intimate Partner Violence in Transgender Populations: Systematic Review and Meta-analysis of Prevalence and Correlates. *American Journal of Public Health*, 110(9), e1–e14. doi:10.2105/AJPH.2020.305774.

Petrullo, J. (2023, January 31). US Has Highest Infant, Maternal Mortality Rates Despite the Most Health Care Spending. *AJMC.* www.ajmc.com/ view/us-has-highest-infant-maternal-mortality-rates-despite-the-most-hea lth-care-spending.

Pew Research Center. (2016). Racial, gender wage gaps persist in U.S. despite some progress. Retrieved November 24, 2023, from www.pewre search.org/short-reads/2016/07/01/racial-gender-wage-gaps-persist-i n-u-s-despite-some-progress.

Pew Research Center. (2023, April). In a Growing Share of U.S. Marriages, Husbands and Wives Earn About the Same. www.pewresearch.org/socia l-trends/2023/04/13/in-a-growing-share-of-u-s-marriages-husbands-and-wi ves-earn-about-the-same.

Pildes, E. & Lessin, T. (2019). *The Janes* [Film]. HBO.

Ramchandani, A. (2018, January 29). There's a Sexual-Harassment Epidemic on America's Farms. The Atlantic. Retrieved December 2, 2023, from www.theatlantic.com/business/archive/2018/01/agriculture-sexual-harassm ent/550109.

Rapp, A. & Kilpatrick, S. (2020, February 4). Changing the Cycle: Period Poverty as a Public Health Crisis. Retrieved December 5, 2023, from http s://sph-webprod.sph.umich.edu/pursuit/2020posts/period-poverty.html.

Risen, C. (2022, December 14). Dorothy Pitman Hughes Dies at 84; Brought Black Issues to Feminism. *The New York Times*. www.nytimes.com/2022/12/14/us/dorothy-pitman-hughes-dead.html.

Ritchie, A.J. (2017). *Invisible no more: Police violence against black women and women of color*. Boston: Beacon Press.

Richie, B.E. (2012). Arrested Justice: Black Women, Violence, and America's Prison Nation. NYU Press. www.jstor.org/stable/j.ctt9qghqn.

Ritman, A. (2015, October 8). London Film Festival: Geena Davis Calls for Gender Equality in Family Entertainment. The Hollywood Reporter. https://www.hollywoodreporter.com/news/general-news/london-film-festival-geena-davis-830623/

Roberts, D. (1998). *Killing the black body*. Vintage Books.

Rosay, A.B. (2016). Violence Against American Indian and Alaska Native Women and Men. *National Institute of Justice Journal*, 277, 38–45. www.ojp.gov/pdffiles1/nij/249822.pdf.

Ross, L. (2006). Understanding Reproductive Justice: Transforming the Pro-Choice Movement. *Off Our Backs*, 36, 14–19. doi:10.2307/20838711.

Rubio, S. (2022, September 30). Governor Signs Rubio Bill Expanding Protections for Revenge Porn Victims. California State Senate. https://sd22.senate.ca.gov/news/2022-09-30-governor-signs-rubio-bill-expanding-protections-revenge-porn-victims.

Sabin, J.A. (2022). Tackling Implicit Bias in Health Care. *New England Journal of Medicine*, 387(2), 105–107. doi:10.1056/NEJMp2201180.

Samuels, A. (2021, May 6). Why Black Women Are Often Missing From Conversations About Police Violence. *FiveThirtyEight*. https://fivethirtyeight.com/features/why-black-women-are-often-missing-from-conversations-about-police-violence.

Sanctuary for Families. (2023, March 10). *The Silent Epidemic of Femicide in the United States*. Retrieved November 29, 2023, from https://sanctuaryforfamilies.org/femicide-epidemic.

Seidman, S. (2023, February 1). Remembering Dorothy Pitman Hughes. Museum of the City of New York. Retrieved December 12, 2023, from www.mcny.org/story/remembering-dorothy-pitman-hughes.

Seifer, D.B., Simsek, B., Wantman, E., *et al.* (2020). Status of racial disparities between black and white women undergoing assisted reproductive technology in the US. *Reprod Biol Endocrinol*, 18, 113. doi:10.1186/s12958-020-00662-4.

Semuels, A. (2017, December 27). Low-Wage Workers Aren't Getting Justice for Sexual Harassment. *The Atlantic*. Retrieved November 29, 2023, from www.theatlantic.com/business/archive/2017/12/low-wage-workers-sexual-harassment/549158.

Sexsmith, K., Reyes, F., & Griffin, M. (2023, July 31). Sexual violence is a pervasive threat for female farm workers—here's how the US could reduce their risk. *The Conversation*. Retrieved December 2, 2023, from https://theconversation.com/sexual-violence-is-a-pervasive-threat-for-female-farm-workers-heres-how-the-us-could-reduce-their-risk-204871#:~:text=Studies%20show%20that%2080%25%20of,of%20sexual%20harassment%20at%20work.

Shonkoff, J.P., Phillips, D.A., & National Research Council (Eds). (2000). *From neurons to neighborhoods: The science of early child development*. National AcademyPress.

SITNFlash. (2020, October 24). Racial Discrimination in Face Recognition Technology. *Science in the News*. https://sitn.hms.harvard.edu/flash/2020/racial-discrimination-in-face-recognition-technology.

Sloand, E.*et al.* (2015). Barriers and Facilitators to Engaging Communities in Gender-Based Violence Prevention following a Natural Disaster. *Journal of Health Care for the Poor and Underserved* 26(4), 1377–1390. doi:10.1353/hpu.2015.0133.

Smith, E.L. (2022). Female Murder Victims and Victim-Offender Relationship, 2021 [Report]. *The Bureau of Justice Statistics*. https://bjs.ojp.gov/sites/g/files/xyckuh236/files/media/document/fmvvor21.pdf.

Smith, M. (2023, October 10). Nobel Prize-winning Harvard economist Claudia Goldin: The gender pay gap will "never" close unless this happens. *CNBC*. Retrieved November 28, 2023, from www.cnbc.com/2023/10/10/nobel-prize-winner-claudia-goldin-the-gender-pay-gap-will-never-close-unless-this-happens.html.

Solá, A.T. (2023, September 18). The wage gap costs women $1.6 trillion a year, new report finds. Here's how to get the pay you deserve. *CNBC*. Retrieved November 29, 2023, from www.cnbc.com/2023/09/18/the-wage-gap-costs-women-1point6-trillion-a-year-report-finds.html.

Strings, S. (2019). Fearing the Black Body: The Racial Origins of Fat Phobia. *The Journal of African American History*, 106(3), 561–563. doi:10.1086/714615.

Sun, S. (2023). National Snapshot: Poverty Among Women and Families [Fact Sheet]. National Women's Law Center. https://nwlc.org/wp-content/uploads/2023/02/2023_nwlc_PovertySnapshot-converted.pdf.

Tam, M.W. (2021). Queering reproductive access: reproductive justice in assisted reproductive technologies. *Reproductive Health*, 18, 1–6.

Taylor, V. (1996). *Rock-a-by Baby: Feminism, Self-Help and Postpartum Depression* (1st ed.). Routledge. doi:10.4324/9780203760437.

The Basic Facts About Women in Poverty. (2020, August 3). Center for American Progress. Retrieved November 28, 2023, from www.americanprogress.org/article/basic-facts-women-poverty.

The National Organization for Women Foundation. (n.d.). Get The Facts. Retrieved December 6, 2023, from https://now.org/now-foundation/love-your-body/love-your-body-whats-it-all-about/get-the-facts.

The Pew Charitable Trusts. (2023, May 16). *Racial Disparities Persist in Many U.S. Jails* [Issue Brief]. Retrieved December 10, 2023, from https://www.pewtrusts.org/en/research-and-analysis/issue-briefs/2023/05/racial-disparities-persist-in-many-us-jails.

Thompson, R.A. (2016). What more has been learned? The science of early childhood development 15 years after neurons to neighborhoods. *Zero to Three Journal*, 36(3), 18–24.

UN Women. (2022, February 28). Explainer: How gender inequality and climate change are interconnected. UN Women–Headquarters. www.unwomen.org/en/news-stories/explainer/2022/02/explainer-how-gender-inequality-and-climate-change-are-interconnected.

US Department of Justice. (2023, March 8). Office of Public Affairs | Justice Department Finds Civil Rights Violations by the Louisville Metro Police Department and Louisville/Jefferson County Metro Government. www.justice.gov/opa/pr/justice-department-finds-civil-rights-violations-louisville-metro-police-department-and.

Villarreal, M. & Meyer, M.A. (2020), Women's experiences across disasters: a study of two towns in Texas, United States. *Disasters*, 44, 285–306. doi:10.1111/disa.12375.

Vogels, E. A. (2021, January 13). The State of Online Harassment. *Pew Research Center: Internet, Science & Tech.* www.pewresearch.org/internet/2021/01/13/the-state-of-online-harassment.

Wailoo, K. (2018). Historical Aspects of Race and Medicine: The Case of J. Marion Sims. *JAMA*; 320(15), 1529–1530. doi:10.1001/jama.2018.11944.

Warner, J. (2017). *Opening the Gates: Clearing the Way for More Women to Hold Political Office.* Center for American Progress.

Washington, H.A. (2008). *Medical Apartheid. The Dark History of Medical Experimentation on Black Americans from Colonial Times to the Present.* Vintage.

Waugh, I. M. (2010). Examining the Sexual Harassment Experiences of Mexican Immigrant Farmworking Women. *Violence Against Women*, 16 (3), 237–261. doi:10.1177/1077801209360857.

Williams, C. 1992. The Glass Escalator: Hidden Advantages for Men in the "Female" Professions. *Social Problems*, 39(3), 253–267.

Wingfield, A.H. (2023). *Gray Areas: How the Way We Work Perpetuates Racism and What We Can Do to Fix It.* Amistad.

Wolff, N., Blitz, C.L., Shi, J., Bachman, R., & Siegel, J.A. (2006). Sexual Violence Inside Prisons: Rates of Victimization. *Journal of Urban Health*, 83(5), 835–848. doi:10.1007/s11524-006-9065-2.

Women's Media Center. (2017, March 22). Divided 2017: The Media Gender Gap. Retrieved December 14, 2023, from https://womensmedia center.com/reports/divided-2017.

Women's Media Center. (2018, November 18). The Status of Women in the U.S. Media 2021. Retrieved December 14, 2023, from https://womensm ediacenter.com/reports/the-status-of-women-in-the-u-s-media-2021-1.

Women's Media Center. (2019, February 7). WMC Investigation 2019: Gender and Non-Acting Oscar Nominations—Full report [Report]. Retrieved December 14, 2023, from https://womensmediacenter.com/rep orts/wmc-investigates-2019-analysis-of-gender-oscar-non-acting-nomina tions-full-report.

Women's Media Center. (2021, September 21). WMC Report: Gender and Race Representation on Five Big Sunday Shows January 1–December 31, 2020—Infographics [Report]. Retrieved December 14, 2023, from https:// womensmediacenter.com/speech-project/online-abuse-101.

Wynn, A.T. (2020). Pathways toward Change: Ideologies and Gender Equality in a Silicon Valley Technology Company. *Gender & Society*, 34 (1), 106–130. doi:10.1177/0891243219876271.

Zamarro, G. & Prados, M.J. (2021). Gender differences in couples' division of childcare, work and mental health during COVID-19. *Review of economics of the household*, 19(1), 11–40. doi:10.1007/s11150-020-09534-7.

Zauderer, C. (2009). Postpartum depression: how childbirth educators can help break the silence. *The Journal of perinatal education*, 18(2), 23–31. doi:10.1624/105812409X426305.

Zheutlin, B. (2023, April 7). The decades-long fight to make child care a national priority. University of California, Berkeley. www.universityofca lifornia.edu/news/decades-long-fight-make-child-care-national-priority.

# 5 How do Feminists Create Change?

This chapter is dedicated to all the tactics, or strategies, that feminists use to create change. Feminists know there is no one mode of "doing feminism." This chapter shows how broad and nuanced feminists are in their approaches to change, and how, as bell hooks wrote "Feminism is for everybody." A large toolkit of feminist tactics makes the movement particularly inclusive and robust, as feminists have many different avenues of activism available to channel diverse interests.

It will not surprise readers, given the heterogeneity of the feminist movement documented throughout this book, that feminists aim to change a variety of entities. These include schools, government, health care systems, policing/legal organizations; public opinion, media and entertainment, music and the arts; communities, marriage, family, and childcare.

Social movements have different targets for change, with one research study finding that women's movement participants more often target public opinion or non-state entities (outside government), rather than formal political institutions (Van Dyke, Soule, and Taylor, 2004). Indeed, feminist activists' targets and tactics vary over time and also by context.

Feminists use a number of tactics to achieve their goals, including feminist art, media, performance, boycotts/girlcotts, protest and civil disobedience, and community organizing/solidarity, to name a few. The point of this chapter is to understand feminists on the ground and to highlight the spectrum of feminist activism they employ. While the tactics are presented separately, note that there is significant overlap.

Key terms presented in this chapter:

DOI: 10.4324/9781003310990-6

- Feminist methods for social change
- Online feminism
- Everyday feminism
- Feminist organizations
- Street protest and civil disobedience
- Consciousness-raising and collective identity
- Feminist legal tactics
- Academia and student activism
- Media
- Art and music

## Feminist Methods for Social Change

Tactics are the actions that social movement participants use to achieve their goals. Tactics vary greatly between and within social movements, and social movement scholars have identified a large range of approaches that activists employ. Movement tactics depend on the goals of activists, as well as the available resources, including time, money, and people power. The methods that activists choose to create change also depend on how receptive a particular target is.

The most useful way of thinking about feminist social movement tactics uses cultural or institutional approaches to change (Taylor and Van Dyke, 2007). Cultural or institutional tactics may result in increasing support of and consciousness of a movement, confronting every day taken-for-granted inequalities, changing organizations from within, and, importantly, creating solidarity among participants. It is important to note that cultural tactics can have significant success and advance a movement in political and cultural ways, and at the same time generate further activism (Taylor et al., 2009).

Tactics that are generally very public and outward-facing, such as street protest, civil disobedience, die-ins or sit-ins, are sometimes thought of in contrast to cultural or institutional approaches to change. While in many ways different and much more visible, they are all members of the same set of tactics that feminists have used over time.

Women's movement scholars have helped us understand that to fully evaluate a social movement, attentiveness to a range of tactics is required. If we think of social movements as only thousands of people marching, we will be missing out on most of the activities of social movement participants. Of having a wide-ranging and inclusive view of strategies and targets, Staggenborg and Taylor (2005) write:

"This approach directs us to look at the ways in which movements build community and change cultural understandings in addition to targeting the state or other elites. It also expands and broadens the boundaries of social movements by focusing on the types of organizational entities that activists consider part of a social movement, including commercial establishments and cultural groups as well as political movement organizations."

(p. 40)

Thus, the constellation of the feminist movement is on a spectrum ranging from everyday feminism to cultural and community-building groups, to large organizations that target state or federal political entities.

A narrow perspective of change might lead us to overlook successes of a movement. Of social movements, write Heather Hurwitz and Verta Taylor (2012): "their most lasting impact may be changes in public attitudes and opinions, the introduction of new cultural tastes and aesthetics, and the legitimation of new identities and cultural practices" (p. 815). These sorts of outcomes take a long time, dedication, and a strong community, rather than sporadic flare ups of highly visible protest. Moreover, while cultural and institutional tactics are often less visible, they are also more ongoing and deeply embedded within a movement, thus sustaining it over time (Staggenborg and Taylor, 2005).

The feminist movement has been successful and continuous, owing in large part to the wide range of tactics that feminists choose to use (Crossley and Taylor, 2015). This breadth and depth means that there are many options for activists to choose from, therefore increasing the likelihood they will find the activity that resonates with them. Another benefit of having a broad range of protest tactics is that movement organizations can be nimble and can respond quickly to the grievances at hand or adjust when necessary (McCammon, 2003).

## Tactic #1: Online Feminisms

Online feminism has been critical to the evolution of contemporary feminism. At different points in the development of Internet technologies feminists have built solidarity and amplified messaging using blogs, comment sections on feminist media sites, and a variety of social media sites including text, photo, and video-based technologies (Keller, 2015).

The platforms used today for online feminism vary widely and have also changed over time, as trends and technologies rapidly evolve.

Prior to the advancement of Internet technologies and popularity of social media sites, feminist organizing and feminist community was more local and in-person, aided by letters and hard copy written communications. Feminist information and resources, while abundant in print form, were not as rapidly available as they are today. That said, the importance of community and solidarity is evident over the entire course of both online and offline feminisms. Because of the difficulty separating our online and offline lives, in many ways online and offline feminism are one and the same. However, there are some distinct features of online feminism that have transformed the movement as we know it.

## *Feminist Consciousness, Community, Platforms*

Online feminism generates feminist consciousness, teaches feminist histories and feminist perspectives on current events, and provides platforms for community-building (Crossley, 2015).

First, online feminism ensures the development of feminist consciousness by exposing new people to feminism. Learning about the feminist movement and understanding the key contours of the movement allows individuals to see how feminism might be relevant to their own lives. Easily accessible online spaces and resources allow wide swaths of people to learn about different approaches to feminism, the history of feminism, and to learn how the movement addresses issues important to them.

Feminist consciousness may be developed online by:

- watching a young person share their personal experiences with gender and racial inequality, leading them to a feminist identity
- reading a feminist historian's take on Black feminism and Black women's participation in protest
- watching a queer person share their experience coming out to their family or followers
- reading an Indigenous woman's view on environmental justice
- reading about how a person realized they were transgender
- understanding that many people share a grievance that you previously thought affected only you

Understanding feminist perspectives allows a person to nurture a feminist consciousness, which facilitates attracting new feminists to the movement, essential to its sustenance. It is possible to obtain this information offline. However, online platforms provide a substantial volume of content instantaneously, speeding up the process of information-gathering.

Second, developing feminist solidarity and feminist community perpetuates feminism. When feminists feel connected to each other, they develop group cohesion, and experience encouragement and validation of their feminist perspectives. Strong online feminist community also shows adversaries or non-feminists there is substantial, impressive support for feminist claims. It also amplifies feminist grievances.

A prominent example of online feminist community development is #MeToo, started by Tarana Burke (long-time advocate for Black women and girls), which called attention to the common experiences of sexual violence. The hashtag was used 19 million times in the period between October 16, 2017 and September 30, 2018 (Anderson and Toor, 2018). Also, "65% of adult social media users in the USA reported regularly seeing content related to sexual harassment and assault" (Drewett, Oxlad, and Augoustinos, 2021). #MeToo succeeded in drawing international attention to the prevalence of sexual assault (a longstanding feminist concern) and the need to hold perpetrators accountable. Through the hashtag, feminists generated solidarity with the realization of how common sexual harassment is, and how, when feminists convene, their goals can be achieved. Arguably one of the most important features of #MeToo was that in banding women together, it served as an entry point to feminism that led to more activism, and stronger and more abundant feminist communities (Mendes and Ringrose, 2019).

Consciousness and community are both vital components of feminism, and have been for generations. The major benefit of having these flourish online is that the same opportunities may not exist offline for many people. Growing up in a family or community that rejects or stigmatizes feminists makes it challenging for someone curious about feminism to access feminist knowledge and networks. Or, if the local library has banned books about feminism and intersectionality, feminist authors will be hard to find. In contrast, online information about feminism is immediately accessible.

Online feminism also constructs a larger platform for diverse feminist voices than was previously available. Writes Feminista Jones (2019): "… Black women's voices have been refreshingly explosive in the self-affirming, self-preserving digital communities we have formed" (pp. 13–

14). Anyone with a social media presence can create and share feminist commentary that is then amplified to huge populations. That powerful a platform was previously reserved for legacy media and well-networked experts to whom legacy media turned. Journalists began quoting tweets or calling on social media figures for commentary, expanding their pool of experts. While there are downsides to this, especially in the age of misinformation, this practice has been particularly beneficial to diversifying the spokespeople for the feminist movement.

**Feminista Jones** is a prolific feminist who got her start on social media and eventually wrote a book called *Reclaiming Our Space: How Black Feminists are Changing the World from the Tweets to the Streets* (2019). Her activism runs the gamut from feminist writing on social media, running a workshop open to the public about the Combahee River Collective and Black feminism, and to a podcast "Black Girl Missing."

*Figure 5.1* Feminista Jones (Colin M. Lenton)

## Hashtags

#MeToo illustrates one major tactic of online feminism: using hashtags on X (formerly known as Twitter) and Instagram. Hashtag campaigns generate awareness, solidarity, and opportunities for users to convene and share their opinions on the same topic, and with the broader public (Jackson, Bailey, and Foucault Welles, 2020). While they typically do not last long, hashtags also generate interest in the topic and the appearance of more hashtags. For example, #MeToo emerged from offline and online organizing, along with a tidal wave of hashtags related to gender-based violence. #Believewomen implored that we hear and believe women who tell their stories of sexual assault, in contrast to the fervent discourse online that questions the truth of women's stories. Writes Rebecca Traister (2020): "The very idea of believing women doesn't have to be an *imperative*; at its most radical, it is a long-overdue *corrective* to the benefit of the doubt that powerful men are given over and over and over again." As a companion to #MeToo, #Believewomen spread interest in this topic and inspired feminist community.

Examples of feminist hashtags:

#whyididntreport
#whyIstayed
#NotYourAsianSidekick
#Solidarityisforwhitewomen
#YouOKSis
#MeToo
#GirlsLikeUs
#theemptychair
#believewomen
#sayhername
#sexworkiswork
#blackgirlmagic
#masculinitysofragile
#YesAllWomen
#NiUnaMenos
#Effyourbeautystandards

Each of these hashtags creates feminist solidarity and promulgates traditional feminist themes online. These themes include: confronting rape culture and gender-based violence, sharing deeply personal stories, learning from others, releasing shame and stigma, reversing the generations of silence around these issues (Keller, Mendes and Ringrose, 2018); as well as allyship (Clark, 2019).

**Research Reflection:** Select one hashtag from the above list. How did the hashtag emerge? What feminist concerns did it address? What feminist themes from this book are illustrated in the hashtag and ensuing conversation?

Feminists do not inhabit a harmonious wonderland. Hashtags also reveal the tensions between feminists of different racial backgrounds, particularly as white women dominated mainstream feminist discourse. There were also moments in which feminist community was challenged or problematized. For example in 2013, #Solidarityisforwhitewomen, started by Mikki Kendall, confronted white feminists who did not stand up to support Women of Color feminists who were being attacked online by a prominent media figure. Kendall (2013) argued that this was part of a long history of white women prioritizing solidarity with each other. This campaign generated a voluminous discussion of feminist inclusiveness and attuned many feminists to issues of privilege and power, and to the realization of how invested they are in discussing and interrogating feminist community.

TikTok has also shaped online feminism, and is another platform that normalizes and sustains feminist language and perspectives. For example, the "me before and after I stopped dressing for the male gaze" and "pov you stopped dressing for the male gaze" phenomena was popularized on TikTok (Shuttleworth, 2022). The "male gaze" is a classic feminist concept that originated in 1973, when film theorist Laura Mulvey explained how women are expected to be attractive and available to the view of heterosexual men, thereby objectifying and sexualizing women. This TikTok trend included short videos of women comparing how they previously dressed for "the male gaze" with how they dressed for themselves after they learned about "the male gaze." In these shorts, the "male gaze" content brought a remarkable feminist concept to a new and young audience, as well as normalized feminist discourse among women.

### Confronting Online Harassment

There is no feminist haven online. As outlined in chapter four, online harassment is particularly heinous towards women and feminism, and online feminists have been found to be monitored and surveilled by men (Megarry, 2018).

Feminists have created a number of organizations like *Heartmob* and *Right to Be* to provide resources and support to those who have experienced online harassment, and to bring the subject out of the shadows. Moreover, there are many overlapping characteristics between offline and online harassment related to power and male privilege. As we think of our online and offline worlds as one in the same, rather than separate, the similarities emerge. Thus, much of the work that feminists do to fight harassment in general, such as provide training about how to respond to harassment, support survivors, and share resources, is also applicable and related to addressing online harassment.

Many organizations now offer resources for those who need help with online harassment, including:

- PEN America's Online Harassment Field Guide
- National Sexual Violence Resource Center's online harassment resource guide

### Tactic #2: Everyday Feminism

Everyday feminism is when an individual incorporates feminist principles and ideologies in their daily lives. Or, in other words, when someone's belief in feminism or desire for a feminist world influences every day, and even mundane activities. As Rupp and Taylor (1987) write, everyday feminism is the "politicization of everyday life, embodied in symbols and actions that connect the members of the group and link their everyday experiences to larger social injustices" (p. 365). The benefit of everyday feminism is that it is easily attainable. It involves thoughtful personal reflection but generally not a lot of outside resources or coordination with other people. Everyday feminism might feel especially rewarding and empowering to feminists because it makes participants themselves feel as though they are effectual, part of something bigger, and contributing to a larger feminist social good.

Why is everyday feminism important to the feminist movement as a whole? Gender and intersectional inequalities are experienced and perpetuated not only in structural, organizational, and institutional ways, but also in interactional and quotidian ways. As such, feminist social change requires both everyday actions as well as agitating for large-scale structural change. Feminists have widely employed "the personal is political." Everyday feminism is a mode of linking the personal to the political.

It is important to note that since experiences with inequality vary significantly by race, class, sexuality, gender identity, and other metrics, everyday feminism will look different for different people. Moreover, the resources that an individual has, whether money, time, networks, or access to education, will also shape what one's everyday feminism looks like. This means that it is best not to judge or police enactments of everyday feminism. The framework presented in this chapter is not meant to be a rigid standard. Instead, it shows examples of everyday feminism and variations in its applications.

Everyday feminism can be practiced in many different ways (Crossley, 2017). Examples include: in interactions with others (language), in relationships, consumption habits, body positivity, and in self-care.

Everyday feminism involves the questioning of or resistance to sexist, racist, or classist language, and embracing inclusive and gender neutral language. As one becomes more knowledgeable about inequality and the way it is replicated through commonly used language, an everyday feminist move would be to confront others' use of sexist, racist, ableist, homophobic or transphobic language. Some people may avoid the practice of using he/man as a universal term to represent all people, or avoid using he/man when gender is unknown or irrelevant. Examples of this are: not assuming a doctor, lawyer, pilot or a leader is a man, or that a nurse, teacher, or domestic worker is a woman. Additionally, we often gender animals or objects as men when it is unknown or irrelevant, thus propping up men as the accepted default. Another example of everyday feminism in the realm of language is using or motivating others to use gender neutral terms in place of male-centered terms, e.g. "chairperson" rather than "chairman." Everyday feminists often think beyond the binary. They use language that doesn't assume someone's gender or sexuality, and that is inclusive of non-binary or transgender people.

Research has also found that feminists report having a "voice in their head" that asks them to consider power dynamics, gender and racial inequalities, and how they as individuals might be able to contribute to positive change in everyday interactions (Crossley, 2017).

In terms of relationships, everyday feminism can be practiced in a multitude of ways. One common way is by being critical of or refuting traditional gender expectations and heteronormativity, in and outside of relationships (Rich, 1980). This might take the form of rejecting the emphasis on heterosexual relationships in a woman's life course, or rejecting heterosexuality completely. Others might commit to their "chosen family" or to relationships with friends or community instead of investing in heterosexual romantic relationships. Everyday feminism might also involve incorporating feminist ideologies within a heterosexual relationship.

Another approach might be to emphasize enthusiastic consent in sexual relationships. While consent should of course be present in all sexual relationships, an everyday feminist approach might be to be particularly sensitive to issues of consent. Research has also found that another example of everyday feminism includes challenging outdated norms such as a man paying for a woman's meal or drink while on a date. This may lead to a power imbalance in which the woman then "owes" something to the man, further preserving power asymmetries.

Everyday feminism might also be practiced by overtly or covertly making typically gendered household/family customs more gender neutral, such as disrupting the expectations that mothers are the primary nurturers or caretakers, or that the home and kitchen are women's domains. Feminists may push for an equitable distribution of household labor based on preferences rather than gendered norms. These would apply to heterosexual relationships. In queer and lesbian relationships the same gendered power dynamics are typically not present.

Another mode of everyday feminism pertains to consumer habits. While such habits are certainly dependent on an individual's financial circumstances, there are many ways in which all feminists can exercise their feminist sensibilities with their dollars. Some feminists might prioritize patronizing Black, women-owned, or cooperative businesses. On the other end of the spectrum is an anti-capitalist or anti-consumption variation of everyday feminism. Those people resist capitalist pressure to participate in conspicuous consumption, and may be particularly conscious of the global inequalities perpetuated by fast fashion, for example. On social media, "no buys" or "deinfluencing" content has been increasing in popularity (Fares, 2023; Green, 2023). While these do not always have to be feminist per se, resisting consumption can be driven by a desire to live a more feminist life.

Some everyday feminists encourage others to refrain from supporting businesses that may promote anti-feminist ideologies, known as a "boycott" or "girlcott." In response to Donald Trump's Access Hollywood tape, Shannon Coulter started #Grabyourwallet (Walters, 2017). This campaign successfully removed Ivanka Trump's fashion brand from Nordstrom and other retailers, and caused loss of business to other Trump-owned stores (he also had a line of chandeliers!).

Are there any girlcotts that you are part of? Or products or businesses that you think should be girlcotted?

Decoupling a person's worth from their appearance is another form of everyday feminism. Feminists may work to convey messages that all bodies are beautiful, or, alternatively that bodies don't need to be beautiful, while challenging the white, thin, youthful stereotype of beauty. Confronting society's obsession with a woman's appearance is both political and feminist. Women's relationships to their bodies are clearly linked to overall physical and mental health. Examples of everyday feminism in this realm include combating fat phobia in social interactions, rejecting conventional beauty norms such as hair removal (Fahs, 2022), and normalizing the healthiness of all different body sizes.

Finally, self-care is another mode of everyday feminism. Self-care is when an individual prioritizes ensuring their well-being, mental health, and contentment. It is particularly important to those who are marginalized and experience the burden of inequality. Self-care is very specific to the individual, as needs and preferences vary greatly. For some it could be having alone time to read or journal, for others it might be sleeping. While self-care is sometimes thought of as a new mode of activism, or a trend, it has actually been linked for decades to having a political and feminist mission. Audre Lorde in 1988 proclaimed that "Caring for myself is not self-indulgence, it is self-preservation and that is an act of political warfare" (p. 130). As a Black lesbian feminist who created art despite the many oppressions she faced daily, Lorde's survival is political in nature. That she was successful and thrived is at its core a statement against white supremacist capitalist patriarchy.

Self-care has become commercialized to some degree, and is in many ways poised to be used as a tool to sell products to women. Tensions arise when self-care is achieved through consumption of consumer goods, the upholding or reifying of traditional feminine beauty norms, and/or on the backs of laboring immigrant women. While still having revolutionary potential, it is important to look at self-care with a critical eye. Some Black feminist scholars and writers have questioned whether the feminist nature of self-care has been watered down (Caldera, 2020).

### Self-care 101

The Nap Ministry, founded by Tricia Hersey, with principles of Black liberation and womanism among others, is an organization and ideology that touts "rest as resistance" (Hersey, 2022). It advocates for napping as a conscious choice that operates in opposition to capitalist impulses that pressure constant production, work, and consumption.

Everyday feminism is sometimes cited for taking away from broader collective organizing, or dismissed as inconsequential, in comparison to marching in the street. However, everyday feminism is significant *precisely because* it allows feminist ideologies to be deeply embedded in the everyday nature of our lives. These are activities that anyone can embrace, all imbued with feminist meaning. Moreover, identifying as feminist and incorporating everyday feminism in one's daily routine might galvanize an individual to participate in a feminist organization or introduce more feminist activity in their lives. In permeating our daily practices, it ensures the endurance of feminist ideologies. It also propels feminism over long periods of time, especially when the wider culture has not been particularly amenable to feminist claims (think the 1950s or 1980s) (Rupp and Taylor, 1987; Whittier, 1995; Taylor and Whittier, 1992; Staggenborg, 1998).

## Spotlight on Sara Ahmed

*Living a Feminist Life* (Ahmed, 2017) is a book written by feminist, queer scholar, and activist Sara Ahmed. Ahmed shows that, owing to the deeply ingrained nature of intersectional inequalities in all aspects of our lives, everyday feminism is critical. With personal reflection and by engaging with the work of feminists such as Lorde and hooks, Ahmed offers an in-depth reflection and analysis of contemporary inequalities and how they shape our lives.

In 2016 Ahmed resigned from her faculty position at Goldsmiths College, University of London:

"I have resigned in protest against the failure to address the problem of sexual harassment. I have resigned because the costs of doing this work have been too high."

Ahmed remains a prolific writer and everyday feminist. See www.feministkilljoys.com.

## Tactic #3: Feminist Organizations

Since the inception of feminism, feminist organizations have created long-lasting feminist change, feminist community, and feminist consciousness. What is a feminist organization? It is a formal structure, in the sense that it has a name, members, norms, and objectives or goals, that meets regularly in an effort to reach a feminist goal (Martin, 1990). Feminist organizations range from large national organizations with local networks and national offices, to small community-based organizations that focus on local feminist grievances. Some organizations are professional and formal, in the sense that they have offices, dedicated staff, and perhaps large budgets. Others run by the work of volunteers dedicated to feminist transformation in their spare time. Some feminist organizations are collectivist in nature, in that they make decisions by consensus, oftentimes being motivated by the feminist ethos of non-hierarchical direction and collective agreement. At the same time, feminist organizations can be bureaucratic and/or hierarchical. This means that there is a structure in which some members (director, president, board) have more power to make decisions than other members. One problem that has plagued feminist organizations is the lack of racial/ ethnic and class diversity, and the white middle-class domination of them. It has been a challenge for feminist organizations to successfully maintain diverse staff and leadership, although some have been successful, namely those that are in a position of service-provision (i. e. shelters and rape crisis centers) (Scott, 2005).

While organizations are not the be all and end all of social movement change, they are crucial in the advancement and development of feminism over time (Staggenborg, 1998). Feminists, in particular, are notable for their organizations and are models for other social movements. As scholar Patricia Yancey Martin wrote:

> "Feminist organizations in the modern, Western women's movements have proved to be extraordinarily prolific, creative, variegated, and tenacious. No other social movement, of the 1960s or later, has produced the rich variety of organizations that the women's movement has."
>
> (Martin 1990, p. 183)

Research has noted the importance of leaders in sustaining movement organizations–training them, retaining them, and finding opportunities for them to connect and learn from each other (Reger and Staggenborg, 2006).

In the 1960s and 1970s many feminist organizations of all sizes sprouted up across the country, in cities, capitals, and small towns. These flourished with feminist energy in response to massive social change in the US. Feminist organizations thrived because they were able to draw in members and secure funding. Also, large audiences were primed to see the importance of feminist organizations.

National feminist organizations are important to the movement because they set a tone for broad feminist issues, motivate and agitate change on a large scale, and also galvanize local chapters to do the work in communities across the country. Examples of these organizations include The National Black Feminist Organization (NBFO), a network of Black feminist groups, and The National Organization for Women (NOW), founded prior to the NBFO by a number of prominent feminists, including Betty Friedan and Pauli Murray. The Third World Women's Alliance (TWWA) emerged in 1968 and grew to national status– it was founded in order to rectify the sexism present in movements for racial justice. TWWA was sensitive to de-centering US and Western feminist concerns, and addressed the injustices of US imperialism and colonialism. At the same time, they were leaders in US-based and domestic Women of Color activism. While they didn't label their ideology as intersectionality, it was a precursor to intersectionality.

More recently, a number of national feminist organizations have addressed the gendered and racial dimensions of prison and carcerality. The organization Surived and Punished mobilizes to support women and trans individuals who have been jailed for defending themselves against abusive partners. The organization establishes mutual aid funds, organizes letters of support to be sent to incarcerated survivors, and hosts in-person convenings to share research and develop community. The related Feminist Anti-Carceral Policy and Research Initiative at University of California, Berkeley "will support efforts to address the lack of research and theory about the criminalization of survivors of domestic and sexual violence, and how gender violence is integral to carcerality." The national organizational energy around anti-carceral feminism has drawn significant attention to the problem, and has provided many opportunities for coalitions, and online and offline organizing.

## Spotlight on an Organization: Environmentalism

Extending the tradition of centering Black women's expertise, Black Girl Environmentalist is an organization founded in 2021 by Wawa Gatheru that addresses how Black women, girls, and gender expansive people are disproportionately affected by climate change and are often excluded from the climate movement. The organization has many programs that empower and support Black women to join environmental leadership and industry, and gathers hubs of supporters across the country. Black Girl Environmentalist is an example of a national organization with small, local groups convening around the country in support of its mission.

Grassroots, or local activism, is also crucial to the wellbeing of the women's movement. While those organizations are certainly impactful, they are typically operating on a small scale, with volunteers supporting the group, often with minimal funding.

Grassroots feminist organizations focusing on reproductive justice have garnered significant attention in the last year. Many of them have existed for a long time, and some have sprung up as major abortion restrictions were put into place and as new community needs were identified. Organizations raising funds for abortions have flourished, collecting money through Venmo and other platforms to then distribute to pregnant people who need to travel for abortion procedures. Feminist organizations are also working to distribute pills that induce abortion. Activists help each other locate the pills (side-stepping some state bans and dubious vendors), share information about using the pills, and who to ask for help if needed (Noor, 2022). Other examples of feminists organizing to ensure accessibility to reproductive health services include those that provide abortion midwifery, which is widely seen as a safe and effective mode of care (Carvajal et al., 2022).

### Spotlight on Organizations: Reproductive Justice

SisterSong, an organization co-founded by Loretta Ross, has had a mission "to strengthen and amplify the collective voices of Indigenous women and Women of Color to achieve reproductive justice by eradicating reproductive oppression and securing human rights."

Mountain Access Brigade is a grassroots abortion fund and doula collective operating in Tennessee, where abortion has been illegal since July 2022, owing to a trigger law. A doula is someone trained in providing physical and emotional support for someone undergoing a medical procedure, such as an abortion.

The organization provides funding to Tennessee residents to travel out of state for abortion care, and solicits donations from the public for their gas and hotel expenses.

**Research Reflection:** Choose two organizations and compare their targets and tactics:

- Incite!
- Bloodroot
- The Black Feminist Project
- The Landesa Center for Women's Land Rights
- Sogorea Te' Land Trust
- Alianza Nacional de Campesinas
- The Afiya Center
- Black Women's Health Imperative
- Black Women for Wellness
- National Black Women's Reproductive Justice Agenda
- New Voices for Reproductive Justice

## Spotlight on an Organization: Period Poverty

Period poverty is fought on state, county, and local levels. The organization No More Secrets Mind Body Spirit (MBS) was founded by Lynette Medley, and is working to eliminate period poverty. The price of tampons and pads has risen dramatically, from 9–10% each year, and in many states, tampons and menstrual products are classified as luxury items and are taxed (Salathe, 2022). No More Secrets MBS addresses the incredible need in poor communities; they have given away over 6 million menstrual products.

Feminist organizations also establish coalitions with each other, to share resources and reach wider audiences. One example of this is the Coalition to Stop Violence Against Native Women, which is based in New Mexico and is a coalition of tribal organizations. Their campaign "MMIWG2S" (Missing and Murdered Indigenous

Women, Girls, and Two Spirit) highlights the lives of the many missing people, shares research and data, as well as takes practical steps when someone goes missing (CSVANW, 2022). Their approach is also steeped in recognition of MMIWG2S as but one recourse to counter ongoing injustices against Indigenous communities, women, and girls.

## Tactic #4: Street Protest and Civil Disobedience

One tactic that may come to mind right away when you think of a social movement might be street protest, such as holding signs in high traffic areas, disrupting traffic, or marching in a crowd. The benefit of this type of tactic is that it is highly visible. It draws the attention that movement activists need, such as news media coverage, so their concerns or demands are amplified. This can attract new protesters and generate enthusiasm for their cause. Although when activists close down a main thoroughfare or bridge it might also anger commuters, thus driving a wedge between protesters and any broader public sympathy.

Traditionally, street protest has been dominated by men. Girls and women typically shy away from a connection to "activist" and "activism" (Taft, 2006; Bobel, 2007). This is not because of any particular essential way women "are" but rather because of the kinds of commitments women have in relationship to men. For example, women have disproportionate responsibilities for care work and household labor, which determine whether they have the spare time to dedicate to this type of protest, or what risks they may be willing to take (Beyerlein and Hipp, 2006; Dalton, 2002; McAdam, 1992). While not all women involved in social movements are feminist, these gendered dynamics in social movements are certainly very influential to feminist movements and the tactics feminists choose (Crossley and Hurwitz, 2023).

That said, women of all races and ethnicities were very visible and active in anti-war, civil rights, and pro-labor organizing throughout the 1900s. Much of the energy for women's public protest in the 1960s and 1970s originated in their disenchantment with and poor treatment by men in mixed gender movements, such as the anti-war, Black power, Chicano Nationalist, and civil rights movements.

The 1968 Miss America uproar might be one of the most well-publicized protests of contemporary feminism. The New York Radical Women's organization staged the action in Atlantic City, NJ, the site of that year's Miss America pageant. The eye-catching flier advertising the event proclaimed "Protest the sexist racist auction-sale pageant! Guerrilla Theater, films, workshops, picketing" (Gay, 2018). At the protest, which the media gleefully publicized, feminists threw objects of women's oppression into "freedom trash cans," symbolizing the desecration of traditional feminine items- such as bras, high heels, and false eyelashes. Nothing was ever burned, owing to the fact that the protest was held on a highly flammable wooden boardwalk. Nonetheless, this was the origin of the feminist myth and slur "bra burner." At the raucous protest, feminists carried "all women are beautiful" signs, and activists performed skits illustrating women's oppression. Famous Black feminist Florynce Kennedy (Flo) "chained herself to a puppet of Miss America" (Gay, 2018). A few activists from the protest sneaked into the pageant venue itself and unfurled a banner that proclaimed "women's liberation" (Gay 2018). Along with the protest, the organizers released a list of demands, objecting to the racism of the historically all-white pageant, to the double standard of femininity in which women pageant participants were expected to be "both sexy and wholesome," to the pageant's representation of "the elevation of mediocrity," encouraging women to be "unoffensive, bland, apolitical" (Gay, 2018).

The outcomes of the protest were exhilarating. The meeting of the New York Radical Women following the protest had over 200 more attendees than usual (Morgan, 2018). The protest drew national attention from the media (although much of the coverage was sexist and dismissive of the activists). It was not only a catalyst for feminist action across the country, but a spotlight on feminists' grievances, for better or worse.

**Reflection:** Do any of the calls for action or demands of the Miss America protest resonate with you? Do they feel dated? Or relevant? Why do you think the "bra burner" myth is so persistent, and do you think it is negative for the feminist movement?

Throughout the 1970s and 80s, feminists across the country held numerous protests advocating for equal rights and the Equal Rights Amendment (ERA), including 100,000 in Washington, DC in 1978 (History of marches and mass actions, 2015). As women's access to reproductive health services began eroding in the 1980s, feminists led and participated in numerous marches for decades. They drew huge crowds, including over 1 million people in Washington, DC in 2004.

Just prior to the 2016 inauguration of President Donald Trump, a record setting event occurred called "The Women's March." 500,000 people marched in Washington, as well as all over the country, with estimates reporting 4.1 million attendees nationwide in over 680 locations (Felmlee et al., 2020). The march in Washington featured a blockbuster number of speakers. Many participants wore pink "pussy hats," in reference to a sexist statement by the president elect. These hats were seen by many as too biological and trans exclusive. There were a number of other controversies about the march and its organizers, many that lingered. While not unimportant, it should be noted that all marches on Washington, because of the scale and number of people and interests involved, are plagued with tension and unrest (Ghaziani, 2008).

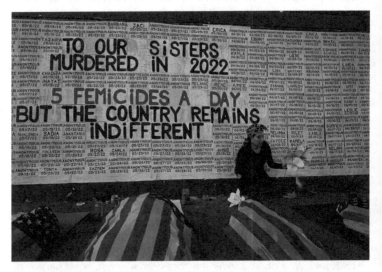

*Figure 5.2* "5 Femicides a Day," Feminist Collages NYC (Chloe Luterman)

Protests are important to activism because they demonstrate to political leaders that these are issues of mass concern to their voting body. They also show the broad population that these are issues to pay attention to. Marches are particularly powerful because they generate a spectacle, often with media contributing striking images of huge crowds and colorful protest signs, and a palpable far-reaching energy.

Feminists also use other ways to publicly protest. For example, an international collective called Feminist Collages uses guerrilla poster campaigns. In the night, activists paste up huge imposing feminist phrases and/or images across cities. Posters include "65% of all trans murder victims are Black women," "abortion is healthcare" and "where are you when your girlfriend is marching for her rights?" and "Challenge notions of masculinity that equate manhood with the ability to exert power over others -bell hooks" (Feminist Collages NYC, n.d.).

## Tactic #5: Consciousness-Raising Groups and Collective Identity

Consciousness-raising (CR) groups are a traditional feminist tactic. CR groups are inwardly focused on the development of its members, with individual and collective consequences. So what is a CR group exactly? It is a small group, typically of all women-identified individuals, who gather together on a regular basis to discuss the challenges and main events of their lives, and to learn from each other. Inevitably, similarities in life experiences emerge across the group. An individual's consciousness is raised in the sense that they come to understand their challenges are not unique, but that their experiences are part of a broader system that often devalues all women. Following in the traditions of the civil rights movement, CR became a central tactic and goal of the feminist movement (Echols, 1989).

## Case Study, CR

Ana is a 23-year-old-member of a CR group made up of women in her Phoenix-area neighborhood. At one meeting, Ana expressed frustration that her boyfriend did not support her in her efforts to graduate from college, worried that her attention to him and their child would diminish. Ana was angry that her boyfriend was so shortsighted.

Through talking with the members of her group, she learned that many of them also experienced tensions between family and career goals, in marriages, in romantic relationships, and in their families of origin. She also learned that this phenomenon was not reserved for personal relationships. Her CR peers said that their work managers also expected them, as women, to be primarily focused on their families. As a result, her peers believed they were not given the same promotions, extra hours, or opportunities for additional pay as their male colleagues were. Together, Ana and her CR group began to understand the numerous ramifications of the expectation that women should be devoted to family above all else. They began to understand how deeply their individual experiences were related to larger social structures.

Women of all backgrounds held CR groups, such as the Radicalesbians group, for example (Stryker, 2017, p. 124); or the Combahee River Collective and the Black Women's Liberation Committee, which formed CR groups that were important to the development of Black feminism (Springer, 2005).

Loretta Ross, a well-known Black feminist and co-founder and former National Coordinator of the SisterSong Women of Color Reproductive Justice Collective, describes CR groups:

"We may have more formally called it 'consciousness-raising' but in essence we were telling each other stories to reclaim ourselves and our humanity. We created a feminist culture with these stories, not through narratives of logic and structure, but by creating verbal snapshots of the lived experiences of women. We didn't have to all tell the same story in order to resonate with each other. Each story was unique but the act of telling our stories created strong bonds among diverse women who worked together to change our realities. We could imagine a world in which women lived in freedom from violence and we set about building rape crisis centers and domestic violence shelters not only to help women who had been violated, but also to project a vision of what a world without violence could look like for women."

(Freedman, 2014)

Ross outlines several of the most important components of CR. First, CR is an individual process in which important relationships are formed and in which women learn from each other. Second, CR groups make the personal, political. They free women to change their realities, and to imagine a world free of inequality. In addition, CR is so powerful because learning happens in a collective manner, as a process, in a non-hierarchical environment. Not by reading a book in a solitary setting, or by sitting in a classroom in front of a teacher. CR is at its core feminist in its principles: one's own experience is the point of departure.

Even though CR groups are not as common as they once were, the tradition continues. The process of CR groups is similar to what occurs in online settings, and scholars have compared conversations, groups, and exchanges on social media to the same processes that occur in offline CR groups (Crossley, 2015; Pruchniewska, 2019).

CR is a tactic, but also a broader contribution to the feminist movement in that it aids in the establishment of feminist collective identity. Collective identity is a significant component of feminist organizing and the continuity of the feminist movement over time, both as a motive of movement participation and as an outcome (Whittier, 1995). Feminist collective identities are created by movement participants understanding their common grievances and goals with a sense of cohesion and solidarity, politicizing everyday life, and establishing boundaries between feminists and others (Taylor and Whittier, 1992; Rupp and Taylor, 1999).

In CR, a person rethinks their own identity and is able to understand their life and personal experience through the lens of feminist ideologies (Whittier, 2017). This leads to a feminist collective identity, a unity with the wider feminist movement. According to Kimberly Springer (2005), the Black Women's Liberation Committee's "consciousness-raising sessions are exemplary of charting the evolution of a Black feminist collective identity that examined race, gender, and class" (p. 119). Strong feminist collective identities propel the movement forward, through organizational change, movement transformation, differences in movement contexts, and even through challenging circumstances. Feminist collective identities even impact other movements, such as peace and anti-war movements (Meyer and Whittier, 1994).

**Reflection:** Do you recognize themes of consciousness-raising in your own social media feeds, in your everyday life and friendships? How so?

There are also many other opportunities for feminists to gather together to share their experiences and perspectives. Women's circles exist across the country, as both informal and formal gatherings of women to develop feminist relationships and community. Another example is the feminist art salon, when feminists gather together to engage around artistic expression. Another variation is feminist networking, wherein feminists meet to talk about strategies, priorities, perspectives, and best practices. One example of this was the *Building an Asian American Feminist Movement Network Gathering* convened by the Asian American Feminist Collective. While not CR exactly, these examples follow in the tradition of feminists gathering to find strength in each other.

## Tactic #6: Feminist Legal Advances

In order to achieve their goals and to confront many of the inequalities outlined in Chapter 4, feminists pursue change through the legal system. This includes creating and advocating for laws that advance equality and reflect the lived experiences of women. It has been an uphill battle for feminists to gain rights for women, and keep them. In addition to this push and pull of change and advancement, feminists are divided on whether women should seek equality with men under the law, or whether we should work toward something else such as a special status because of fundamental differences between men and women (Hoff-Wilson, 1987). The entire law career of the late Supreme Court Justice Ruth Bader Ginsburg reshaped and transformed the legal landscape for gender equality and solidified equal protection under the law on the basis of sex, such as Moritz vs. Commissioner of Internal Revenue (argued prior to ascending to the Supreme Court).

The Equal Rights Amendment (ERA), states "Equality of rights under the law shall not be denied or abridged by the United States or by any state on account of sex." For over 100 years, feminists have fought, and continue to fight for this clause to be added to the US constitution. Proponents of the ERA believe this is a way to guarantee equality for all women. Opponents of the ERA include political conservatives who do not want to grant women equality through laws and/or who believe that women need to be protected because they are essentially different from men. Historically, there were also many progressive people and feminists who organized against the ERA. Labor feminists, represented primarily by Black and white women, were an early group who fought against the ERA. They believed that women in the workplace, unlike men, needed special treatment such as breaks, limits on working hours, and how much weight they could lift (Novara, 2023).

More recently, the repeal of Roe v. Wade has galvanized a new generation of feminists who believe that the passage of the ERA could guarantee the right to abortion. Previously in the fight for the ERA, abortion was largely sidestepped as a strategy to draw in as many supporters as possible. However, now that Roe is gone, high-school and college-student groups like Generation Ratify are rallying with renewed energy to pass the ERA. A news article in the *19th* writes:

> "Generation Ratify, which was formed in late 2019, sees a space for policymakers, particularly Democrats, to better communicate to the public the power of the ERA — the proposed text would explicitly state the Constitution does not discriminate on the basis of sex. Some legal experts believe that would protect not just abortion rights but prevent discrimination on the basis of gender identity and sexual orientation in several areas of life, including in the workplace and in cases of sexual assault."
>
> (Rodriguez, 2022)

Thus, with heightened attention to bodily autonomy in the wake of the repeal of Roe, new opportunities for feminist activism related to the law have emerged.

Interested in learning more about the contemporary landscape of the ERA?
  See: The ERA Project at Columbia
  The ERA coalition

Another important feminist legislation is the Equal Pay Act, passed in 1963. It "prohibits sex-based wage discrimination between men and women in the same establishment who perform jobs that require substantially equal skill, effort and responsibility under similar working conditions" (The Equal Pay Act of 1963, n.d.). While there is still a vast wage gap, the Equal Pay Act has been part of the landscape that has allowed women to advance economically. As addressed in Chapter 4, the wage gap persists, as a result of many other factors that are not addressed in the Equal Pay Act, such as women confined to lower wage occupations and the gendered responsibility for care work. Additional policies and laws that could further aid in the narrowing of the wage gap include the Paycheck Fairness Act, salary history ban laws, increasing the minimum wage, and making childcare and carework a federal priority that warrants infrastructure and significant investment (Khattar and Estep, 2023).

**Research Reflection:** What are some of the policy approaches to achieving equality that seem most effective to you? Why?

The Violence Against Women Act (VAWA) was signed into law by President Clinton in 1994. VAWA designates federal funds to address and prevent violence against women, and also to support and serve survivors. Research has found that VAWA reduced the rate of intimate partner violence (Modi et al., 2014), reduced social service costs (such as police response and victim services) (Clark et al., 2002), and fundamentally changed the way we as a society address violence against women. President Biden signed the VAWA Reauthorization Act of 2022, with the largest funding package to date. Among a wide range of provisions, the reauthorization provides funding to address violence in Indigenous and Native communities, to implement culturally specific aid to queer and underserved communities, and to counter online harassment and violence.

There are some feminists who argue that increased involvement of law enforcement and monitoring of women through VAWA-funded programs is not the answer to gender-based violence. There are the risks of further perpetuating gendered racial hierarchies and funneling more people into the prison pipeline and other state-sanctioned surveillance. Other scholars argue that the benefits of VAWA are not evenly distributed. Black women may experience negative consequences given VAWAs expansion of police presence in domestic violence cases, in light of the racial and gender bias baked into criminal justice systems (Shinde, 2021).

Title IX was another major victory for feminists. Passed in 1972, it states "No person in the United States shall, on the basis of sex, be excluded from participation in, be denied the benefits of, or be subjected to discrimination under any education program or activity receiving Federal financial assistance" (Title IX and sex discrimination, n.d.). Because most schools receive some federal funding, it was a watershed moment in education. At first, it was largely interpreted as targeting sports, addressing the uneven distribution of resources between men and women in athletics. However, in 1977 Catherine MacKinnon brought forth the argument that sexual harassment was also a violation of Title IX because it interfered with a survivor's education and could be interpreted to exclude or deny women full participation in education programs. A Yale law student at the time, MacKinnon advised students and wrote the argument for the case *Alexander vs. Yale* that sexually harassed students were also experiencing sex discrimination. The plaintiffs were not seeking financial recourse, but rather that Yale would institute a process for responding to sexual harassment. The lasting legacy would be for Yale and hundreds of other schools to institute such processes that had previously never existed (Kingkade, 2014).

Many sexual harassment lawsuits in the early 1970s brought attention to the problem at a national level. While sexual harassment law is sometimes thought of as white women's terrain, in fact African American women brought some of the earliest sexual harassment cases to the Supreme Court (Mechelle Vinson) and the federal court of appeals (Paulette Barnes) (Baker, 2004).

**Laws in Action**

The state of California is paying reparations to those who experienced forced sterilization while incarcerated. A survivor can receive $15,000, with the state budgeted $4.5 million to distribute. This is an example of a state law being passed that especially benefits women and Women of Color. Other states have implemented similar laws.

Indeed, lawsuits are a way in which feminists can gain and protect rights for women, and be remunerated for injustices. There are many ongoing lawsuits at the state level to protect bodily autonomy and abortion. For example, a 2021 lawsuit challenged SB8 in Texas, a law that allowed everyday citizens to enforce a ban on abortion. In 2023 in Alabama, where abortion is nearly entirely outlawed, abortion proponents filed suit against the state's attorney general who insinuated that he may prosecute individuals who help pregnant persons travel out of state to get an abortion. This is a rapidly shifting landscape.

In regards to the wage gap, lawsuits have been used to target employers. Recently, women faculty at Vassar College sued for pay discrimination. Their statement read:

"Since at least as early as 2008, and consistently since then, female professors have internally elevated concerns to the Vassar administration about unequal pay within the college's ranks. Instead of remedying its gender pay gap, Vassar responded by decreasing the level of transparency about faculty salaries, in an apparent attempt to mask its decades-long pattern of underpaying of women."

(Salam, 2023)

The faculty involved argue that there is a 10% difference in pay gap between full professor men faculty members and full professor women faculty members at the college, which perhaps ironically was one of the "seven sisters" colleges founded to provide educational equality to women (Nittle, 2023). The Equal Employment Opportunity Commission enforces federal laws related to workplace discrimination, and has provided recourse for many women whose employers were violating the Equal Pay Act.

Finally, a series of lawsuits related to sexual assault occurred at the end of 2023, a result of New York State's "Adult Survivors Act." This act, signed by New York Governor Kathy Hochul, temporarily lifted the statute of limitations for survivors to file a sexual assault complaint. As a result of this, more than 2,500 lawsuits related to the act were filed, many against high-profile alleged perpetrators. When Hochul signed the act, she said:

> "Today, we take an important step in empowering survivors across New York to use their voices and hold their abusers accountable," and "The fight against sexual assault requires us to recognize the impact of trauma within our justice system. I am proud to sign this legislation, which is part of our collective responsibility to protect one another and create an environment that makes survivors feel safe. While our work is not done, eradicating sexual assault begins with our ability to bring the perpetrators of these heinous acts to justice and this legislation is a historic step forward."
>
> (*Governor Hochul signs Adult Survivors Act*, 2022)

While not all feminists will agree that the solution to gender-based violence is lawsuits against perpetrators, the language of the act comes from generations of feminists drawing mass attention to and working to eradicate gender-based violence. The language was normalized during #MeToo, when women across the world shared accounts of gender-based violence.

To rectify the dearth of women and people of color in elected office, many organizations have sought ways to expand the pipeline of women running for office, educate potential leaders, introduce them to political mentors, and secure voter rights.

A number of grassroots organizations exist to encourage and propel women into the political sphere. One is called Ignite!, which started as a small organization in Oakland, California, and that now has trained 20,000 women and girls in leadership skills, political efficacy, and political engagement. Others include Asian

American Women's Political Initiative, She Should Run, and Emily's List.

**Research Reflection:** Research the elected officials who represent you. Who are they? Are there any organizations in your community and state that encourage the election of underrepresented people?

## Tactic #7: Academia and Student Activism

Feminist organizing in academia established women's studies departments, some ethnic studies departments, and women's centers. They increased women's enrollment and opportunities in academia, and built support for women and underserved students, faculty and staff. Feminist tactics have transformed higher education.

A major goal of feminist movements was for women to gain access to higher education (Gelb and Palley, 1996). A student, someone who might be interpreted as bettering herself and her community, investing in herself and her career, is a marked distinction in a woman's identity outside of the home, family, or even a job. Women's entry into higher education symbolized an important turn in gender dynamics in the US, and even an oppositional role for women (Solomon, 1985). This varied among and between communities of women, with white women gaining access before most Women of Color. African American women were largely excluded from white colleges and universities and African American schools such as Fisk and Howard (Crocco, 1999, p. 63; Solomon, 1985, p. 76). However, some African American women were able to enroll in higher education to become teachers, such as Anna Julia Cooper, African American scholar and educator who fought her entire life for educational access for underrepresented populations.

One could easily regard women's studies programs and departments as institutional branches of the feminist movement. Founded in the 1960s from the energies of the women's movement, civil rights, gay and lesbian rights, and peace movements (Taylor, 1989; Rosen, 2004), women students of all different backgrounds began to understand their lives in new ways, through the lens of inequalities and the lens of the intersectional nature of oppression. This included the organizing by feminist students and faculty members to dedicate intellectual and physical campus space to women's issues- from classes with a gender perspective, to gender research, and to communities for women academics to establish networks and solidarity.

The first women's studies department was founded in 1970 at San Diego State College (now San Diego State University), and was deeply embedded in the feminist movement and feminist tactics. Their initial vision included a day care center, information sharing on abortion and family planning, and a research and cultural center (Orr, 1999). While their radical vision had to be tempered for the institutional context, the interconnected traditions of feminist tactics and women's studies departments remained. As Boxer (1998) writes, women's studies drew "on the ground rules of consciousness raising, which prescribed equal opportunity for self-expression and validation of each woman's experience" (p. 21). In addition, the courses that were offered centered women's experiences and realities (Bart et al. 1999, p. 257).

Early women's studies departments paid most attention to white women's lives (Hull, Scott, and Smith 1982). While women's studies departments were being started, social movement participants were also forming Black studies and Chicano/Chicana studies. This meant that feminist activist attentions were likely diffused within area studies, and also likely that racist and exclusionary practices kept Women of Color from being full participants in the discipline of women's studies (Crossley 2017, p. 587). Black women's studies emerged, closely linking the academy and Black women's lives more broadly (Guy-Sheftall, 1992; Hull, Scott, and Smith, 1982). Over time, women's studies departments at many universities and colleges changed to "Feminist Studies" and other similar names, and many also became more diverse and expansive in the research areas and classes taught.

Additionally, research centers across the country focus on race, gender, and sexuality research. They are often dedicated to conducting and publishing research that centers interdisciplinary and intersectional approaches.

Academia has also been an important site for key inflection points in the feminist movement. For example, the 1982 "The Scholar and The Feminist Conference" or the "Barnard Conference on Sexuality" as it is known, ignited fierce and long-standing debates about sex and sexuality, as well as the lines between feminism inside and outside academia (Corbman, 2015). Also supported by Barnard College, the 2012 gathering and subsequent report #FemFuture (about the future of online feminism) was the catalyst for substantial tension and arguments about inclusion and exclusion in online feminism.

**Research Reflection:** Conduct an online analysis of the feminist landscape at a college or university located near you, or at the college or university you are enrolled in. Is there a gender research institute or gender and ethnic studies departments? Are there feminist organizations run by students, staff, and faculty? Are there organizations that serve students who have been historically marginalized in higher education? How do the offerings at the school fit in with the goals and historical development of feminism in higher education outlined in this chapter?

Feminist student activism on college campuses has also created institutional change, from demands related to student safety, to courses and faculty that reflect the racial and ethnic diversity of the student body, and to institutional accountability related to gender-based violence on campus (Bovill et al., 2021). Student organizations of all varieties contribute to feminist campus organizing. Chicana student activists, for example, continue to be an important part of transforming campus cultures as well as propelling the Chicana feminist movement broadly (Crossley, 2017). Feminism is also propelled on campus in multicultural sororities, which may focus on leadership skills and mentorship in order to advance women (ibid). Feminist student organizations may have long histories on campus, be affiliated with national feminist organizations, or be in startup mode.

Other student activists have been specifically vocal about Title IX. Student survivors of gender-based violence have created organizations both locally and nationally, and have even partnered with President Obama. Student led and/or campus organizations related to sexual assault include: *End Rape on Campus, Know Your IX,* and *It's On Us.*

Student activists have had many successes in holding perpetrators and institutions accountable for rape cultures, allocating resources to assault-survivors, creating systems of accountability, and listening to survivors. Some of this activism was focused inward and toward student activists' particular colleges, and some was agitating for broader change outside their universities through state and national laws and policies.

These student activists across the country have connected online to learn about each other's tactics and organizing strategies. Online networking has made their activities more effective and has also shown connections and similarities across campuses (Pérez-Peña, 2013). They amplify voices sharing stories of gender-based violence, and, in some cases, stories of how students' cases were mishandled by universities. When these accounts gain traction, often through cross-campus networks, colleges are pressed to respond to and in some cases amend their attributes and processes in managing gender-based violence.

Student activists must balance their school work and the cycle of the school year, possible obstacles to maintaining activist momentum and institutional knowledge of activism over time. Moreover, additional challenges to student activism are the structural and resource restraints that shape all mobilization. For example, students who are receiving scholarships, and immigrant or undocumented students, may not feel that they can either report gender-based violence or become involved in campus organizing for fear of losing financial support (Berastaín, 2017). Similarly, queer students, and others who have faced gender-based violence may choose to hide their stories or feel excluded from the often heteronormative narratives of gender-based violence

There is great variation across campuses, in both enactments of feminism and support of student feminists. Many colleges are not progressive or hospitable to feminist ideologies, shaping feminist student activist communities in significant ways. Reger (2012) shows that, for example, members of feminist groups at a conservative college campus find great meaning and support from their communities. In contrast, on a campus that is more progressive with greater engrained feminist ideologies, feminism is less of a salient unifier and identity, given the expected nature of feminism across the campus (Crossley, 2017). This is but one more example of the variations in feminism given the local context.

**Research Reflection:** Research the experiences and lives of these anti-sexual assault advocates: Chanel Miller, Emma Sulkowicz, Kamilah Willingham, Andrea Pino.
   What did their activism look like? What were their tactics? What change did they create?

## Tactic #8: Media

Feminists aim to create a mediascape that is representative of all people. Feminists advocate for the inclusion of women and other marginalized groups in both leadership and representation: in executive, director, and producer leadership roles, and as nuanced subjects of news coverage, and entertainment story lines.

### *Film, Television, and Print Media*

A number of Black women in Hollywood have made important advancements in diversifying entertainment media. Shonda Rhimes, for example, created television shows Grey's Anatomy, Scandal, and Bridgerton, among others, and has won numerous major awards. Rhimes purposefully features women, people of color, and those who otherwise are marginalized in entertainment. She said:

> "The entire world is skewed from the white male perspective. If you're a woman, they have to say it's a female-driven comedy. If it's a comedy with Latinos in it, it's a Latino comedy. 'Normal' is white male, and I find that to be shocking and ridiculous."
>
> (Myers, 2022)

In response, Rhimes concentrates on the professional and personal lives of women and Black women in her work. Black women in her shows are national leaders, royalty, regular working people and everything in between. In what Rhimes calls "the most iconic feminist moment" (Myers, 2022) on TV, Rhimes has actor Viola Davis remove all her makeup and her wig, revealing her stripped-down and most vulnerable self, a side rarely shown in entertainment media.

Ava DuVernay has also been immensely successful in her film and television career. She is the first Black woman director to be nominated for a best film Oscar (Selma) and in 2023 the first Black woman to direct a feature in the prestigious Venice Film festival. For her series Queen Sugar, produced with Oprah Winfrey, DuVernay hired only women directors, a radical act. Of the women she hired, she said "Can you believe that these women had directed films that had played at film festivals around the world—many had won—yet they couldn't get hired in Hollywood for one episode of television?" (BUST Magazine, 2017).

### Spotlight on Lily Gladstone

Gladstone made history in January 2024 as the first Indigenous actor to win a Golden Globe award, and the first Indigenous woman to be nominated for an actress in a leading role Academy Award. She won the best actress award for the film *Killers of the Flower Moon*. Previously, Gladstone's role in *The Unknown Country* (2022) was also critically acclaimed. Gladstone is a member of the Blackfeet Nation of Montana.

### Spotlight on Ali Wong

Wong made history in January 2024 as the first Asian American actor to win a best actress in a limited series at the Golden Globes, as well as the first Asian woman to win an Emmy for best lead actress in a limited series or movie. Both awards were for her performance in the series *Beef.*

Film Fatales, The Geena Davis Institute, and the Women's Media Center are three organizations that address the lack of diversity in Hollywood by conducting outreach and convening programs to mitigate bias. Davis, an actor who has won two Academy Awards, focuses on sharing her research with Hollywood principals. Of her work, she said: "As a colleague, I can go directly to the creators. And once they have the research, they're appalled....Sixty-three percent of creators we talked to said our research had impacted two or more projects" (Wappler, 2015). Davis also organizes a film festival every year to screen the work of individuals who have been marginalized in film, and guarantees that the winners of the festival will have their work distributed. The Women's Media Center, founded by Jane Fonda, Gloria Steinem, and Robin Morgan, works broadly to diversify media, gathers data about media inequality, and runs leadership and media training programs to expand the pools of "experts" featured in the media. Other examples of organizations diversifying the film world are: The Sojourner Truth Festival of the Arts, which has, since 1976, honored Black feminist art and filmmaking (Lee, 2023), and the Athena Film Festival at Barnard College.

*Ms. Magazine* is the oldest national feminist publication in the US, and has been distributed for over 50 years. Of its origins, co-founder Gloria Steinem wrote: "There was no national voice for those of us who had the radical idea that women are people" (Steinem, 2023). Its first issue in spring of 1972 sold out nationwide in eight days. That first issue included articles such as: "The housewife's moment of truth," "Welfare is a Women's Issue," Can Women Love Women?" and a petition for legalizing abortion, "We Have Had an Abortion" (Steinem, 2023) Founding editors include: Patricia Carbine, Joanne Edgar, Nina Finkelstein, Mary Peacock, Letty Cottin Pogrebin, Gloria Steinem. Alice Walker, early editor of *Ms. Magazine*, recently wrote of the magazine's early coverage of abortion:

> "I'm very grateful for the strength of the argument for abortion that was in the magazine...once you really open people's awareness to a situation, it's very difficult for them to slide back altogether. If the magazine and the women in the movement had not stood firmly all those years ago, I shudder to think how young women would be feeling today. They would have no backup, no history to look back to. So I really applaud the women's movement and the magazine for standing really firm on abortion."
>
> (Bennett, 2022)

The magazine has had its ups and downs financially and otherwise, and struggled with racism. Alice Walker resigned because she didn't feel it was inclusive of her as a Black woman, primarily because the majority of its covers had featured white women (Pogrebin, 2019). *Ms. Magazine* is now owned by The Feminist Majority Foundation, publishing a majority of its content online, with 2.8 million page views in 2021.

## Discussion Prompt

**Michele Goodwin** is Georgetown University's Linda D. and Timothy J. O'Neill Professor of Constitutional Law and Global Health Policy. She focuses on issues of race and reproductive justice in her scholarship and writing. In addition to being a faculty member, she is also a contributor to *Ms. Magazine* and hosts its podcast.

With a classmate or friend, choose one of Goodwin's "On the Issues" podcast and both listen to the same episode. Take notes of the three key points Goodwin makes. Compare your key points with your classmate or friend, and discuss the following questions: What is Goodwin's argument and perspective? Who is the expert? What did you learn?

*Ms. Magazine* was the only national non-profit feminist magazine on the scene for decades. *Bitch Magazine* (1996–2022) and *BUST Magazine* (1993–2022) circulated for many years as feminist publications for younger audiences. But because online feminist outlets (e.g. Feministing and Jezebel) were able to produce content more rapidly and cost-effectively than print magazines, and as magazine circulations dropped in general, *Bitch* and *BUST* eventually didn't make sense financially (Schwedel, 2022).

*Essence Magazine*, a commercial publication for Black women audiences, was first published in 1970 and continues to circulate. While distinct from *Ms. Magazine* as a commercial and for-profit operation, there was crossover between the two magazines, with Marcia Ann Gillespie editor-in-chief of both (Floyd, 2017). *Essence* is in many ways a conventional glossy women's magazine. Instead of questioning mainstream beauty standards, like *Ms. Magazine*, for example, it touts models and advertisements for beauty products, skin care, and makeup. However, *Essence* features Black models and all its content is for Black women. This is radical in the milieu of mainstream women's magazines, which would rarely if ever feature Women of Color. In a study of *Essence Magazine's* content, scholars found that it was largely a "liberating feminist text" that challenged stereotypes of Black womanhood (Woodard and Mastin, 2005, p. 264). *Essence* forged new ground in feminist media by being a commercial enterprise, and also by presenting content that portrayed women with nuance.

### Ever heard of a Zine?

Zines are handmade and printed packets, basically a homemade magazine, distributed by mail. They were predominantly associated with feminists of the 1990 and early 2000s with Riot Grrrl culture. Zines explored issues including intersectionality, gender identity, sexuality, bodily autonomy, sexual violence, often with striking images and detailed collages. An inexpensive alternative to mainstream media, zines normalized feminist language and created feminist communities (Piepmeier, 2009).

Other smaller feminist print magazines, news sources, and newsletters were always important to feminists, communicating their ideas to a variety of stakeholders and engaging new supporters. *Off Our Backs* was a radical feminist print magazine operating from 1970 until 2008, the longest-printed feminist newspaper in the US. *Sojourner* was a feminist newspaper based in Boston, and the Third World Women's Alliance newsletter *Triple Jeopardy* was another feminist media source (discussed in Chapter 2). The 19th, an independent news outlet named after the 19th amendment founded in 2020, continues many themes salient throughout the development of feminist news and media.

### Protest Spotlight

"On March 18, 1970, about a hundred women stormed into the male editor's office of Ladies' Home Journal and staged a sit-in for eleven hours, demanding that the magazine hire a female editor-in-chief. Says feminist activist-writer Vivian Gornick, 'It was a watershed moment. It showed us, the activists in the women's movement, that we did, indeed, have a movement'" (Pogrebin, 2019).

*Feminist blogs*

In the late 1990s to early 2000s feminist blogs proliferated such as Feministe, Feministing, Racialicious, Crunk Feminist Collective, and Jezebel. These outlets were staffed with feminist writers who produced cutting-edge, serious, and often humorous feminist content. Their wide-ranging feminist commentary included heterogeneous material from journalists of diverse backgrounds. Each of the blogs had a different tone and many developed impressive followings. A sense of community was generated on many of these sites through regular readership and comment sections. At times blog posts drew significant hits, and mainstream/legacy media picked up on their stories as well, blurring the line between feminist blog and legacy media content.

Jezebel, one of the longest-lasting feminist blogs (which was recently closed and then re-opened), ran a contest in its early days. It awarded $10,000 for the best unretouched cover photo, to dispute by comparison the prevalent airbrushing of models' and celebrities' photos. The contest winner was an unretouched photo of country singer Faith Hill, the same photo that was on the cover of *Redbook* magazine in a highly airbrushed version. Comments on the contest blew up all across the Internet and mainstream media. The contest and accompanying photos screamed how even a thin, white, blonde, conventionally attractive woman gets airbrushed for a cover. Of the contest, a Jezebel post written by Jennifer responded "it's hard to escape the fact that women, if you believe the media, are increasingly expected to look like female avatars" (2007). When Jezebel did this contest again in 2014 and an unretouched *Vogue* magazine cover photo of Lena Dunham won, it didn't go over as well, and indeed represented tensions in feminism at the time. Jezebel also launched the careers of numerous feminist authors, including Lyz Lenz, Jia Tolentino, Irin Carmon, Dodai Stewart, and Emma Carmichael.

In a *Rolling Stone* obituary for Jezebel in November, 2023, Erin Gloria Ryan wrote: "Jezebel was an important political voice, treating women's concerns like serious, vital issues....Jezebel played an outsized role in mainstreaming the ongoing fight for reproductive rights, from TRAP laws in Texas to Todd Akin's senate campaign-derailing 'legitimate rape' comments to the catastrophic Supreme

Court appointments of the Trump administration to the death of Roe, and ensuing and ongoing political galvanization of American women." Through the contrast of the Faith Hill controversy and the reproductive rights coverage, we can see that feminist blogs also served to normalize feminist perspectives, to apply feminist perspectives to all types of current events, and to take feminist issues seriously.

Feminist blogs shifted the content that was available online and in media in general, revealing the sexism and racism inherent in much of the mainstream women's media. Additionally, what was particularly interesting about blogs is that they posted popular culture criticism (which in and of itself is an important feminist endeavor) and political commentary from a feminist's view.

Feminist blogs showed the success of this model. They drew huge page views. Writers on feminist blogs also started contributing to other places online like *Salon*, *Cosmo*, and eventually outlets like *The New York Times, The Guardian*, and *The New Yorker*. These are not necessarily feminist outlets, but they were meeting the demand and popularity of feminist perspectives. Feminist podcasts such as Call Your Girlfriend (2014–22), and website The Toast (2013–18) also were central to the development of feminist media.

The arrival of social media and changes in the feminist movement dramatically altered the feminist media landscape after the feminist blog heyday of the 2000s. Into the 2010s as social media sites like Facebook, Twitter, and Instagram became central to online information dissemination, and as there became many more outlets for feminist expression, the need for the collective ethos of feminist blog communities diminished. The popularity of the individual "influencer" began to rise. Moreover, when larger non-feminist media companies realized how much interest and money there was in reaching feminist audiences, they started their own feminist sections, hiring many former feminist bloggers. Especially in the 2010s, feminist content became more common on sites like *Teen Vogue, Harpers*, and other mainstream media outlets. Since then, most feminist blogs have shuttered. However, their content in many ways lives on in the incorporation of feminist viewpoints throughout the media.

**Spotlight on Roxane Gay**

Roxane Gay is a writer, professor, and social commentator whose views and analysis have transformed contemporary feminism and informed a new generation of feminists. Gay's sharp perspectives on current events, her humor, and her productivity have made her one of the most sought-after feminist writers and thinkers today. Moreover, she has had enormous success in infusing feminist views into legacy media, such as *The New York Times* (where she is a contributing opinion writer), and *Marvel* (where she wrote *World of Wakanda*), and in her numerous bestselling books.

## Tactics #9: Music and Art

Feminist artists and musicians have, for generations, created feminist change. This includes feminists who express grievances, power, and solidarity with other feminists through visual art and music. Music and art are tactics to create community, to make cultural and political change, and to spread information about feminism.

Feminists have simultaneously critiqued the art world and revolutionized it (Reckitt and Phelan, 2001). Famous feminist visual artists include:

- Faith Ringgold, whose painting, writing, and mixed media artwork have been critically acclaimed.
- Barbara Kruger's collages offer sharp-edged feminist criticism and have been shown on a large scale across the world.
- Jenny Holzer is known for her public art, including electronic light installations, with phrases that are thought-provoking and political in tone.
- Visual artist Judy Chicago's famous "dinner party" work is an imposing installation of a triangular table featuring place settings for influential women throughout civilization.
- Kara Walker employs thought-provoking feminist themes in her artwork, which has been shown internationally.

Each of these artists challenges notions of conventional womanhood and family, political systems that uphold the patriarchy, and intersecting axes of identity and oppression.

**Research Reflection:** Choose an artist from the above list and examine their work online. What feminist themes emerge? How is their art a feminist tactic?

While women visual artists have predictably been sidelined by major museums, some feminists and women have broken through that barrier. In 2007 a large feminist retrospective was shown at the Los Angeles Geffen Contemporary MOCA, called "Wack! Art and the Feminist Revolution." Judy Chicago has a major show at the New Museum in New York City in 2023–24. And on the other side of the country, The Oakland Museum of California recently had an exhibit all about feminists in Oakland and the Bay Area, called "Hella Feminist."

**Research Reflection:** Is there a feminist art exhibit being shown at a museum in your area? What is it? Or, search online for a feminist art exhibit shown in the last year. Where is it held? How does it promulgate feminist priorities, as described in this book?

Online and offline exhibits also call attention to feminist themes of bringing that which is silenced into the light. The *What Were You Wearing* exhibit is a recent example of feminist tactics in art. This traveling show was founded by Dr. Mary Wyandt-Hiebert and Ms. Jen Brockman and has been shown at college campuses around the US. The exhibit includes displays of clothing of what student-survivors wore while they were sexually assaulted, responding to the fact that so many survivors of gender-based violence are questioned about what they wore at the time. In essence, with this question, victims are implicitly blamed for their assault because of their attire rather than questioning the violence of the perpetrator. The exhibit, with statements by survivors and clothing on display, paints a fuller picture of gender-based violence, unmasks assumptions about assault, and empowers survivors to share their experiences.

A recent online feminist exhibit is called *The Abortion Project*. An award-winning documentary filmmaker Heather started the project to "demystify and destigmatize medical abortions by showing what they actually look like" (The Abortion Project, n.d.) The online photo exhibit features women in various stages of pregnancy termination in their homes, and shows mundane, painful, and relieved emotions that are all a part of ending a pregnancy: "Her work shines light on the realities and beauty of the processes experienced by her participants. She's made it her mission to dispel feelings of fear, shame, ugliness, or dirtiness that society has cast onto these seasons of life" (The Abortion Project, n.d.). Given the Pew 2023 statistic that in 2020 there were anywhere between 600,000–900,000 legal abortions in the United States (the exact number being difficult to measure) (Diamant and Mohamed, 2023), and that since Roe vs. Wade was overturned the overall number of legal abortions in the US actually increased (Millman, 2023), destigmatizing this very common medical procedure could benefit hundreds of thousands of women.

Feminist musicians address themes of power and intersectionality (also see Chapter 2). Genres such as blues were particularly important to the development of Black feminism (Brooks, 2021), illustrating the cross over and dynamism in cultural production with music both reflecting and shaping communities. Queen Latifah has been classified as a feminist rapper who transformed hip hop, especially "Ladies First" (Rose, 1994). Recent musicians and performance artists who have highlighted feminist perspectives include H.E.R., who addresses themes of Black women's rage and feminism (Peralta, 2021) and Noname, who raps about issues related to white supremacy and gender (Cea, 2018). Rapsody's "Eve" album addresses issues related to Black femininity and the intersections of race and gender.

It is clear that all of the feminist art and music discussed here is political in nature, in the sense that the artists are confronting power imbalances and hierarchies, and creating alternative communities through their art and music. Scholars Reger and Heintz (2023) specifically argue that music shapes collective identity of a lesbian feminist community, both in opposition to homophobia and the heterosexual male dominated mainstream music world, and in celebration of lesbian community. Indeed, many songs have become feminist anthems performed by artists such as Beyoncé, Dolly Parton, Lady Gaga, Janelle Monae, MIA, Cardi B, and Megan Thee Stallion.

---

### Feminist Anthem R-E-S-P-E-C-T

Aretha Franklin famously recorded Otis Redding's "Respect" in 1967, and it became a rallying anthem for feminist and civil rights movements. It also won many awards and became an iconic song for generations of women. Franklin, a Black woman musician with strong ties to civil rights organizing, was deeply intersectional in her approach, and affirmed women's strength at a time when women en masse were recognizing their power (North, 2018).

**Reflection:** listen to Franklin's "Respect". Do the lyrics resonate with you? Why do you think it was so influential at the time, and why do you think it continues to be so iconic? Can you think of any other songs that project similar themes, either current or historic?

---

## Chapter 5 Mini Toolkit: Guerrilla Girls

This toolkit highlights the work of the Guerrilla Girls. Founded in 1985, the Guerrilla Girls are an international group of women artists and activists. Their goal is to diversify the art and film world, particularly related to race and gender. They draw attention to the white male domination of museum collections and leadership, disseminate the art of Women of Color and white women to broad audiences, and educate the general public about feminism. They do this around the world by giving talks, staging protests, writing books, creating exhibitions, buying billboard space, and wheatpasting posters.

Called Guerrilla, as in guerrilla tactics, they wear gorilla masks when they speak and perform. This is humorous, but necessary because many of the members of this organization are themselves employed at museums and are active in the art world; they don't want to jeopardize their jobs by revealing their identities.

To learn more about the Guerrilla Girls and get involved:

Conduct online research on Guerrilla Girl campaigns related to racism and sexism in Hollywood and the art world.

- What are their primary tactics? Have they changed over time?
- Have the Guerrilla Girls been to your town? Are they coming?
- What did the Guerrilla Girls do in Venice, Italy?
- What feminist tactics of the Guerrilla Girls are striking to you?

Check out the books:

Guerrilla Girls, *The Art of Behaving Badly*
Guerrilla Girls, *Bedside Companion to the History of Western Art*
Guerrilla Girls, *Code of Ethics for Art Museums*

## Chapter 5 Dive Deeper

- *Liner Notes for the Revolution* (Daphne Brooks)
- *Feminist Fight Club* (Jessica Bennett)
- *Weightless: Making Space for my Resilient Body and Soul* (Evette Dionne)
- *Sharing the Work: What My Family and Career Taught me about Breaking Through (And Holding the Door Open for Others)* (Myra Strober)
- *This American Ex-Wife: How I Ended My Marriage and Started My Life* (Lyz Lenz)
- *Men Explain Things to Me* (Rebecca Solnit)
- *Sexual Justice: Supporting Victims, Ensuring Due Process, and Resisting the Conservative Backlash* (Alexandra Brodsky)
- *Glitch Feminism: A Manifesto* (Legacy Russell)
- Film: On the Basis of Sex
- Film: Knock Down the House
- Film: Moxie

## References

*The Abortion Project*. (n.d.). The Abortion Project. www.theabortionp roject.com.

*Additional online harassment resources.* (n.d.). *Online Harassment Field Manual.* https://onlineharassmentfieldmanual.pen.org/additional-online-harassment-resources.

Ahmed, S. (2016, May 30). Resignation. *feministkilljoys.* https://feministkilljoys.com/2016/05/30/resignation.

Ahmed, S. (2017). *Living a Feminist Life.* Duke University Press.

Anderson, M. & Toor, S. (2018). How social media users have discussed sexual harassment since #MeToo went viral. Pew Research Center.

Andreasen, M.B. (2020). Feminist/activist responses to online abuse. *The International Encyclopedia of Gender, Media, and Communication*, 1–8. doi:10.1002/9781119429128.iegmc021.

Baker, C.N. (2004). Race, Class, and Sexual Harassment in the 1970s. *Feminist Studies*, 30(1), 7–27. www.jstor.org/stable/3178552.

Bart, P.B., Bentz, L., Clausen, J., Costa, L., Froines, A., Golan, G., Grant, J.M., Orwin, A.S., Ryan, B., & Sarker, S. (1999). In sisterhood? Women's Studies and activism. *Women's Studies Quarterly*, 27(3/4), 257–267. www.jstor.org/stable/40004495.

Bennett, J. (2022, June 16). Opinion | Gloria Steinem on 50 years of Ms. Magazine and the feminist movement. *The New York Times.* www.nytimes.com/2022/06/16/opinion/gloria-steinem-ms-magazine-feminism.html.

Beyerlein, K. & Hipp, J. 2006. A Two-Stage Model for a Two-Stage Process: How Biographical Availability Matters for Social Movement Mobilization. *Mobilization*, 11, 299–320.

Berastaín, P.R. (2017, April 1). Sexual assault in universities: those excluded from the dialogue. *HuffPost.* www.huffpost.com/entry/sexual-assault-in-univers_b_9552014.

Blackwell, M. (2003). Contested histories: Las hijas de Cuauhtémoc, Chicana feminisms, and print culture in the Chicano movement, 1968–1973. In *Chicana Feminisms*. Duke University Press. doi:10.1215/9780822384359-003.

Bobel, C. (2007). 'I'm not an activist, though I've done a lot of it': Doing activism, being activist and the 'perfect standard' in a contemporary movement. *Social Movement Studies*, 6(2), 147–159. doi:10.1080/14742830701497277.

Bovill, H., Mcmahon, S., Demers, J., Banyard, V., Carrasco, V., & Keep, L. (2021). How does student activism drive cultural campus change in the UK and US regarding sexual violence on campus? *Critical Social Policy*, 41(2), 165–187. doi:10.1177/0261018320913967.

Boxer, M.J. (1998). *When women ask the questions: Creating Women's Studies in America.* John Hopkins University Press.

Brodsky, A. *Sexual Justice: Supporting Victims, Ensuring Due Process, and Resisting the Conservative Backlash.* Henry Holt and Company.

Brooks, D.A. (2021). *Liner Notes for the Revolution: The Intellectual Life of Black Feminist Sound*. Harvard University Press.

*BUST Magazine*. (2017, November 3). Ava DuVernay on why she only hires female directors. *BUST Magazine*. https://bust.com/ava-duvera y-interview.

Caldera, A. (2020). Challenging capitalistic exploitation: A Black feminist/ womanist commentary on work and self-care. *Feminist Studies*, 46(3), 707–716. https://doi.org/10.1353/fem.2020.0049.

Carvajal, B., White, H.K., Brooks, J., Thomson, A., & Cooke, A. (2022). Experiences of midwives and nurses when implementing abortion policies: A systematic integrative review. *Midwifery*, 111, 103363. doi:10.1016/j.midw.2022.103363.

Cavender, E. (2021, October 30). TikTok wants you to stop dressing for the male gaze. *Mashable*. https://mashable.com/article/male-gaze-tiktok-trend-pov.

Cea, M. (2018, September 17). How Noname is pushing back against myths about women in hip-hop and 'conscious' rap. *Billboard*. www.billboard.com/music/rb-hip-hop/noname-room-25-anti-cardi-b-female-rappers-con scious-rap-8475474.

Clark, K.A., Biddle, A.K., & Martin, S.L. (2002). A Cost-Benefit Analysis of the Violence Against Women Act of 1994. *Violence Against Women*, 8 (4), 417–428. doi:10.1177/10778010222183143.

Clark, M.D. (2019) White folks' work: digital allyship praxis in the #BlackLivesMatter movement. *Social Movement Studies*, 18(5), 519–534, doi:10.1080/14742837.2019.1603104.

Corbman, R. (2015). The scholars and the feminists: The Barnard sex conference and the history of the institutionalization of feminism. *Feminist Formations*, 27(3), 49–80. doi:10.1353/ff.2016.0010.

Crocco, M.S. (1999). The Price of an Activist Life: Elizabeth Almira Allen and Marion Thompson Wright. In M. Smith Crocco, P. Munro, & K. Weiler (Eds), *Pedagogies of Resistance: Women Educator Activists, 1880–1960*, pp. 47–80. New York: Teachers College Press.

Crossley, A.D. (2015). Facebook Feminism: Social Media, Blogs, and New Technologies of Contemporary U.S. Feminism. *Mobilization*, 20(2), 253–269.

Crossley, A.D. (2017). Women's activism and educational institutions. In *The Oxford handbook of U.S. women's social movement activism*. Oxford University Press.

Crossley, A.D. & Hurwitz, H.M. (2023). Women's Movements. In D.A. Snow, D. Della Porta, D. McAdam, & B. Klandermans (Eds), *The Wiley Blackwell Encyclopedia of Social and Political Movements* (2nd ed.).

Crossley, A.D. & Taylor, V. (2015). Abeyance cycles in social movements. In *Movements in Times of Democratic Transition*, pp. 64–88. Temple University Press. doi:10.2307/j.ctvrf893j.6.

CSVANW. (2022, May 23). MMIWG2S. *CSVANW—Coalition to STOP violence against women*. www.csvanw.org/mmiw.

Dalton, R. (2002). *Citizen Politics: Public Opinion and Political Parties in Advanced Industrial Democracies*. London: Chatham House.

Diamant, J. & Mohamed, B. (2023, January 11). Abortion in the U.S.: What the data says. Pew Research Center. www.pewresearch.org/short-reads/2023/01/11/what-the-data-says-about-abortion-in-the-u-s-2.

Dionne, E. 2022. *Weightless: Making Space for my Resilient Body and Soul*. New York: Ecco.

Drewett, C., Oxlad, M., & Augoustinos, M. (2021). Breaking the silence on sexual harassment and assault: An analysis of #MeToo tweets. *Computers in Human Behavior*, 123. https://doi.org/10.1016/j.chb.2021.106896.

Echols, A. (1989). *Daring to be Bad: Radical Feminism in America, 1967–1975*. University of Minnesota Press.

*The Equal Pay Act of 1963*. (n.d.). US Equal Employment Opportunity Commission. www.eeoc.gov/statutes/equal-pay-act-1963.

Fahs, B. (2022). *Unshaved: Resistance and revolution in women's body hair politics*. University of Washington Press.

Fares, O.H. (2023, July 9). The deinfluencing trend reflects a growing desire for authenticity online. *The Conversation*. https://theconversation.com/the-deinfluencing-trend-reflects-a-growing-desire-for-a uthenticity-online-208828.

Felmlee, D., Blanford, S., Matthews, S.A., & MacEachren, A.M. (2020). The geography of sentiment towards the Women's March of 2017. *PLOS ONE*, 15(6), e0233994. doi:10.1371/journal.pone.0233994.

*Feminist Anti-Carceral Policy & Research Initiative*. (n.d.). Berkeley Center for Race and Gender. https://crg.berkeley.edu/feminist-anti-carceral-poli cy-research-initiative.

*Feminist Collages NYC*. (n.d.). Chloe Luterman Photography. www.chloe lutermanphotography.com/work/projects-with-feminist-colla ges-collective-nyc.

Floyd, S. (2017, February 2). Magazine Trailblazer Marcia Ann Gillespie Talks Luck & Legacy. Black Enterprise. www.blackenterprise.com/tra ilblazer-marcia-ann-gillespie.

Freedman, J. (2014). Tools of the movement: Democracy, community and consciousness raising. In *Boston University Women's, Gender and Sexuality Studies Program. A revolutionary moment: Women's liberation in the late 1960s and 1970s*. www.bu.edu/wgs/files/2013/10/Freedman-A-Ne w-Era-of-Consciousness-Raising.pdf.

Gay, R. (2018, January). Fifty years ago, protesters took on the Miss America pageant and electrified the feminist movement. *Smithsonian Magazine.* www.smithsonianmag.com/history/fifty-years-ago-protestors-took-on-miss-america-pageant-electrified-feminist-movement-180967504.

Gelb, J. & Palley, M.L. (1996). *Women and public policies: Reassessing gender politics.* University of Virginia Press.

Ghaziani, A. (2008). *The dividends of dissent: How conflict and culture work in lesbian and gay marches on Washington.* University of Chicago Press.

*Governor Hochul signs Adult Survivors Act.* (2022, May 22). Governor Kathy Hochul—New York State. www.governor.ny.gov/news/governor-hochul-signs-adult-survivors-act.

Green, F. (2023, March 23). Is "de-influencing" worth it? The trouble with Tiktok's controversial new trend—BUST. *BUST Magazine.* https://bust.com/deinfluencing-tiktok-controversy.

Guy-Sheftall, B. (1992). Black Women's Studies: The interface of Women's Studies and Black Studies. *Phylon (1960−),* 49(1/2), 33–41. doi:10.2307/3132615.

Hayssen, S. (2020, March 9). What #BelieveWomen really means. Women's Media Center. womensmediacenter.com/fbomb/what-believewomen-really-means.

Heinze, J. (2022, March 2). Online harassment resources. *NSVRC Blogs.* www.nsvrc.org/blogs/online-harassment-resources.

Hersey, T. (2022). *Rest is resistance: A manifesto.* Little, Brown Spark.

Hoff-Wilson, J. (1987). The Unfinished revolution: Changing legal status of U.S. women. *Signs,* 13(1), 7–36. doi:10.1086/494384.

Hull, G.T., Bell-Scott, P., & Smith, B. (1982). *All the Women are White, All the Blacks are men, but some of us are brave: Black Women's Studies.* The Feminist Press.

Hurwitz, H. & Taylor, V. (2012). Women's cultures and social movements in global contexts. *Sociology Compass,* 6(10), 808–822. doi:10.1111/j.1751-9020.2012.00502.x.

Jackson, S.J., Bailey, M., & Foucault Welles, B. (2020). *#HashtagActivism: Networks of Race and Gender Justice.* MIT Press.

Jones, F. (2019). *Reclaiming Our Space: How Black Feminists Are Changing the World from the Tweets to the Streets.* Beacon Press.

Keller, J. (2015). *Girls' Feminist Blogging in a Postfeminist Age.* New York: Routledge.

Keller, J., Kaitlynn Mendes & Jessica Ringrose (2018) Speaking 'unspeakable things': documenting digital feminist responses to rape culture. *Journal of Gender Studies,* 27(1), 22–36. doi:10.1080/09589236.2016.1211511.

Kendall, M. (2013, August 14). #SolidarityIsForWhiteWomen: Women of Color's issue with digital feminism. *The Guardian.* www.theguardian.com/commentisfree/2013/aug/14/solidarityisforwhitewomen-hashtag-feminism.

Khattar, R. & Estep, S. (2023, June 8). What to know about the gender wage gap as the Equal Pay Act turns 60. *Center for American Progress*. www.americanprogress.org/article/what-to-know-about-the-gender-wage-gap-as-the-equal-pay-act-turns-60.

Kingkade, T. (2014, June 10). How a Title IX harassment case at Yale in 1980 set the stage for today's sexual assault activism. *HuffPost*. www.huffpost.com/entry/title-ix-yale-catherine-mackinnon_n_5462140.

Lorde, A. (1988). A burst of light: living with cancer. In *A burst of light*. Firebrand Books.

Lee, T. (2023, February 23). Sojourner Truth Festival to bring together generations of Black women filmmakers. The University of Chicago Division of Humanities. https://humanities.uchicago.edu/articles/2023/02/soujourner-truth-festival-bring-together-generations-black-women-filmmakers.

Lenton, C.M. (2017, September). [No title].

Lenz, L. (2024). *This American Ex-Wife*. Penguin Random House.

Luterman, C. (2022, November 1). 5 Femicides A Day.

Martin, P.Y. (1990). Rethinking feminist organizations. *Gender & Society*, 4(2), 182–206. doi:10.1177/089124390004002004.

McAdam, D. (1992). Gender as a mediator of the activist experience: The case of Freedom Summer. *American Journal of Sociology*, 97(5), 1211–1240. doi:10.1086/229900.

McCammon, H.J. (2003). "Out of the parlors and into the streets": The changing tactical repertoire of the U.S. women's suffrage movements. *Social Forces*, 81(3), 787–818. www.jstor.org/stable/3598176.

Mendes, K. & Ringrose, J. (2019). Digital Feminist Activism: #MeToo and the Everyday Experiences of Challenging Rape Culture. In B. Fileborn & R. Loney-Howes (Eds), *#MeToo and the Politics of Social Change*. Cham: Palgrave Macmillan. doi:10.1007/978-3-030-15213-0_3.

Megarry, J. (2018) Under the watchful eyes of men: theorising the implications of male surveillance practices for feminist activism on social media. *Feminist Media Studies*, 18(6), 1070–1085. doi:10.1080/14680777.2017.1387584.

Meyer, D.S. & Whittier, N. (1994). Social movement spillover. *Social Problems*, 41(2), 277–298. doi:10.2307/3096934.

Millman, J. (2023, October 24). Abortions increased the year after Roe was overturned. *Axios*. www.axios.com/2023/10/24/abortion-increase-roe-wade-state-ban.

Modi, M.N., Palmer, S., & Armstrong, A. (2014). The role of Violence Against Women Act in addressing intimate partner violence: a public health issue. *Journal of women's health (2002)*, 23(3), 253–259. doi:10.1089/jwh.2013.4387.

Morgan, R. (2018, October 9). I Was There: The 1968 Miss America Pageant Protest (A. McNearny, Interviewer). History. www.history.com/news/miss-america-protests-1968.

Mulvey, L. (1975). Visual pleasure and narrative cinema. *Screen*, 16(3), 6–18. doi:10.1093/screen/16.3.6.

Myers, R. (2022, February 10). Shonda Rhimes on power, feminism, and police brutality. *ELLE*. www.elle.com/culture/career-politics/q-and-a/a30186/shonda-rhimes-elle-interview.

Nittle, N. (2023, September 7). Vassar College pays its women professors less than men in similar roles, new lawsuit alleges. *The 19th*. https://19thnews.org/2023/09/vassar-college-women-professors-gender-pay-gap-lawsuit.

Noor, P. (2022, May 8). The activists championing DIY abortions for a post-Roe v Wade world. *The Guardian*. www.theguardian.com/us-news/2022/may/07/abortion-pill-at-home-activists-future-roe-v-wade.

North, A. (2018, August 17). The political and cultural impact of Aretha Franklin's "Respect," explained. *Vox*. https://www.vox.com/2018/8/17/17699170/aretha-franklin-2018-respect-song-otis-redding-feminism-civil-rights.

Novara, E. (2023, July 27). The centennial of the Equal Rights Amendment (ERA): Origins and early debates. *Library of Congress Blogs*. https://blogs.loc.gov/manuscripts/2023/07/the-centennial-of-the-equal-rights-amendment-era-origins-and-early-debates.

Orr, C.M. (1999). Tellings of our activist pasts: Tracing the emergence of Women's Studies at San Diego State College. *Women's Studies Quarterly*, 27(3/4), 212–229. www.jstor.org/stable/40004489.

Peralta, S. (2021, November 21). HER Narrative: An analysis of feminism and Black rage in contemporary R&B. *Medium*. https://medium.com/the-grey-space/her-narrative-an-analysis-of-feminism-and-black-rage-in-contemporary-r-b-4ea31cb449b5.

Pérez-Peña, R. (2013, March 19). Activists at colleges network to fight sexual assault. *The New York Times*. www.nytimes.com/2013/03/20/education/activists-at-colleges-network-to-fight-sexual-assault.html?pagewanted=all&_r=0.

Piepmeier, A. (2009). *Girl Zines: Making Media, Doing Feminism*. NYU Press.

Pogrebin, A. (2019, April 11). An Oral History of 'MS.' Magazine. *New York Magazine*. https://nymag.com/news/features/ms-magazine-2011-11.

Pruchniewska, U. (2019). "A group that's just women for women": Feminist affordances of private Facebook groups for professionals. *New Media & Society*, 21(6), 1362–1379. doi:10.1177/1461444818822490.

Reckitt, H., & Phelan, P. (2001). *Art and Feminism*. Phaidon.

Reger, J. (2012). *Everywhere and Nowhere: Contemporary Feminism in the United States*. Oxford University Press.

Reger, J., & Heintz, S. (2023). The power of song: music and the construction of a politicized lesbian identity. *Sexuality & Culture*. doi:10.1007/s12119-023-10104-z.

Reger, J., & Staggenborg, S. (2006). Patterns of Mobilization in Local Movement Organizations: Leadership and Strategy in Four National Organization for Women Chapters. *Sociological Perspectives*, 49(3), 297–323. doi:10.1525/sop.2006.49.3.297.

Rich, A. (1980). *Compulsory Heterosexuality and Lesbian Existence. Signs*, 5(4), 631–660. www.jstor.org/stable/3173834.

Rodriguez, B. (2022, August 17). Key Equal Rights Amendment activists long avoided tying it to abortion. A group of teenagers is changing that. *The 19th*. https://19thnews.org/2022/08/young-equal-rights-amendment-activists-abortion-rights.

Rose, T. (1994). *Black noise: Rap music and Black culture in contemporary America*. Wesleyan University Press.

Rosen, R.L. (2004). *Women's studies in the academy: Origins and impact*. Prentice Hall.

Russell, L. (2019). *Glitch feminism: a manifesto*. Verso Books.

Rupp, L.J. & Taylor, V.A. (1987). *Survival in the doldrums: The American women's rights movement, 1945 to the 1960s*. Oxford University Press.

Rupp, L.J. & Taylor, V. (1999). Forging feminist identity in an international movement: A collective identity approach to twentieth-century feminism. *Signs*, 24(2), 363–386. doi:10.1086/495344.

Ryan, E.G. (2023, November 11). Jezebel Is Dead. Long Live Jezebel. www.rollingstone.com/culture/culture-features/jezebel-shuts-down-womens-media-1234875520.

Salam, E. (2023, October 4). Female professors at Vassar accuse college of paying them less than men. *The Guardian*. www.theguardian.com/us-news/2023/oct/04/vassar-female-professors-pay-gap-lawsuit.

Salathe, S. (2022, November 19). Inflation adds cost to menstrual products on top of the "pink tax" and pandemic. *Yahoo News*. https://news.yahoo.com/inflation-menstrual-products-more-expensive-182737880.html?guce_referrer=aHR0cHM6Ly93d3cuZ29vZ2xlLmNvbS88&guce_referrer_sig=AQAAABatv2wldp2Sg7r7tJvnEyGoy_6yYIgNzVcnKQmlj167HWjm4DAh6ZR6iHwf5XxerFTFfJ_xqYHjnM3aW_M889AnEIlT2rvoR8_IirUZk37945QtIj-UM3sXN4GSlOxALg9ZEFWD0ly6qHFdZIwEA4LJv7erryLSd90pfC_rAt2e&guccounter=2.

Schwedel, H. (2022, May 12). Bitch Media's co-founder explains why Bitch Media had to fold. *Slate Magazine*. https://slate.com/business/2022/05/bitch-magazine-feminist-publishing-non-profit.html.

Scott, E.K. (2005). Beyond tokenism: The making of racially diverse feminist organizations. *Social Problems*, 52(2), 232–254. doi:10.1525/sp.2005.52.2.232.

Shinde, R. (2021). Black Women, Police Brutality, and the Violence Against Women Act: How Pro-Arrest Policies Facilitate Racialized and Gendered Police Violence. *Georgetown Journal of Gender and the Law*, 22(2). www.law.georgetown.edu/gender-journal/wp-content/uploads/sites/20/ 2021/01/Final_Black-Women-and-VAWA_Rhea-Shinde_Issue-2.pdf.

Shuttleworth, C. (2022, February 1). How young women are facilitating and challenging feminist discourse on TikTok. *Mashable*. https://mashable. com/article/tiktok-feminism-male-gaze.

Solnit, R. (2015). *Men Explain Things to Me*. Haymarket.

Solomon, B.M. (1985). *In the company of educated women: A history of women and higher education in America*. Yale University Press.

Springer, K. (2005). *Living for the revolution*. Duke University Press.

Staggenborg, S. (1998). Social movement communities and cycles of protest: The emergence and maintenance of a local women's movement. *Social Problems*, 45(2), 180–204. doi:10.2307/3097243.

Staggenborg, S. & Taylor, V. (2005). Whatever happened to the women's movement? *Mobilization*, 10(1), 37–52. doi:10.17813/ maiq.10.1.46245r7082613312.

Steinem, G. (2023, September 20). We are Not Alone: 50 years of Ms. Magazine. *Literary Hub*. https://lithub.com/we-are-not-alone-50-yea rs-of-ms-magazine.

Strober, M. (2016). *Sharing the Work: What My Family and Career Taught Me about Breaking Through (and Holding the Door Open for Others)*. MIT Press.

Stryker, S. (2017). *Transgender history: The roots of today's revolution*. Seal Press.

Taft, J.K. (2006). "I'm not a politics person": Teenage girls, oppositional consciousness, and the meaning of politics. *Politics & Gender*, 2(03). doi:10.1017/s1743923x06060119.

Taylor, V. (1989). Social movement continuity: The women's movement in abeyance. *American Sociological Review*, 54(5), 761–775. doi:10.2307/ 2117752.

Taylor, V. & Van Dyke, N. (2007). Get Up, Stand Up: Tactical Repertoires of Social Movements. In D. Snow, S. Soule, and H. Kriesi (Eds), *The Blackwell Companion to Social Movements*, pp. 262–293. Oxford: Blackwell.

Taylor, V., Kimport, K., Van Dyke, N., & Andersen, E.A. (2009). Culture and mobilization: Tactical repertoires, same-sex weddings, and the impact on gay activism. *American Sociological Review*, 74(6), 865–890. doi:10.1177/000312240907400602.

*Title IX and sex discrimination.* (n.d.). U.S. Department of Education. Retrieved December 3, 2023, from www2.ed.gov/about/offices/list/ocr/ docs/tix_dis.html.

Traister, R. (2020, February 26). You Believe he's Lying? *The Cut*. https://www.thecut.com/2020/02/chris-matthews-elizabeth-warren-believe-women.html?utm_campaign=thecut&utm_source=tw&utm_medium=s1.

Van Dyke, N. (2017). Movement emergence and research mobilization. In *The Oxford handbook of U.S. women's social movement activism*. Oxford University Press. doi:10.1093/oxfordhb/9780190204204.013.18.

Van Dyke, N., Soule, S.A., & Taylor, V. (2004). The Targets of Social Movements: Beyond a Focus on the State. In D.J. Meyers & D.M. Cress (Eds), *Authority in Contention, Volume 25 of Research in Social Movements, Conflict and Change*, pp. 27–51. Oxford: JAI Press.

Walters, J. (2017, December 2). Ivanka Trump boycott campaign #GrabYourWallet claims retail victory. *The Guardian*. www.theguardian.com/us-news/2016/nov/18/ivanka-trump-grab-your-wallet-shoes-com-bellacor.

Wappler, M. (2015, October 15). Geena Davis has a simple way to fix the gender bias in Hollywood. *ELLE*. www.elle.com/culture/movies-tv/interviews/a31285/in-a-league-of-her-own.

*What Were You Wearing? Installation*. (n.d.). KU Sexual Assault Prevention & Education Center. https://sapec.ku.edu/wwyw.

Whittier, N. (1995). *Feminist Generations: The Persistence of the Radical Women's Movement*. Philadelphia, Pennsylvania: Temple University Press.

Whittier, N. (2017). Identity politics, consciousness-raising, and visibility politics. In *The Oxford handbook of U.S. women's social movement activism*. Oxford University Press. doi:10.1093/oxfordhb/9780190204204.013.20.

*Women Strike for Equality*. (n.d.). Women & the American Story. https://wams.nyhistory.org/growth-and-turmoil/feminism-and-the-backlash/women-strike-for-equality/#single/0.

Woodard, J.B. & Mastin, T. (2005). Black Womanhood: Essence and its Treatment of Stereotypical Images of Black Women. *Journal of Black Studies*, 36(2), 264–281. doi:10.1177/0021934704273152.

# 6 What is the Future of Feminism, and How Can I Live a Feminist Life?

One of the most important takeaways from this book is to recognize the immeasurable number of individuals and groups who are working toward feminist goals. In all different settings, online and off, formal and informal, quiet and clamorous, feminists are constantly advancing the movement.

Feminists are not working in lockstep. The competing interests and many forms of feminism don't necessarily lead to harmony. If we think back to the metaphor of waveless feminism, we are reminded that feminism keeps flowing forward, through tributaries, trickles and gushes of water.

The final chapter poses two main questions. One, in taking stock of the material in the book, what might the future of feminist organizing look like? Second, given research about feminist strategies and tactics, how may an individual live a feminist life? The book concludes with a description of the feminist lens.

## Visions for Feminist Futures

There are a few key themes that are vital to building a feminist future.

### Feminist Community in the Midst of Backlash

There is consensus that we are in a period of feminist backlash. This is not its first appearance. Support for the feminist movement and advancement of feminist goals ebbs and flows, and backlash has often followed a period of feminist gains. What is important is that during times of low-level support of feminists and feminist

DOI: 10.4324/9781003310990-7

backlash, such as in the 1950s and 1980s, the main avenues through which feminism persisted were feminist networks, communities, and a sense of cohesion. They have always sustained the movement.

As we look forward to the future of the movement, the maintenance of and further development of feminist communities will be critical to advancing the movement. Throughout the book, you have learned about feminist networks and solidarity. They will not disappear. They might change, resources might be scant, but feminist networks will always run deep.

Since the last widely recognized phase of backlash in the 1980s, we now have the added tactic of online feminism. Research has shown this to be a critical source of feminist community-building and information sharing. Feminists online might be forced to change their strategies during backlash, make communities more private, voice their feminist sentiments more quietly. Despite this, feminists are adaptable online, and any outlets for feminist solidarity will be crucial to the continuity of the movement.

*Figure 6.1* Feminist community and collectivity has always fueled the movement. Resistance Revival Chorus at the Women's Convention, October 28, 2017, Detroit, MI

What would your feminist future look like? For you as an individual? For your community? For your country and the world? What would be different or the same? Think big and small!

## Obliterating the Obituaries

The narrative that feminists have disappeared or died is part of the backlash phenomenon. This cycle of feminist obituaries is crystal clear: the media calling the movement dead, displaying ignorance to the ways that feminism is actually ongoing, stigmatizing feminists, and then the movement inevitably surges again. With an understanding of this pattern, feminists can get ahead of it to help with the movement's continuity and robustness. While not downplaying the reversals of success, nor ignoring how feminism may become negatively viewed in a period of low support, there is always room to demonstrate feminisms' persistence and speak out against the false feminist death syndrome (Pozner, 2003) in networks, friend groups, organizations, online and offline. With active resistance to the narrative that feminism is dead, perhaps the effects of the obituaries can be tempered, so when the time comes for feminism to surge again, less work is needed to correct the narrative.

A feminist future is one in which feminists and allies pay particular attention to (read: fund, support and join) all the different ways feminism is swirling around us. A feminist future is one in which all different types of feminisms are acknowledged and valued as signs of feminist life and progress.

## Intersectional Feminisms Beyond the Binary

Intersectionality is and always has been a strength of the feminist movement. To make it in the future, feminist activists will continue to take into account the intersecting axes of oppression that shape women's experiences, and the intersectional outlook that will make mobilization adaptable. What does this look like? It means recognizing how women experience oppression and privilege differently, and being sensitive to and inquisitive about women's experiences. It means that feminists will not speak on behalf of all women. Intersectional feminist perspectives will make the movement as strong and long-lasting as it can be.

The future of feminism must also wholly include trans and non-binary communities and individuals. Being inclusive and relevant, we will develop communities and connections together– cis and trans women, and gender queer women. The more we can draw in and raise each other up, the more powerful feminist organizing will be. Feminism is not about putting tall fences with barbed wire around who is a woman or who is not a woman. It never will be (MacKinnon, 2023). Feminism is about dismantling social and political systems that oppress all women and girls, not about defining who must be in the category of women. As MacKinnon (2023) points out, it is not women's biology that is the basis of being oppressed, it is social structures that devalue nearly everything women do. For sure there are some important moments in which we need to discuss the meanings of sex and gender, but attacking or questioning women is counterproductive.

### Feminist Alliances

A feminist future will have alliances across social justice organizing of all stripes. Since feminism is intersectional, feminist activism belongs to anti-poverty groups and racial justice groups, for example. Environmental degradation and global warming will have the most deleterious effects on women and girls; so too is feminist activism a part of environmental organizing. We have learned from this book that feminist organizing poses a solution to all of these social problems.

While experts argue that we face an overwhelming set of inequalities– global warming, war, poverty, pandemics–gender scholars also know it is very likely that these phenomena will disproportionately affect women and girls, people of color, and under-resourced communities. We know also, however, that in order for any type of activism to be effective, it must be shaped by the needs of the people organizing and those served. Feminist activism might call for transnational and global alliances, alongside local feminist alliances. Feminists, given their intersectional and impactful organizing, should be leaders and spokespeople in the fight for egalitarianism in all sectors of our society.

## Living a Feminist Life: Quotidian Feminisms

Achieving feminist futures requires both broad structural and small everyday changes. As we have learned from historical and current feminist organizing, even when it feels like a feminist future is far out of reach, feminists persist and focus on all manner of changes. Here are some research-informed feminist approaches to living a feminist life (Ahmed, 2017).

To begin, one challenge that plagues feminists is the enormous change required to advance social justice. It can be tempting to feel that in order to make meaningful change, our current institutions and structures need to be built from scratch. As you have learned, the framework of "everyday feminism" illuminates the significance of small, everyday actions for change. Another strategy is the "small wins" model for change (Correll, 2017). According to Shelley J. Correll, Lori Nishiura Mackenzie, and Caroline Simard of the VMware Women's Leadership Innovation Lab (2020), "our research shows that 'big bets' can't be achieved without breaking them down into achievable, smaller goals, and staying the course." Thus, any meaningful change, whether in an organization such as a workplace or school, or in our cultures and languages, cannot happen without small, dedicated, and deliberate action. In fact, one culprit that thwarts change is setting too lofty a goal that ends up in frustration when not achieved. The "small wins" model confronts the notion that the path to social change is grand and ideal: "the changes we can realistically make in any one instance are often small and imperfect" (Correll 2017, p. 727). Yet that is not reason to toss overboard our hope for change, but rather is an emboldening and realistic plan for action.

Second, for generations feminists have broken the silence on issues of relevance to women and gender marginalized populations. Feminism's progress has relied on "speaking truth to power," which for many means talking about difficult issues that are related to power hierarchies. Topics often silenced by society and then addressed by feminists include: gender-based violence, sexual harassment, heterosexism, mental health, miscarriage, abortion, and the racial and gendered dimensions of climate change. Secretiveness around these issues creates isolation and carries on the notion that women individually are responsible for society's structural failings. Future feminists will not shy from speaking and spreading the truth.

**Gloria Steinem** recently reflected on the inception of *Ms. Magazine*, the nation's first feminist magazine, on its 50th anniversary. She said that the magazine sold out quickly and they were shocked at its success. They received bags and bags of mail from readers of all different ages. One common theme was "At last, I know I'm not alone." Of which, Steinem writes (2023): "A movement is a contagion of truth telling: at last, we know we are not alone."

Third, feminists have sought to live their lives in a way that is consistent with their values and priorities. Often this is contrary to what is stereotypically expected of women. Feminists interrogate structures, relationships, and institutions that are taken for granted. The point is to not judge women for their choices, but to acknowledge the constraints that shape them, and support each other in moving beyond them.

Fourth, research has documented that despite an increasing amount of feminist media content available, women and people of color's perspectives are consistently missing from media, news, and entertainment sources. There are many ways that gender and racial hierarchies are propped up through the media. Indeed, biases are built into most all forms of media content. We may not even recognize it!

### Feminist Media Literacy Reflection

- Are you reading or viewing any news sources regularly?

   a  If yes, what sources? Do they cover issues of importance to you? Whose perspectives are considered "neutral"?
   b  If you do not read or view news sources regularly, why not?

- Whose perspectives and story lines are emphasized in your favorite shows or movies?
- Whose views are normalized in your social media feeds? What views are they?
- Do you consume any feminist media content that normalizes feminist and intersectional discourses? If so, what?

Fifth, online feminism has expanded the podium of who can be a feminist spokesperson. Many feminists prioritize amplifying the work of other feminists as part of expanding the movement and making it more reflective of a diverse set of voices. Feminists support other feminists, uplift other feminists, learn about them, understand the histories and legacies of different forms of feminism.

## A Feminist Lens

Research has shown that possessing a feminist lens is one fundamental mode of feminist activism. Like an anchor, it provides stability, grounding, and assurance during all types of weather. A feminist lens is particularly useful because it costs nothing, is easily available, and is flexible. It requires just your brain. A feminist lens is a worldview that is sensitive to gender inequalities and all interrelated inequalities. It is attuned to power and privilege. It is the perspective that undergirds all feminisms described in this book, and can be applied to any aspect of an individual's life or organizational culture.

Looking through a feminist lens means being critical of the de facto or "neutral" stance. Looking through a feminist lens allows recognition of the racial and gender dynamics in a room, classroom, or social setting. Looking through a feminist lens encourages a vigilance in any setting, towards whose voice is present, and whose is missing.

Based on what you have learned in this book, you now have a full picture of the feminist movement and feminist activism. Here are some additional resources for you to continue on the journey.

## Chapter 6 Dive Deeper

*Black Futures* (Kimberly Drew)
*Colonize This! Young Women of Color on Today's Feminism* (Daisy Hernandez, Bushra Rehman)
*The Feminist Utopia Project: 57 Visions of a Wildly Better Future* (Alexandra Brodsky and Rachel Kauder Nalebuff)
*Unapologetic: A Black, Queer, and Feminist Mandate for Radical Movements* (Charlene A. Carruthers)
*Living a Feminist Life* (Sara Ahmed)
Blackfeminisms.com
Film: We are the Radical Monarchs

# References

Ahmed, S. (2017). *Living a Feminist Life*. Duke University Press.

Carruthers, C. (2018). *Unapologetic: A Black, Queer, and Feminist Mandate for Radical Movements*. Beacon Press.

Correll, S.J. (2017). Reducing Gender Biases In Modern Workplaces: A Small Wins Approach to Organizational Change. *Gender and Society*, 31(6), 725–750.

Correll, S.J., Nishiura Mackenzie, L., & Simard, C. (2020, January 31). Small Wins Quarterback: A Winning Strategy. *Poets and Quants*.

MacKinnon, C. (2023). "Exploring Transgender Law and Politics" with Finn Mackay, Mischa Shuman, Sandra Fredman, and Ruth Chang. *Signs*. https://signsjournal.org/exploring-transgender-law-and-politics.

Pozner, J.L. (2003). The 'big lie': False feminist death syndrome, profit, and the media. In *Catching a wave: Reclaiming feminism for the 21st century*, edited by R. Dicker & A. Piepmeier. Boston: Northeastern University.

Steinem, G. (2023). We Are Not Alone: 50 Years of Ms. Magazine. *Lithub*. https://lithub.com/we-are-not-alone-50-years-of-ms-magazine.

# Index

Note: Page numbers in *italics* refer to figures.

abeyance theory 83–86
abortion medication 120
abortion midwifery 168
*The Abortion Project* 195
academia 182–185
Acevedo, Elizabeth 62
"Adult Survivors Act" 181
Aflalo, Yael 95
African American Policy Forum
 (AAPF) 27
Ahmed, Sara: *Living a Feminist Life* 165
Ailes, Roger 135
Alexander, Michelle 123
*Alexander vs. Yale* 179
Alfrey, L.M. 127
Aly E. 68
Amoruso, Sophia 95
anti-abortion laws 120
anti-Black racism 49
anti-carceral feminism 167
anti-gender-based violence 81
anti-Vietnam war movement 47
anti-war movements 45
Anzaldúa, Gloria 36, 58, 61
Aronson, Pamela 95
Asian American and Pacific Islander
 (AAPI) 45, 48
Asian American communities
 48, 49

Asian American Feminist Collective
 (AAFC) 45, 47, 48, 176
Asian American feminisms 45–49;
 groups 47; movement 45, 47;
 organization 49
Assisted Reproductive Technologies
 (ART) 116

Barrara, Elma 60
Bear, Tillie Black 53
#Believewomen 158
Benard, S. 105
Berkeley feminists 47
Beyoncé 44, 196
Biden, Joe 44, 80, 178
Black, Indigenous 37–39
Black feminism 39–42, 85, 174, 195
Black feminist collective identity 175
Black feminist communities 48
Black feminist organizations 42, 44
Black Feminist Project 98
Black feminist thought 48
Black Joy Farm 98–99
Black Liberation 70
Black Lives Matter 68, 96
#Blacklivesmatter 41
Black Mamas Matter Alliance 41
Black Power movement 41
"Black queer feminism" 41
Black resistance movements 41

Blackwell, Maylei 59
Black Women Radicals 42, 45, 85
Black Women's Liberation Committee 174
Body Mass Index (BMI) 118
Boxer, M.J. 183
Boylorn, Robin M. 44
Brant, Beth 56
Braun, Joye 55
Brave Bull Allard, LaDonna 57
Brockman, Jen 194
Brömdal, A. 123
Brown, Michael 26
*Building an Asian American Feminist Movement Network Gathering* 176
Burke, Tarana 156

Carbine, Patricia 188
Carll, E.K. 130
Carlson, Gretchen 135
Carmichael, Emma 191
Carmon, Irin 191
Castillo, Ana 61
Center for American Women in Politics 132
Center for Intersectionality and Social Policy Studies (CISPS) 27
Cervantes, Lorna Dee 61
Chavez, Denise 61
Cheung, Kylie 97
Chicago, Judy 193, 194
Chicana activism 59
Chicana feminism 58–62
Chicana feminist issues 62
Chicana feminist movement 59
Chicano communities 60
Chicano Nationalist Movement 58–61
Chicano Youth Liberation Movement 59
childcare insecurity 125–126
Chow, E.N.-L. 46
Christopher Street Liberation Rally 69
Chrystos 56; "I Walk in the History of My People" 56

cisgender 10
Cisneros, Sandra 61
civil disobedience 170–173
civil rights movements 38, 45
Clarke, Cheryl 39
climate change 124–125
Clinton, Bill 178
Coalition to Stop Violence Against Native Women 169
Cole, Elizabeth 14
collective identity 173–175
Collins, Patricia Hill 34, 40
colonization 46
Combahee River Collective 7, 27, 39–41, 66, 174
community activism 99
community-based organizations 48
consciousness-raising (CR) groups 173–176
Cooper, Anna Julia 182
Cooper, Brittney C. 44; *Feminist AF: A Guide to Crushing Girlhood* 44
Correll, Shelley J. 105, 127, 211
Crenshaw, Kimberlé 27, 44
Crunk Feminist Collective 43–44
Cullors, Patrisse 41
cultural tactics 153

Dakota Access Pipeline 54
Davis, Angela 12, 44
Davis, Viola 186
Deer, Sara 52; *The Beginning and End of Rape: Confronting Sexual Violence in Native America* 52
Denetdale, J.N. 50
Depp, Johnny 93
Dick, Kirby 111
"doing feminism" 152
domestic violence 111, 113
Donegan, Moira 94
Dunham, Lena 191
DuVernay, Ava 187

Eavis, Peter 109
Edgar, Joanne 188

endometriosis 118
environmental degradation 210
environmental inequalities 124–125
environmentalism 167–168
environmental toxins 54
Equal Employment Opportunity Commission 109, 180
Equal Pay Act 178, 181
Equal Rights Amendment (ERA) 172, 177
everyday feminism 160–165, 211

face recognition technologies 128
false feminist death syndrome 91–92, 209
Faludi, Susan: *Backlash: The Undeclared War Against American Women* 93
Farmer, Ashley 41
"fatherhood bonus" 105
Feinberg, Leslie 64
feminism, definition of 5–6
feminist activism 82, 99, 210, 213
feminist alliances 210
Feminist Anti-Carceral Policy and Research Initiative 167
feminist art and music 195
feminist backlash 93–95
feminist blogs 191–192
feminist coalitions 35
"Feminist Collages" 173
feminist collective identities 175, 176
feminist communities 66, 98–99, 155–157, 207–208, *208*
feminist consciousness 155–157
feminist emergence 35
feminist identities 14–18
feminist legal advances 176–181
The Feminist Majority Foundation 189
feminist methods for social change 153–154
feminist movements 1, 11, 14, 25, 34, 37, 61, 63, 67, 79, 83, 87, 88, 92, 120, 154, 161, 182, 183, 192, 213
feminist organizations 165–170

feminist platforms 155–157
feminist poetry 70
feminist social change 161
feminist social movement tactics 153
feminist student: activism 184; organizations 184
feminist tactics 183
feminist wave framework 86, 88–91, 99
feminization of poverty 108
Finkelstein, Nina 188
"5 Femicides a Day" 172
Floyd, George 26, 96, 123
Fonda, Jane 188
Ford, Christine Blasey 113
Fradella, Henry 13
Franklin, Aretha 44, 196
Frazier, Demita 39
Friedan, Betty 67, 167

García, A.M. 37, 59, 66
Garza, Alicia 41
Gay, Roxane 44, 193
gay rights movement 65
Gearon, J. 50, 56
Gelman, Audrey 95
gender-based violence 52, 109–114, 122, 124, 130, 134, 181, 185, 194
gender binary 51
gendered expectations 127
gendered language 118–119
gender egalitarian community 50
gender equality 38, 39
gender inequalities 5, 12, 20, 38, 84, 125, 126, 161, 213
GenFoward's research (2018) 17
Gillespie, Marcia Ann 189
Ginsburg, Ruth Bader 176
Girl Boss feminism 96–97
Gladstone, Lily 187
global feminisms 24–26
global warming 210
Glynn, Sarah Jane 106
Goeman, M.R. 50
Goldin, Claudia 107
Gonzalez, Estella 62

Goodwin, Michele 189
Gorman, Amanda 44
Gornick, Vivian 190
grassroots feminist organizations 168
Guerrilla Girls 196–197

Haynie, Kerry L. 134
Haley, Nikki 133
Haney, Tyler 96
Hardnett, Sukari 113
Harris, Kamala 133
Hawaiian sovereignty movement 54
health disparities 114–121
Heard, Amber 93, 94
Heintz, S. 195
"Hella Feminist" 194
heteronormative 68
heteronormativity 162
heteropatriarchy 51
"hierarchy of oppressions" 8
Hill, Anita 112, 113
Hill, L. 116
Hochschild, Arlie Russell 106
Hochul, Kathy 181
Holzer, Jenny 193
hooks, bell 18–20, 44, 165
Hootch, Lenora 53
household labor 162
"How We Talk About Trans
    Inclusion Matters" 68
Hughes, Dorothy Pitman 126
Hull, Akasha 39
Hurwitz, Heather McKee 11, 154

Ifill, Gwen 12
imperialism 46
Indigenous feminisms 49–57
Indigenous Feminist Organizing
    School 55
inequality in technology 127–129
Institute for Women's Policy
    Research (IWPR) 104, 108
institutional tactics 153
International Women's Day 25
interpersonal violence 111, 113
interrelated inequalities 5

intersectional feminisms 1, 8–12,
    24, 64, 68, 96, 97, 209–210
intersectional feminists 11, 20;
    approach 24; campaign 10, 12,
    27; framework 5; perspectives 12
"intersectional imperative" 11
intersectional inequalities 14, 80,
    116, 161
intersectionality 7–8

Jackson, Ketanji Brown 133
*Jacobin* (2022) 25
Jane Collective 121–122
Johnson, Marsha P. 69
Jones, Feminista 85, *157*
Jordan, June 44, 45

Kavanaugh, Brett 113–114
Kendall, Mikki 159
Kennedy, Florynce 171
Kingston, Maxine Hong 48
Kington, S.G. 54
Korey, Steph 95
Kruger, Barbara 193

LaDuke, Winona: *All Our
    Relations: Native Struggles for
    Land and Life* 53
Lady Gaga 196
*The Lancet* 108
Las Hijas de Cuauhtémoc 61
Latifah, Queen 44
Lauer, Matt 112
"lavender menace" 67
Lemon, Don 133
Lenz, Lyz 191
lesbian 64–70
lesbian feminist community 195
lesbian separatist organizations 66
LGBTQ: communities 65;
    mobilization 65
Liddell, J.L. 54
Lindsey, Treva 41
Lorde, Audre 8, 39, 41, 44, 64, 70, 164
Lovett, Laura L 126
low-wage jobs 112

Mackenzie, Lori Nishiura 211
MacKinnon, C. 179, 210
Martin, Patricia Yancey 166
Mason, C. Nicole 109
Mayo Clinic Health System 117
McCray, Chirlane 39
McLaughlin, H. 112
McMillan Cottom, Tressie 85
McRobbie, Angela 94, 95
media 186–192; inequality
    130–132, 188
"medical exceptions" 121
Medley, Lynette 169
men and feminism 22–23
#MeToo movement 26, 135, 156, 158
Miller, H.E. 121
Missing and Murdered Indigenous
    Women, Girls, and Two Spirit
    (MMIWG2S) campaign 169–170
Missing white woman syndrome
    12–14
Monáe, Janelle 44, 196
Moraga, Cherríe 8–9, 34, 36, 61, 64,
    70; *This Bridge Called My Back* 61
Morgan, Joan 43
Morgan, Robin 188
Morris, Susana M. 44; *Feminist
    AF: A Guide to Crushing
    Girlhood* 44
"motherhood penalty" 105
Mountain Access Brigade 168
movement tactics 153
Mukhopadhyay, Samhita 97
Mulvey, Laura 159
Murray, Pauli 167

National Asian Pacific American
    Women's Forum 48
National Black Feminist
    Organization (NBFO) 39,
    85, 167
National Black Women's Health
    Project 40
national feminist organizations 167
National Institutes of Health
    (NIH) 117

National Intimate Partner and
    Sexual Violence Survey 111
National Organization for Women
    (NOW) 24, 66,167
native feminisms 50, 53
New York Radical Women 171
No More Secrets Mind Body Spirit
    (MBS) 169
non-disclosure agreements (NDA)
    134–136
"Not Murdered, Not Missing:
    Rebelling Against Colonial
    Gendered Violence" 51

Obama, Barack 80, 184
occupational segregation 105
Okazawa-Rey, Margo 39
online abeyance structures 85
online feminisms 26, 42, 154–160,
    184, 208, 212
online feminist community
    development 156
online harassment 127–129, 160
online "misogynoir" 43
organizational climate 110

Paik, I. 105
pandemic inequalities 96
Parton, Dolly 196
Paycheck Fairness Act 178
Peacock, Mary 188
Peitzmeier, S.M. 113
period poverty 169
persistence of feminism 80–83
Phillips, Layli 42
Pogrebin, Letty Cottin 188
police violence and brutality 26
political opportunity 80, 81
political representation 132–134
postfeminism 93–95
postpartum depression (PPD)
    116, 117
Pozner, Jennifer 91
prison industrial complex 122–124
"public health crisis" 115
Putin, Vladimir 25

queer and trans feminisms 64–70
Quintero, Isabel 62
quotidian feminisms 210–213

racial tension in feminism 63
racism 9, 37, 40
Radicalesbians 64, 65, 174
Ramirez, Deborah 114
Red Canary Song 49
Reger, Jo 98, 185, 195
reproductive health care 118–120
reproductive justice 118–120
"reproductive rights" framework 120
Rhimes, Shonda 186
Ringgold, Faith 193
"risk assessment" algorithms 123
Ritchie, Andrea 27
Rivera, Sylvia 69, 70
Rodger, Elliot 82
Roe *vs.* Wade 120, 121, 177, 195
Romano, Aja: *Vox* 93
Ross, Loretta 168, 174, 175
Ross, Luana 52
Roth, Benita: *Separate Roads to Feminism* 37
Rothberg, Emma 69
Rupp, L.J. 26, 160, 165, 175
Rushin, Donna Kate 36
Ryan, Erin Gloria 191

Sanchez, Erika 62
Sandberg, Sheryl 18–20; *Lean In: Women, Work, and the Will to Lead* 18–21
Sandoval, Chela 86
#SayHerName 26–28
secretiveness 211
self-care 164
sexism 40
sexual assault 130
sexual harassment 10, 11, 112, 134–135; law 179
Simard, Caroline 211
Simpson, Leanne Betasamosake 51
Sims, Marion 114
SisterSong 168

Slakoff, Danielle 13
"small wins" model 211
Smith, Barbara 5–6, 39, 41, 64, 70
Smith, Beverly 39
Smith, Bridget 96
Smith, Stacy 132
social change, feminist methods for 153–154
social justice groups 68
social justice movements 68
social movements 16, 91, 152, 153, 170; abeyance 84; activity 81; communities 81
Sojourner Truth Festival of the Arts 188
Speak Out Act 135
Springer, Kimberly 85, 89, 90, 175
Staggenborg, S. 82, 153, 154, 165, 166
Stallion, Megan Thee 44
Steinem, Gloria 188
Stewart, Dodai 191
Stonewall Inn 65
Stonewall Uprising 65
street protest 170–173
Street Transvestite Action Revolutionaries (STAR) 69
Strike for Women's Equity Day 63
Strings, Sabrina 118
Stryker, S. 65–67
student activism 182–185
Sullivan, Mecca Jamilah 41

tactics 153
Tanner, Chanel Craft: *Feminist AF: A Guide to Crushing Girlhood* 44
Taylor, Breonna 124
Taylor, V. 16, 64, 84, 154, 160, 165, 175; *Rock-a-by Baby: Feminism, Self-Help and Postpartum Depression* 117
Third World feminist movements 48
Third World Women's Alliance (TWWA) 36, 167
*This Bridge Called My Back: Writing by Radical Women of Color* 36, 46, 56, 61

Thomas, Clarence 112, 113
*To Be Real: Telling the Truth and Changing the Face of Feminism* 89–90
Tolentino, Jia 191
Tometi, Ayọ̀ 41
toxic masculinity 110
toxic waste 124
traditional feminist tactics 68
traditional gender expectations 162
Traister, Rebecca 158
trans-exclusive radical feminists (TERFS) 24
transgender 24; individuals experience 111
trans-inclusive feminism 24
transnational feminist networking (TFNs) 25, 26
transnational feminist networks 26
TRAP laws 191
Trask, Haunani-Kay 54
"trigger laws" 120
"Triple Jeopardy" 61
Trump, Donald 172, 192

US Department of Justice 111

varieties of feminisms 34; Asian American feminism 45–49; Black, Indigenous, Asian American, and Chicana feminisms 37–39; Black feminism 39–41; Chicana feminism 58–62; Indigenous feminism 49–57; lesbian, queer and trans feminisms 64–70; Lorde, Audre 70; Whitewashed feminisms 62–64; Women of Color feminisms 35–37
VAWA Reauthorization Act of 2022 178
Vidal, Mirta 59

Violence Against Women Act (VAWA) 178; funded programs 179
VMware Women's Leadership Innovation Lab 211
*Vox* (Romano) 93

wage gap 107; and trucking 109; wages and 104–109
Walker, Alice 15, 16, 188; *The Color Purple* 42
Walker, Kara 193
Walker, Rebecca 89
waveless feminism 79, 86–89, 95, 207
Weinstein, Harvey 81, 112
Weiss, Emily 95, 96
white feminism 1, 16, 92
white-led feminist organizations 63
white supremacist society 63
Whitewashed feminisms 35, 62–64
Whittier, Nancy 16, 64, 165, 175, 176
Williams, Christine L. 106
"The Woman-Identified-Woman" 64
womanism 15, 16, 42
Womanist Working Collective 42
Women of Color 7, 10, 11, 13–15, 35–37, 40, 42, 43, 46, 62–64, 89, 123, 127, 128, 182, 183, 190, 196
"women's liberation" 171
working-class movement 61
workplace sexual harassment 134
Wyandt-Hiebert, Mary 194
Wynn, A.T. 127

Yale law 179
Yamada, M. 46; *This Bridge Called My Back* 46
#Yesallwomen movement 82

Ziering, Amy 111
Zucker, Alyssa 14